FIGURES OF TIME

THOUGHT IN THE ACT
A series edited by Brian Massumi and Erin Manning

FIGURES OF TIME

AFFECT AND THE TELEVISION OF PREEMPTION

Toni Pape

DUKE UNIVERSITY PRESS
DURHAM AND LONDON
2019

© 2019 Duke University Press
All rights reserved

Text design by Adrianna Sutton
Cover design by Matthew Tauch
Typeset in Sabon and Din by Copperline Books

Earlier versions of excerpts from this book have previously been published in "Temporalities on Collision Course: Time, Knowledge, and Temporal Critique in Damages," in *Time in Television Narrative: Exploring Temporality in Twenty-First-Century Programming*, edited by Melissa Ames (Jackson: University of Mississippi Press, 2012), 165–77; and "Preemptive Narratives, Modes of Attention, and the Politics of Perception," *Spectator* 34, no. 2 (2014): 63–71.

Library of Congress Cataloging-in-Publication Data
Names: Pape, Toni, [date] author.
Title: Figures of time : affect and the television of preemption / Toni Pape.
Description: Durham : Duke University Press, 2019. | Series: Thought in the act | Includes bibliographical references and index.
Identifiers: LCCN 2018040995 (print) | LCCN 2018055093 (ebook)
ISBN 9781478004653 (ebook)
ISBN 9781478003731 (hardcover : alk. paper)
ISBN 9781478004035 (pbk. : alk. paper)
Subjects: LCSH: Television programs—Political aspects—United States. | Television programs—Social aspects—United States. | Television broadcasting—United States—Influence. | Time on television. | Television programs—Plots, themes, etc. | Future, The, in popular culture. | Political culture—United States.
Classification: LCC PN1992.6 (ebook) | LCC PN1992.6 .P36 2019 (print) | DDC 791.45/6581—dc23
LC record available at https://lccn.loc.gov/2018040995

Cover art: *Life on Mars*, BBC, credit sequence with motion blur.

CONTENTS

INTRODUCTION
Preemptive Narratives and Televisual Futures | 1

1. **THE SERIAL MACHINE**
   Toward Figures of Time | 38

2. **THREE REPRESENTATIONS AND A FIGURAL**
   Bergsonian Variations on Metric Time, the Virtual, and Creative Becoming | 73

3. **LOOP INTO LINE**
   The Moral Command of Preemption | 109

4. ***DAMAGES* AS PROCEDURAL TELEVISION** | 142

   AFTERWORD
   Anarchival Television | 176

Acknowledgments | 183
Notes | 185
Works Cited | 203
Index | 215

INTRODUCTION

PREEMPTIVE NARRATIVES AND TELEVISUAL FUTURES

The television series *Breaking Bad* (AMC, 2008–13) opens on Walter White's frenzied, dramatic escape in an RV through the New Mexican desert. After a few brief opening shots, the image places us inside the RV's microcosm of mayhem: scantily clad in his briefs and a steamed-up gas mask, the driver barely manages to control the vehicle; in the seat beside him lies an unconscious passenger who is also wearing a gas mask; in the "recreational" space behind him, test tubes are breaking and falling into a toxic brew that laps across the floor; in it, two bodies slide from side to side. Going at full speed, the RV begins to swerve across the desert roads and ultimately crashes into a ditch. The driver frantically leaves the vehicle and takes off his mask. As he gasps for air, the stench of chemicals makes him bend over and retch. After nervously putting on his green dress shirt, he pulls out a video camera and records a confession. The image trembles as the driver looks directly into the camera and identifies himself as Walter White (Bryan Cranston). While Walter speaks to his family through the shaky camera, asking for understanding if not exactly forgiveness, sirens are wailing in the distance and slowly increasing in volume. The speed run was, in all appearances, a chase and the followers are closing in. Walter pulls a gun out of his briefs, places himself squarely in the middle of the desert road, and, in a somewhat iconic shot, points his gun at his arriving pursuers. Right then, after three and a half minutes of high-octane pursuit: cut! The opening titles intervene to suspend our attention at this moment of imminent escalation. After the title sequence, however, we do *not* return to this moment. Instead, we see the most conventional establishing shot: a residential house, Walter's, with the subtitle "three weeks earlier" (see figures 1.1–1.3).

What has just happened? *Breaking Bad* begins with a loop through the future in the sense that the juxtaposition of disjunct moments in time

2 | INTRODUCTION

Figure I.1. *Breaking Bad*: Walter White (Bryan Cranston) before imminent confrontation with his presumed pursuers.

Figure I.2. *Breaking Bad*: opening sequence.

Figure I.3. *Breaking Bad*: establishing shot "three weeks earlier."

triggers a perceptual movement that makes us see the present through the future.[1] The series anticipates a dramatic chase across the desert and an impending stand-off *before* it provides a proper exposition to introduce characters, settings, and themes. Now, *after* the flash-forward and the opening titles, we learn what will have caused the previewed calamity in an emphatic da capo. Thus, as we receive the necessary background information, we are already poised for the future to return. Narrative progression is now a matter of catching up with the foretold showdown. As we see Walter, a responsible teacher and family father, go through the depressing routine of his everyday life, we already wonder what could possibly turn this person into a hunted criminal within only three weeks . . . And in this particular case, we do not need to wait long for the answer: *Breaking Bad* catches up with its first preempted future within the pilot episode. In the meantime, we learn that Walter's transformation was triggered by a personal prophecy of doom that anticipates the ending, or *an* ending, of the series as a whole: a terminal cancer diagnosis. So by the time the pilot of *Breaking Bad* has closed its first episodic loop through the future, it has already drawn up another dark horizon that looms over the entire show. Throughout the series, these episodic loops through the future will return to such an extent that they have become part of *Breaking Bad*'s recognizable signature style (see Logan 2013; Sánchez-Baró 2014).[2] Indeed, while the series explicitly tells us, by way of a subtitle, in its first two episodes that we have jumped in time, we are subsequently expected to understand how the narrative operates without any such indication. When the sixth episode, "Crazy Handful of Nothin'," preempts its ending again without any subtitle, we have attuned to the ways in which the series moves through time. In this way, *Breaking Bad* fosters and expects a certain level of media literacy in its audience. But what do these loops effectuate? Surely, *Breaking Bad* uses what I call the preempted ending as a means to create suspense, but what kind of suspense is this exactly? If the series repeatedly anticipates events that are bound to happen, it is to make felt the inevitability of a calamitous future and, as a consequence, the precariousness of the present. In the case of *Breaking Bad*, the inevitable is the steady corruption of Walter White. We are made to feel the inexorable erosion of the American middle class within an increasingly harsh society, where healthcare is a luxury and a high school teacher has to supplement his income with a side job at the carwash and, soon enough, as a meth cook (see Logan 2013, 2016). The suspense created here does not follow a logic of revelation—*what will happen?*—because we already know, at least to a certain extent, what will happen. Rather, suspense emerges from the interval between the present and the foretold future, from the intensely vibrant joy and the felt certainty that every step along the way will inevitably lead to the announced calamity.[3] The thrilling question is that of *how* things will have come about.

The answer to that question does not always come as quickly as in *Breaking Bad*'s pilot episode. On other occasions, the series takes much longer to catch up with its foreboding visions, most notably in its second season when it lassoes eerie shots from a more distant future into the preemptive movement. The season opens on the desaturated image of an empty residential backyard accompanied, again, by the wail of a siren. After a few disjoint shots of the backyard, the camera is placed inside the pool and captures an eyeball that is slowly sucked into the water drain. Color first enters the image when a bright-pink teddy bear drifts into the frame. As the stuffed bear circles through the water, we come to see that it is half-charred and missing one of its (plastic) eyes (see figure I.4). This damaged toy is the attractor that pulls the narrative toward its cataclysmic end, intentionally setting off a series of speculations on the

Figure I.4. *Breaking Bad*: portentous pink teddy bear in pool.

part of the viewer. Has there been a meth lab accident at the White residence? Has one of Walter's enemies taken revenge on him and his family? Throughout the season, *Breaking Bad* repeatedly loops these future moments into our experience of the narrative, keeping perception in the thrall of the eerie, inevitable ending.[4] In this way, the series never lets us forget that Walter White's existence teeters on the brink of collapse.

This narrative loop through the future is television's new refrain, that is, a consistent and repeatable "gathering of [discursive, aesthetic] forces" that brings existential territories into existence (Bertelsen and Murphie 2010, 145).[5] Given how often TV series currently preempt their own futures in ways similar to *Breaking Bad*, this narrative device seems to have a particular consistency and force that make for powerful storytelling that is, moreover, capable of expressing certain future-related concerns of our time. *Figures of Time* explores the aesthetic force of the preempted ending, suggesting that its strength lies in the affective responses it elicits in viewers. It is worth noting that, in the case of *Breaking Bad*, it is the viewers themselves, not the fictional characters, who have visions of the future that influence their perception of a narrative present. So whatever preempted endings do, they do it to and with the viewer. Although the examples discussed in this book vary substantially in their treatment of the future visions (including fictional characters who see their own future), the focus here will be on the viewer's embodied experience, in particular the suspense, effectuated by the loop through the future. This is the first reason why I call this particular aesthetic movement a "refrain": the preempted ending must be thought as a nonrepresentational motif that orders how we perceive the represented stories in the first place. As I have briefly suggested in my opening example, *Breaking Bad* repeatedly preempts its future to make us sense the slow but steady decline into precarity of the American middle class. In this particular example, then, the aesthetic movement reinforces the series' representational project. But this is not always the case: nonrepresentational aesthetic movements can just as well undermine or counteract the explicitly stated project of a series. In order to understand the wide variety of effects that this refrain of the future can have, this book will draw on aesthetic theories of the *figural* because it is in the nonrepresentational, affective dimension of the figural that preempted endings acquire the consistency of a refrain. Secondly, preempted endings constitute a refrain because the ordering of perception they accomplish is politically relevant. As Gilles Deleuze and Félix Guattari suggest, refrains express territories (1987, 310–16). Indeed, the political argument of *Figures of Time* suggests that television's loop through the future participates in the recent shift toward preemption politics. This political resonance is what distinguishes television's new refrain from previous refrains of the future.

250 Years Earlier

The territory of the future has been actively charted and contested for at least two centuries. The period we call modernity alone has given us a variety of refrains of what is yet to come. Consider the argument for necessary progress that relied, among other things, on a concept of linear, teleological time that has legitimized a remarkable series of social utopias. Support for this manageability of enlightened social teleologies came from the domain of science where classical mechanics, which considers time reversible, articulated the comforting idea of a calculable, foreseeable future. Introduce a cause here and observe the desired effect there. It does not surprise, then, that utopias set in the future as well as time travel narratives, which rehearse these concepts of time for a lay audience, emerge as literary genres at roughly the same time, in the late eighteenth century (see Hausmann 2009). The discovery of entropy in the nineteenth century shook this confidence: as the now notorious second law of thermodynamics formulates, entropy implies that time is irreversible and the future uncertain. And, sure enough, the late nineteenth century feared "general entropy" as a state of complete energy dissipation that would put an end to progress, as numerous fin-de-siècle dystopian narratives confirm.[6] When H. G. Wells's time traveler rushed millions of years into the future, he found "a steady twilight brood[ing] over the earth, a twilight only broken now and then when a comet glared across the darkling sky." To his dismay, "the sun, red and very large, halted motionless upon the horizon, a vast dome glowing with a dull heat, and now and then suffering a momentary extinction" (Wells 1975, 99). This fear of extinction due to the dissipation of energy was not merely a popular adaptation of powerful scientific concepts. The opposite is true: art appropriates these notions of time to express a conceptual territory that cocreates social and political realities (see Deleuze and Guattari 1987, 316).[7] Power is in the transversal relations between the heterogeneous fields of science, philosophy, and art. Today television, as any other art, articulates refrains of the future that help bring today's political territories into existence. These futures are not or not only represented or mediated; refrains of the future are first and foremost aesthetic movements that eventfully lift off from moving images and are directly sensed by the viewer. Television is an aesthetic vector of subjectivation. Given this nonrepresentational efficacy of the aesthetic and the fact that political theory and practice of recent decades have actively harnessed and weaponized perception, the aesthetic is considered immediately political in the present account. *Figures of Time* explores one of the contemporary connections between aesthetics and politics by tracing how the nonlinear complexity of fictional television, understood here as an artful mode of expression, crafts preemptive movements into the audience's perception.

Territories being contestable, art never simply confirms the political territories it helps establish but continuously tests their potentials and traces their limits. Here is another familiar version of the future, this time from the realm of finance: Economies of credit bank on the future, trusting that a debtor will be able to pay for what has already been purchased. Credit's sidekick, the insurance industry, guarantees that the money value of an as-yet-unpaid commodity is upheld even if that commodity is lost or broken at some point in the future. Although these are surely useful achievements, cinema and television know the fine print that comes with an ensured future. Countless once-loved spouses, estranged siblings, and geriatric great-aunts have had to bite the dust on the screen for the price tag attached to the loss of their life. The commodity to be broken and reimbursed might as well be you, goes one future-tending audiovisual refrain that resounds from *Double Indemnity* to *The Widower* and through countless episodes of crime television.[8] Art offers counterrefrains to destabilize territories, temporal and otherwise, to sound out the existential loopholes in their reassuring provisions. Accordingly, *Figures of Time* does not read the television series under study here in a mode of critique. Instead, the book sets out to engage with televisual aesthetics as a mode of thinking in its own right. The arguments that aesthetic movements unfold over time may lead in various philosophical, political, and ethical directions, sometimes confirming powerful doctrines and sometimes slowly unraveling them from within. *Figures of Time* proposes an encounter with television's aesthetic thinking in motion to intervene in the debates around a contemporary politics of perception.[9]

In all of this, the future exerts its ontogenetic power not so much through representations of itself (even though it is often represented). It works through affect. Third refrain, this time from the realm of politics: The twentieth century fostered the politics of prevention and deterrence, both of which consist in taking measures so that a certain future does *not* materialize. As we will see, this is what clearly distinguishes them from the doctrine of preemption.[10] Prevention proceeds by empirically assessing the causes that will lead to the threatening future, devising methods to counteract or eliminate these causes, thus solving the problem at its root. This is of use in the management of a population's health, for instance. Deterrence, dominant during the Cold War era, is a strategy for averting catastrophe when prevention has failed. When both the US and the Soviet Union were in possession of sufficient amounts of nuclear weapons to destroy each other, the only thing that prevented nuclear war was the scenario of mutually assured destruction itself. For this scenario to act as a deterrent, it requires an equilibrium between the adversaries' destructive powers. Since each side must continuously make sure that its weaponry is up to par, the equilibrium is necessarily dynamic. Deterrence fuels an arms race for the sake of peace. Two of the audiovisual refrains that grafted this duplicitous dynamic into the bodies of the audience are the Doomsday Clock and the fictional Red Button (or Red Telephone) to launch the nuclear missiles. The doomsday clock's frightening suggestion that it might be just about too late is also an injunction to make sure that the clock never strikes twelve. The fear that we are running like clockwork into catastrophe is complemented by the conservative desire to stop time. The red button expresses a similar ambivalence. Operated through the smallest physical effort, possibly at a whim, it articulates the fragility of the status quo and intensifies apprehension through the embodied knowledge that the forbidden button is also the most tempting one. The affective singularity of these refrains consists in an ambiguity that oscillates between a suspense that pulls toward the coming catastrophe on the one hand and, on the other, fear and the imperative of moral superiority that push away from it. The politicality of uncountable Cold War narratives consists in rehearsing the balancing act of deterrence in the affective mode. That the red button in the Oval Office does not actually exist is of little consequence. Art *fabulates* fictional refrains whose affect feeds back into "real" politics, regardless of their truth-value.[11] *Figures of Time* investigates such affective refrains and their political resonance. More specifically, the book looks at recent serial dramas and argues that a remarkable number of TV series of the last two decades have developed and circulated a new, properly televisual refrain of the future. The political doctrine that these narratives support aesthetically is neither that of prevention nor that of deterrence. It is the doctrine of preemption.

Politics: Preemption and Narrative

That the future should still be a resource for political action today is not beyond dispute. In fact, thinkers from various fields hold that the future has run its course as a driving force for social progress. Historian François Hartog suggests that the acceleration of life and the proliferation of crises over the twentieth century have produced a new order of time that he calls *presentism*, the contemporary experience of an "omnipresent present" (2015, xviii). In this view, the modernist notion of a continuous social progress toward the future is no longer adequate to the ways in which history can be thought in a globalized, late-capitalist world. The future is outdated. Franco Berardi concurs in *After the Future* that "a progressive model for the future" is no longer credible. Consequently, "when the collective imagination becomes incapable of seeing possible alternatives to trends leading to devastation, increased poverty and violence," the future appears as "a threat" (Berardi 2011, 58–59). Hartog and Berardi are right. But to say that the future has become a "threat" is far from declaring it obsolete. It is to say that it continues to shape our present through affective charges.

A new refrain—preemption—resonates through our contemporary political territories and it draws on this affective force of threat as a present futurity. Preemption does not respond to an actual danger in order to thwart it as prevention or deterrence would do; it evokes an indeterminate threat in the future in order to modulate and potentialize the present. If preemption does not counteract a preexisting danger, it is because it does not know the future in the same way that prevention and deterrence do. Today, our future is so uncertain, so indeterminate, that one cannot possibly rely on rational calculation and fact-based purposive action. "Terrorists and terror states do not reveal [their] threats with fair notice, in formal declarations—and responding to such enemies only after they have struck first is not self-defense, it is suicide," the presidential refrain begins (Bush 2003). The alternative is to harness that very uncertainty and evoke an indeterminate threat on which to act. "Saddam Hussein *could* build a nuclear bomb within months *if he were able* to obtain fissile material," the tune continues (White House 2002, emphasis added). This conditional logic—would have, could have—is at the heart of the refrain. Since the factual basis for preemptive action is affective in nature, there will never have been any hard evidence to prove the necessity for preemptive action. You must therefore insist that the threat *would have* fully materialized by itself if you *had not* taken measures on time. This means that preemption is always and openly based on a lack of knowledge and factual evidence. It operationalizes an epistemology (lack of knowledge) and an ontology (the mere potentiality of the threat) in order to potentialize the present. The hard facts do not matter; what counts is fear as an "affective fact" that piggybacks your action plan into existence (Massumi 2015, 189). "The security of the world requires disarming Saddam Hussein *now*," the cadence falls (Bush 2003, emphasis added). The vague threat of a potential future attack has leveraged a real invasion of foreign territory in the present. Preemptive politics is what happens in the interval between the present and the future catastrophe that could be. Its goal is not to prevent but to make a vague threat materialize in one way or another so that, at least, one has something to respond to.[12]

If this rings a bell, it is because preemption operates in ways similar to the more familiar prophecy of doom. A prophecy consists in predicting a catastrophe in the future so that we can take measures in the present to prevent that catastrophe. Based on the affective state of fear triggered by the prophecy, its recipients will then take countermeasures. If all goes well, the predicted catastrophe will not happen. Note that, following this logic, a "good" or "efficient" prophecy is one whose predicted catastrophe never occurs. In other words, a "good" prophecy will turn out to be false; it falsifies itself, as it were. Consider this to be not a mere side effect but an integral part of the process: the efficiency of a prophecy of doom *depends* on its capacity to falsify itself. This also means that, if the prophecy is efficient, there will not be any proof that the measures taken actually needed to be taken. In fact, the very lack of proof can be recast as proof that whatever was done must have been appropriate. After all, the catastrophe did not come about. It is clear why this is possible and unproblematic within a theological view of the world: the biblical god who imparts the prophecy also stands in as a transcendent guarantor of a truth that cannot be verified in this world. That this should also be the modus operandi of contemporary secular politics is worrisome, to say the least. Preemption sanctions virtually any kind of concrete action (including war) by means of a hypothetical conditional proposition and, yet, contemporary political thinkers hold that we *should* tackle future threats and uncertainties in the same way as biblical prophecies do.[13] The limitation of such arguments is that they continue to consider the future a purely epistemological problem, neglecting the possibility that the infamous known and unknown knowns that the future holds are deployed to produce immediately felt, affective realities. As I further explain in chapter 1, arguments that insist on rational scenario planning tend to neglect the active role that contemporary media play in the dissemination of fearful "doomsday" scenarios and, more specifically, the way in which they can help undermine rational, deliberative politics.[14] Indeed, preemption's ecology of fear firmly relies on the mediation of potential future catastrophes through news and current affairs media as well as fiction programming. As the example of *Breaking Bad* has already shown, the narrative loop through the future gives primacy to the affective force of moving images and subordinates their referential or communicative content; for contemporary media the future is not or not primarily an epistemological problem.

Staging an encounter between television studies and cultural theory, *Figures of Time* explores one way in which contemporary media culture has adapted to the increasing geopolitical uncertainty of our time by drawing on affective facts to *create* futures. The book argues that the creation and modulation of affective states in the mode of preemption rely first and foremost on the nonlinear temporal movement described above and the specific aesthetic experience it enables. More specifically, the book's aim is to show that contemporary TV fiction contributes to this modulatory, ontogenetic dynamic through what I call *preemptive narratives*. Preemptive narratives are fictional television series that infuse their stories with glimpses of a daunting future and, in this way, prime viewers to interpret the present in light of a worst-case scenario. As a result, I contend, television normalizes preemption and attunes us to its functional principles. These narratives produce an embodied and affective experience of contemporary future politics, a popular preemptive nonconscious as a complement to official preemption-based policies. While other media certainly participate in this process as well (notably news media), I contend that fictional television series are particularly conducive to a differentiated negotiation of preemption politics because of their extended narratives with many internal tensions, their serial structure, and the relative freedom that fiction affords.

Preemptive narratives have proliferated in recent years. Examples include several seasons of *Revenge* (ABC, 2011–15), *How to Get Away with Murder* (ABC, 2014–present), *Bloodline* (Netflix, 2015–2017), *Quantico* (ABC, 2015–2018), and *Big Little Lies* (HBO, 2017–present).[15] While preemptive narratives exist in many different genres and many cultural contexts, the corpus of the present study has been restricted to Anglophone serial dramas belonging to various subgenres of crime fiction. Furthermore, the fictional programs discussed more closely in this book—*Damages* (FX/Audience Network, 2007–12), *Life on Mars* (BBC, 2006–7), and *Flashforward* (ABC, 2009–10)—deploy this temporal movement as the functional principle of their narrative project in that they persistently anticipate their own (season) endings. As a result, the entire narrative is structured around the loop through time. Each of these series preempts or predicts its catastrophic outcomes and only afterward returns to the beginning, now imbued with the gloom of the foretold disaster; the narrative then slowly unfolds the events leading up to that disaster over the duration of an entire season. These series thus activate the interval between the present moment and the foretold ending as the domain where reality is generated, where time is made: ontogenesis. This means that the future is by no means a purely epistemological problem; it does not provide excess information in a straightforward way, to merely add meaning. Most of *Breaking Bad*'s flash-forwards confuse and disconcert the viewer instead of providing useful information that would allow her to assess the narrative present in light of its foretold future (see Connelly 2015). The seemingly objective presentation of the future *creates* meaning for the purpose of leading and misleading the viewer in the present; it makes and unmakes sense in the now of watching; it triggers affective responses that color the perception of the present moment. It is crucial in this context that, by way of genre, many of these future-tending narratives relate to issues of justice, law, and law enforcement.[16] They are crime dramas like *Breaking Bad*, police procedurals like *Life on Mars*, legal thrillers such as *Damages*, or FBI action-adventures as in the case of *Flashforward*. All these genres have their own powerful refrains with established social and political commitments. Usually taking off from a disruption of the social order, these narratives conduct an investigation into the crime or other offense at hand to arrest the offender or dispense punishment and thereby mend the social fabric. Clearly, then, the preemptive temporalities that so often occur in the series belonging to these genres are relevant to the ways in which we conceive social relations and order through fiction. The question is *how* they are relevant. What happens when crime fiction's measured legato toward harmonic resolution is syncopated by preemption's commanding loop phrase? *Figures of Time* argues that the preempted ending provides a narrative counterpoint that transforms the basic narrative schemes of the cop show or the court drama, including the underlying notions of justice and law enforcement. The inspectors, agents, and litigators of preemptive narratives no longer investigate a crime as a preexisting reality waiting to be uncovered. Rather, they interfere with the attending world to create a milieu conducive to their exercise of power. By emphasizing the affective factuality of the future, for instance through persistent flash-forwards to the coming disaster, these narratives and their dubious heroes exploit these felt realities to leverage ethically questionable action plans, stratagems, or policies. Fear is instrumentalized to impose tight security measures as comforting protection. Hate is fueled to foster support for "enhanced interrogation techniques." Uncertainty is propagated to bring the population in line with those who pretend to know. In this way, the preempted ending renders the ontogenetic force of a felt future to generate what comes to count as real and true in the present.

But preemptive narratives can also carry a critical impetus. When the second season of *Breaking Bad* proliferates future visions and weaves them into each other—the returning pink teddy bear, a dead body lying next to Jesse's bouncing red lowrider, anonymous men wading through a river and finding Hank's trophy of kingpin Tuco's teeth grill enclosed in glass—the loop through the future circles in and puts pressure on the precarious present of the middle class. The preempted endings make felt that the status quo is highly unstable, that minor decisions or deviations from plan can lead to utter devastation, and that it is always almost-too-late for course corrections. As suggested earlier, the depressing affect of *Breaking Bad*'s preemptive movements brings the bare survival of middle-class Americans into perception. One of the achievements of contemporary television and preemptive narratives in particular is that they negotiate their political concerns in the same way as policy makers: through sensation. And yet the critical dimension of *Breaking Bad*'s ominous pink teddy bear is seriously undermined when it turns out in the season finale that it has barely anything to do with Walter White's immediate situation. It did not bode of a lab explosion in the White residence that might have put the entire family in danger, nor was there an attack organized by one of Walt's increasingly numerous enemies. The teddy bear literally fell from the sky—*ursulus ex machina*. Numerous viewers felt underwhelmed and manipulated by a resolution that was all but tangential, especially because these inauspicious glimpses of the future created much of the suspense that the second season ran on. We were made to fear for the Whites—and for nothing. Such TV moments as this one bring into awareness our participation in the popular preemptive nonconscious mentioned earlier and make clear that the real affective dynamic of preemption may operate autonomously from a relevant factual basis.[17] In the face of such a realization, one important question is what other effects our affective engagement has helped leverage in the meantime. In other words, how do television series operationalize such affective facts? The following chapters provide a range of different answers to these questions. Preemptive narratives can obviously participate in a politics of fear, as I will argue for *Flashforward* in chapter 3. But they can also launch philosophical investigations into the nature of time, as does *Life on Mars*, which I consider in chapter 2, or propose ethico-aesthetic solutions to the problem of preemption like *Damages*, as I further explore in chapters 1 and 4. It must be noted, then, that the core dynamic of preemption can give rise to a variety of perceptual movements that can potentially be constructive or destructive, enabling or restrictive.

The book's focus on affective realities and their efficacy is the reason why the various stories narrated in these TV shows, though they will be discussed in due measure, are not the main focus of this book. It is a particularity of preemption that, while it continuously modulates representations, it is not in the mode of representation that its force operates. Rather, it acts directly on the senses, as an attack on perception induced by evoking a future threat. Consequently, an engagement with preemptive narratives must pass through their aesthetic investment in time and the politically relevant experiences of time they create. Throughout this book, I argue that the central insights concerning preemption are articulated *by* the image as well as its movement through time, and not so much *in* the image, or on the level of story and content. While television's new refrain of the preempted ending certainly does tell us many stories, this refrain, by virtue of its sheer frequency, acquires its own consistency and becomes "autonomous from the dramatic action" (Deleuze and Guattari 1987, 319).

Such an endeavor makes it necessary to think what media might be as an assemblage in motion. *Figures of Time* offers a theory of televisual time—constructed around the concept of the *figural*—that adequately describes the aesthetic experience of time in preemptive narratives. And to first of all understand the emergence of these narratives in the twenty-first century—to understand why television is capable of producing such aesthetic experiences—the book thinks television itself as a machinic assemblage of heterogeneous elements (technical, social, political, ethical) that co-compose our lived experience of TV. Finally, the book tries to offer an innovative way of scholarly engaging with television that begins precisely there, in lived experience. This method is indebted to William James's radical empiricism and the aesthetic theories it has influenced, including those of Gilles Deleuze, Brian Massumi, Thomas Lamarre, Anna Munster, Erin Manning, and Alanna Thain. James insists that a thinking that intends to be radically empirical "must neither admit into its constructions any element that is not directly experienced, nor exclude from them any element that is directly experienced" (2003, 22). This means that a radically empirical study of our encounter with television must not reduce its field of investigation to a research object or "text," to a production "context" or a technological "apparatus." It must engage with the field of relations as such, thinking the connections between all the elements that factor into an experience. Thus, in order to think with television in radically empirical fashion one must ask: What is seen, heard, and felt through a program's images and sound? What exactly comes into sensation? How does this experience come into existence? How exactly does it engage the body? These questions will be the starting points for the analyses in the following chapters.

In the remainder of this introduction, I provide a more detailed framework for the book's main fields of engagement. Besides the political engagement with the doctrine of preemption, *Figures of Time* is grounded in theories of *technics*, *aesthetics*, and *ethics*. While each of these fields will be introduced separately, it will become clear that they are deeply connected. Simplifying a bit, one could say that the new technical capacities of television give rise to a new televisual aesthetic that, in turn, allows for new political resonances and requires appropriate ethical consideration. As I will shortly lay out in the following sections, each of the main chapters also focuses on one of these areas: chapter 1 explores the technics of television as an enabling condition for new aesthetic movements while chapter 2 provides a first in-depth reading of figural aesthetics in serial television. The third chapter engages the implications of preemption politics head-on and prepares chapter 4's investigation into a possible ethics for preemption and the control society.

Technics: Television as Abstract Machine

According to this book's core argument, fictional television participates in the shift of political culture away from a model of rational deliberation and representation to a politics of preemption. This hypothesis regarding the politicality of contemporary televisual aesthetics cannot be argued without engaging the notion of televisual time itself.

Conventionally, the medium's temporality is defined through the transient but persistent present of the live broadcast, which later produces more general notions of *flow*.[18] Given the requirements of programming, this is by no means an open, undetermined movement through time. Rather, "televisual time is programmed and scheduled as precisely as possible, down to the last second. Television's time is a time which is, in effect, wholly determined" by its mode of distribution (Doane 1990, 237).[19] Thus, the focus on the technological deployment of the moving image and on its linear organization in broadcasting schedules produces a concept of time as the linear, steady, and determined passage from instant to instant. Subsequently, the sequential progression of the apparatus is generalized into "the" time of the medium. Inadequacies arise when such a general concept sneaks into discussions not just of a medium's technological substratum but also of narrative structure and even the aesthetic experience of time. Consider, for instance, the various attempts at thinking a certain strand of recent narrative cinema and television that are characterized by anachronisms, temporal loops, parallel and crossing timelines, repetitions, and so forth. A list of examples would surely include such films as *Butterfly Effect*, *Eternal Sunshine of the Spotless Mind*, *Memento*, *Inception*, and *Edge of Tomorrow* as well as many TV series, including those discussed here. It has been suggested that such narratives take us "*out* of time" and make moving images "*a*temporal" (McGowan 2011). But why would one call repetitions, loops, and anachronisms *a*temporal if not because one has already conceptualized time as a linear, homogeneous chronology? At the beginning of such an argument stands an impoverished concept of time that does justice neither to aesthetic experience nor to contemporary politics. If, however, one begins with a different concept of time—based on notions of, say, topology, becoming, and emergence—one would actually have to consider these films all the more "temporal" for their strange loops and nonlinear timelines. They take you *into time* rather than out of it. Their quirky temporalities speak not to a dismissal of "real" time but, quite the contrary, to a serious engagement with time as an aesthetic, political, and ethical problem. In order to think those engagements, it is necessary to develop and hone a practice of what Bliss Cua Lim (2009) calls "temporal critique," or a practice of reading that can think such irreducibly heterogeneous and nonlinear temporalities or "immiscible times" as cinema or television's very own temporalities. In order to think the effects of these temporalities, it is moreover crucial to go beyond strictly narratological accounts of temporal structures that are provided by a lot of recent work on "narrative complexity." Instead of an apparatus, mode of distribution, or narrative structure, this book therefore takes *aesthetic experience* as its starting point to build a more appropriate concept of televisual time.

If such an approach to television is not entirely new, it nonetheless attempts to fill a considerable gap within the available research. While cinema has since its very beginnings been considered for the strong aesthetic experiences it creates, television has often been described as a notoriously anaesthetic medium. Here, the term *anaesthetic* must be taken in at least two senses. First, television as both an entertainment and a mass medium is considered utterly uninteresting from an aesthetic viewpoint, providing only formulaic and shallow junk to its audience. Second and more importantly, it is understood as the medium of distraction par excellence. Its continuous onslaught of images thwarts our capacity for attention and numbs our senses like a powerful anesthetic, so that eventually we perceive it as little more than white noise. Given these general views of the medium, it is little wonder that strong aesthetic theories of television have not existed for a long time and only become available quite recently (see, e.g., Butler 2010; Caldwell 1995; Cardwell 2013 and 2014; Jacobs and Peacock 2013).[20] The dismissal of television as an anaesthetic medium is one of the main reasons that, while much ink has been spilled on the time-images or "pure optical and sound situations" of cinema, one is hard pressed to find accounts within television studies that would consider TV equally capable of such intensive aesthetic experiences (see Deleuze 1986, 1989). *Figures of Time* argues that television is indeed capable of the feat and that therefore we require approaches that allow us to think the medium's aesthetic potential.

To do this, however, it is not necessary to reject the technological aspect of moving-image narratives. On the contrary, technological innovations and the techniques of viewing they enable have made a significant contribution to the creation of new and more complex temporal experiences in television series. Such aesthetic experiences are *co-conditioned* (rather than determined) by a range of factors that, in the case of television, include but are not limited to network systems, digital technologies, production companies, distribution sites and practices, writing processes, reception practices, and politics. These factors are not discrete entities that enable or preclude certain processes as on a switchboard. Rather, they must be thought as elements of a "functional ensemble" (Guattari 1995, 35) that sustains "a process of mutual stimulation that exceeds what they are as a set" (Fuller 2005, 1). What comes into being or, rather, into thinking, then, is a dynamic network of differential relations between the various components. Félix Guattari gives a name to this dynamism that animates and differentiates the assemblage of concrete components over time: *abstract machine*. Because the differential push-and-pull of the abstract machine at the same time *sustains* the assemblage and *differentiates* it in time, it gives rise to an *auto*poietic *hetero*genesis, a *self*-creating becoming-*other*. If subjectivity is processual, continuously produced at the intersection of various, heterogeneous components, then there is no stable subject whose perception of (televisual) time is determined by an apparatus; there is only collective self-differentiation (see Guattari 1995, 33–57). Not incidentally, this way of emphasizing the collective becoming of the assemblage is, as Jussi Parikka notes, "a fundamentally and radically *temporal* way of looking at the world" (2010, 81, emphasis added).[21]

It becomes possible then to think the concrete components of today's television assemblage—be they technological, industrial, economic, or other—in terms of their creative potential and to articulate the ways in which they collectively effectuate singular movements of sensation (see also Rizzo 2015). One way of conceptualizing this way of bringing in abstraction, potential, and sensation without isolating them from concrete matter and assemblages is to think in terms of *technics*, understood as the complex of technology and the techniques it enables. The goal of the first chapter is precisely to articulate this relation between the concrete technologies of TV fiction and television's potential for creating innovative techniques and aesthetic movements, some of which are invested in a politics of perception aligned with the doctrine of preemption. In chapter 1, I define the *serial machine* as the singular abstract machine that animates the diagrammatic relations between the various components of contemporary television and that allows for a new aesthetic of television seriality to emerge. The chapter explores how the technology of television (with its new modes of production, distribution, consumption, etc.) has coevolved with a number of expressive machines, such as new genres, season formats, episode structures, long-arc narratives, complex temporalities, and more.[22]

The concept of the abstract machine also allows the continuities and discontinuities, the confluences and differentials within processes of becoming to be addressed in equal measure. For machines are as much about "conjunctions, connections, couplings, transitions, concatenations" as they are about "interruptions, ruptures, refractions, fragmentations" (Raunig 2010, 8, 9). Consider the genre of the soap opera as a brief example. The waning popularity of the soap opera is due in part to the fact that it does not connect with digital technologies in the same way other genres and formats do. Soap operas are not segmented into seasons and they are not made for rewatching. For these and other reasons, they hardly ever make it to the DVD market (except for the occasional special collection). This example, to be considered in more detail in the following chapter, indicates that the productivity of abstract machines is by no means a matter of flow and continuity alone. The serial machine sustains itself by disconnecting from other, henceforth minor genres of the serial format. But it also establishes new connections, which is particularly clear in the case of *Breaking Bad*. It has been repeatedly stated that the series would not have been successful without Netflix. Vince Gilligan, creator of the show, went so far as to say that "Netflix kept [*Breaking Bad*] on the air" (Sim 2016, 192; see also Landau 2016, 313). How can this be explained? The short answer is that video-on-demand services have opened up a new distribution window for content and, through this additional revenue, made edgier, more provocative programs intended for niche audiences financially viable. This explanation is certainly right but it also reduces *Breaking Bad*'s success to a matter of finding the right audience for the right program. *Figures of Time* intends to trace the more interesting follow-on and feedback effects that shift the television's machinic assemblage as a whole and allow for new modes of expression to emerge. For instance, one of the important achievements of digital TV networks and services like Netflix consists in overcoming TV studios' dependence on syndication, or the distribution of content to other, mainly local network affiliates for reruns. Syndication was a necessary industry component during the broadcast era because it allowed studios to make relatively large revenues on their mainly deficit-financed programs. But an attractive syndication deal comes with a number of requirements: a program should have accumulated a sizeable catalog of at least eighty episodes and ideally more than one hundred. It also helps if the episodes do not rely too much on continuous story arcs as the audience for reruns consists of mostly casual viewers. It does not surprise then that the most successful shows in syndication are sitcoms such as *Seinfeld* and *Friends*. In this way, syndication as a distribution strategy produces feedback effects on the kind of television content that gets produced in the first place.[23] It becomes clear also that a series like *Breaking Bad* hardly meets these requirements given its shorter seasons and its heavy reliance on an ongoing storyline. If *Seinfeld* is the classic case of a syndicated show, *Breaking Bad* is a prominent example of bingeable content. Binge-watching, in turn, makes for more attentive audiences and thus also allows for innovative, more complex storytelling (Tryon 2015, 110). Written and distributed in such a way as to enable continued watching, *Breaking Bad* illustrates that a singular aesthetic experience always comes into experience at the crosscurrents of various conditioning factors.

This insight feeds into the radically empirical approach chosen here. As James explains, "Against [the] rationalistic tendency to treat experience as chopped up into discontinuous static objects, radical empiricism protests. It insists on taking conjunctions at their 'face-value,' just as they come" (2003, 124). Thus, to understand the technics of contemporary TV, *Figures of Time* traces the entanglements of both enabling and deactivating relations within the assemblage of contemporary television. Crucially, this approach allows me to go beyond the stale and general discussions around "consumer agency." Recent discussions around this topic rely heavily on a conceptual framework that was developed in response to the introduction of remote control devices (RCDs) in the 1970s and 1980s. Critics believed that RCDs were a "subversive technology" because they wrested power away from the dominant networks and gave it to the viewer (Bellamy and Walker 1996, 1). While power was earlier understood in terms of choice and control alone, the list has more recently been extended to five c's, now including convenience, customization, and community (Lotz 2007, 245).[24] Either way, power is presented as something that can be possessed or lost, something that one wants to keep or take away from somebody. This book sets out to push against these discourses by showing that power is in the complex relations of an assemblage. Via the works of Michel Foucault and Gilles Deleuze, power is here conceived as relational, nonlocal as well as operational or ontogenetic.[25] As the brief examples of soap operas and the *Breaking Bad*–Netflix connection show, what can or cannot be done is not determined by any single party that "has" the power. What is and is not possible depends on a constellation of conditioning factors that are in turn transformed by the singular ways in which they relate as well as by that which they bring into the world. As much as *Breaking Bad* depended on a confluence of innovative practices in writing, production, and distribution, its success has also fed back into network management as a lesson on how initially low-rating programs can be turned into critical and commercial successes. This nonlinearity is why the serial machine and its components are continuously emergent: their ways of relating to one another produce them as provisional terms of a relation.

Chapter 1 thus shows how today's technics of television allows for a figural aesthetic. While the majority of *Figures of Time* is grounded in close reading and aesthetic analysis, this first chapter explores some of the key industrial and technological conditions for preemptive narratives. The chapter also defines the concept of the figural in a first engagement with *Damages*. Within the ecological framework for TV as a transformed medium, two of the book's central questions are: What is television capable of today? What are the new social and political potentials of contemporary TV? In *Figures of Time*, I understand television—a medium many of us live with on a daily basis—as a vector of subjectivation that inflects our individual and collective existence. If television as a medium is undergoing considerable changes, then we must ask how the transformations feed back into the wider context of contemporary culture. The recent transformations of the medium have allowed it to participate in the development of new modes of perception, particularly as regards the aesthetic experience of time. More specifically, then, chapter 1 explores in depth to what extent television's contribution to a popular preemptive nonconscious is conditioned upon a number of technical factors. The overall claim defended throughout the book is that television has a new propensity to create singular experiences of time—to *make time*—which also allows it to participate in the political operationalization of time and, in particular, of the future. What's more, my exploration of the serial machine will show that this push toward complex temporalities is particular to television, if not exactly unique to it. Looking at the genealogy of preemptive narratives, we will see that they are firmly grounded in televisual conventions and innovations. So, to the question occasionally raised as to whether television still matters in a postnetwork era, whether it even still exists, I respond that it does and that the medium's continuing relevance lies in the shifting political alliances that it forms in a highly mediated world, the innovative and singular modes of expression that it gives rise to, and the qualitatively new aesthetic experiences it enables.

Aesthetics: Making Time

It is evident that a particular concept of time is already at work in the technics of the serial machine. If I subsequently think narrative, politics, and ethics along the same lines, this is not, however, because the approach taken here is as determinist as that of certain conceptions of "cinematic" or "televisual" time. The decisive difference is that, in this approach, it is not the apparatus that comes first but time itself. For if time is thought as the creative self-differentiation of a topological world, then *everything* discussed in this book—from media technics to preemption politics and then on to the control society—must fall within the purview of this concept. This claim rejoins the earlier contention that, in this thinking, there is no "out of time." We shall see, in fact, that we can let go of distinctions between inside and outside altogether and simply say that everything *is* time—*space-time*—and, more precisely, spacetime in the making.[26]

What does it mean to say that a television series "makes" time and gives it to perception? First, the way in which contemporary television makes time goes beyond mere representations of time. As an example, consider the British television series *Life on Mars*. It is an interesting show to engage with in this respect because it offers three different representational logics for its story. A present-day police inspector has an accident and, when he comes to, finds himself in 1973. Has he traveled in time, is he in a coma, or is he mad? Each of these premises—time travel, (un)consciousness, and madness—resonates with a specific concept of time or an aspect thereof. Interestingly, though, the three representations of time in *Life on Mars* are mutually exclusive: if you look at the story through one representational logic, you temporarily cancel out the other two. More importantly, no single representation can account for what is actually going on in the image; time is irreducible to any one representation. If one forces it into a representational logic nonetheless, one aspect of it or another is bound to be lost. Eventually, the continuous oscillation between the different premises undermines an increasingly unstable narrative and foregrounds the processual form-taking of the image. So while *Life on Mars* takes the viewer out of various representations of time, it does not take her "out of time." An aesthetic theory that wants to account for the creativity and efficacy of perception cannot begin with notions of coded signification or representation because images—televisual, filmic, or otherwise—are not already bound up with a meaning or a *signifier* to form stable, repeatable signs (in the way that the sound and signifier \'trē\ is bound up with the little drawing of a tree in Ferdinand de Saussure's notorious model of the linguistic sign). Instead, "the image *gives rise* to signs" (Deleuze 1986, 69, emphasis added). Moving images employ their available resources (color, contrast, depth, focus, sound, etc.) to create meaning, to make sense, potentially differently each time. This is a way of approaching moving-image narratives that does not discredit representation; rather, it takes a conceptual step back to see *what else* there is and to integrate representation as one way of making sense among many.

What else is there, then? There is sensation, irreducible to the sense perception of images and sounds alone. The experience of audiovisual material does not exhaust itself in an appeal to eyes and ears: it melts the senses into one another. We see and hear, obviously. But we also have goose bumps, cringe and flinch, gasp and cry.[27] The important point is that when, for instance, a horror film or series scares us out of our seat, our reaction does not pass through signification, representation, or reflection. The horror film's orchestral stab, often used to do the job, carries its name for a reason: it is a signal that directly hits the senses and produces a visceral reaction. From this vantage, the "spectator is no longer passively receiving optical information, but exists as a bodily being, enmeshed acoustically, senso-motorically, somatically, and affectively in the film's visual texture and soundscape" (Elsaesser and Hagener 2010, 10). This, then, is what I mean by *aesthetics*: not the poetic codes of a genre or format, nor the current set of "narrative devices" in TV fiction, but rather the perceptual dynamics and intensities of sensation specific to a given media ecology.[28] *Figures of Time* explores these dynamics between television series and the viewer, between the medium and the body as forms of knowing, as modes of thought. The contention is that television series trigger experiential movements through time that bring something to expression that is not thought representationally.

These suprarepresentational forces of expression of the image will be called *figures of time*, following Gilles Deleuze's notion of the figural developed in his consideration of Francis Bacon's paintings. As the following chapter explores in detail, the figural is a concept for thinking beyond the figura*tive*, to speak of the ways art has of "capturing forces" and "*directly* relating them to sensation" (see Deleuze 2004b, 31). What comes into focus then is the *immediate* experience of the medium, not what is represented in or mediated by the image but how the image itself is experienced. While this immediate aspect of experience may be fairly easy to grasp in the above-mentioned example of the orchestral hit, it is much less evident how we may think the visceral sensation of an aesthetic movement that is not startling and bloodcurdling but is painted into a still canvas or slowly unfolds over hours of viewing. The challenge is to think the direct or immediate without reducing it to the fast and easy. The figural impact of one of Bacon's paintings can slowly grow on the spectator just as the figural movement of the TV shows considered here slowly builds from the interval that is opened up between the preempted ending and the present moment. This book proposes the concept of the *figure* and a method of figural analysis to think TV's serial movements through time as an abstract shape slowly but directly crafted into sensation and that must be understood as an important site for the image's political efficacy. In chapter 1, figures are conceived as the singular aesthetic experiences that "lift off" from a narrative assemblage co-conditioned by the innovative serial machine (Massumi 2011, 19–20).[29] Figures, as they are defined here, are neither rhetorical strategies nor formal elements of moving images but *events* or *effects* produced in the encounter between moving images and the viewer.[30] Figures are fundamentally *relational* because they emerge within a favorable constellation of conditioning factors, and *processual* because they occur over time, feed into other processes, and eventually fade. Finally, figures are *asignifying* because the way in which they make sense is not reliant upon coded and conventionalized signification; instead, figures require and foster what Guattari calls "non-discursive, pathic knowledge," a kind of thinking directly through the senses (1995, 25). Grounded in such a concept, figural analysis is a method for studying the procedural modulation of affective forces running through moving-image narratives. As Alanna Thain puts it in her engagement with cinema: "This figural form of analysis gets us productively lost in the medium via *attention to passage itself*, taking a lost highway rather than the royal road of narrative analysis. Being lost in the medium subjects us to these *de-ranging effects of reading time against the grain*. . . . The figural attunes us to the *plastic temporality* of film figures as the unique materiality of the film as audiovisual image and the mutable, even 'virtual' side of film" (2017, 51–52, emphasis added). Figural analysis emphasizes the audiovisual materiality of moving-image narratives and asks how the images and sound we perceive are not already *in* time but create a singular experience of time in the first place. In conjunction with its specific argument regarding preemption politics, *Figures of Time* intends to make a valuable addition to nonrepresentational methodologies by analyzing the political impact of narrative media through a particular focus on temporal movements. It is worth noting that while the argument of this book requires a strong focus on preemption politics and warrants a select corpus of programs relating to themes of crime and justice, the method proposed here can be productive across the boundaries of academic disciplines. In other words, and as the important precursors in the fields of literary theory, art theory, and film studies suggest, figural analysis is a transdisciplinary approach to media. If in this book I develop an aesthetic theory of *televisual* figures of time in particular, this is because the resulting method of figural analysis allows me to unfold the various aspects of this book's central political argument regarding preemption as a mode of televisual aesthetics. This focus on the aesthetic experience of time and figural analysis is also the reason why *Francis Bacon: The Logic of Sensation* and *Bergsonism* are my central reference points within Deleuze's work. Other relevant texts such as *The Logic of Sense* and its preoccupation with serialization support the argument intermittently but do not provide its backbone. And although the *Cinema* books are an important reference point throughout the following chapters, some readers may find that they do not figure quite as prominently as they might expect from a book as indebted to Deleuze's thinking as this one. This is again because this book draws on Deleuze's engagement with the nexus of aesthetic experience, time, and affect across his entire oeuvre (including the *Cinema* books) but also because of a certain dissatisfaction with the inflationary and thus less productive use of terms like the time-image in what is sometimes dubbed Deleuze studies.

Focusing on what moving-image assemblages effectuate, *Figures of Time* attempts not to pin down all their formal qualities with descriptive accuracy but to see what they *do*, what they give to experience. Such a "functionalist conception" of aesthetics, which "only considers the function a quality fulfills in a specific assemblage, or in passing from one assemblage to another," focuses on the ways in which, in the present case, the production of temporalities is ecologically carried by a relational field in which a technic (in itself complex) intersects with modes of media consumption, social and political ecologies, and other attending existential domains (Deleuze and Guattari 1987, 306).[31] For instance, binge-watching, enabled by serial repetition as well as long narrative arcs and technologically supported by distribution on DVD and through on-demand platforms, is a functional component of the serial machine that facilitates a figural aesthetic. The intensive engagement and sustained temporality of long viewing sessions create a new sensitivity to the aesthetic idiosyncrasies and minor perceptual movements of television's long serial narratives. Binge-watching is functional in the present account in that it creates an attentional disposition that allows the concrete materiality of serial narratives to take figural effect.

How, then, can we describe the figure of time that *Breaking Bad*'s media ecology composes for? What does it effectuate? How does it make sense without signifying? One might be tempted to say that Walter

White's precarious present is experienced as a hopeless deadlock that makes escape impossible (see, e.g., Freeley 2014, 48–50). But precariousness is not synonymous to a lack of potential. On the contrary, Walter's case makes it amply clear that a precarious present—precisely because there is no security to be found in tried-and-tested solutions—makes previously unimaginable paths of action conceivable. What comes into sensation when we glimpse the innocent teacher's future as a meth cook in the pilot is the interval between these two moments in time, an interval open wide with the potential for radical change. First, then, the preemptive movement brings into sensation that precarity is potentializing in the most unpredictable ways. Moreover, *Breaking Bad*'s repeated loops through the future make felt that a precarious present, far from being an impasse of imposed immobility, *compels* to action. When Walter declares to Jesse that he will only cook the meth and refuses to have anything to do with its distribution, we already—by way of the image's intercutting between present and future—see him walk away from the scene of an accident, blood-smeared moneybag in hand ("Crazy Handful of Nothin'"). The preemptive loop relentlessly pushes the precarious present toward the limit of permanent collapse, a limit from which one only returns by way of yet another reluctant self-differentiation. *Breaking Bad*'s temporal movement conveys the extent to which Walt's existence has become a continuous act of enforced self-transformation that serves the sole and sad purpose of saving him from one near-impossibility to the next. In this way, the series crafts a figural movement—co-conditioned by the complex set of innovative writing, production, distribution, and viewing practices described earlier—that articulates the temporality of neoliberal subjectivation as an enforced propensity toward flexible self-differentiation in the midst of a present atremble with inauspicious potentialities.

Figures of Time explores the political import of such temporal movements in and of narrative. Along the way, it is hoped, the book becomes a proposition for watching television differently, *productively*, by which I mean once again that we engage with television as a vector of subjectivation in a variety of ways, attuning to or inflecting the directions in which it takes us. This book is itself the product of such an attunement that thinks with television's preemptive narratives to create an aesthetics, a politics, and ultimately an ethics of time. If the narrative movement of the preemptive loop intersects with a political ecology, then how do we engage with it? The answer will potentially have to be different in each case because each program inserts itself differently into the existing ecology of media, culture, and politics. And each program engages the viewer differently. Chapter 2 engages with *Life on Mars* to illustrate the subjectivating force of participatory viewing, which should not be understood as the active production of meaning by the viewer. Rather, we will see that the viewer co-composes—in concert with the narrative—the making and unfolding of immediately felt time. Furthermore, the chapter teases out important differences between the concurring concepts of time that it puts into play, ultimately arguing for an understanding of time as creative becoming.

Conceived in this way, figures of time are more than fictional models of what Richard Grusin has called *premediation* to describe the relation between media and affect. Grusin shows that, after 9/11, American news networks have tapped into the "affectivity of anticipation" to develop "a form of medial pre-emption" (2010, 4, 2). Media no longer only mediate preexisting content. In a globalized and accelerated world characterized by uncertainty and fear, they cover possible future events as much as the past, potentialities as much as actualities. His example is once again the war in Iraq, which was mediated at least a year before it started: "The mediation of war and its aftermath always preceded the events themselves, . . . such real events as war and its aftermath occurred only after they had also been premediated by networked media, by government spokesmen, and by the culture at large" (45). In the logic of premediation, the main goal of media is not to convey reliable information but to attune the public to a shared affective state of fear and to create the felt necessity for security measures.[32] This is a valuable reminder that the political must not be thought in terms of nation-states and governments alone. The dynamics of preemption make clear that "Big Politics" cannot be disentangled from the micropolitical, from individual or shared affect, and that their entanglement passes through the media. In this book, the political is understood as just such a complex articulation of the macro and the micro. In the end, however, my focus on aesthetics, sensation, and affect is also the reason why the term *premediation* itself rarely makes it into my own writing even though the logic it describes is pervasive in the preemptive TV series addressed in this book. It is because preemptive figures of time are *directly* felt, *immediately* sensed, that this project is less interested in what is re- or premediated than in what is "immediated"(Thain 2017, 2, 11–12).[33] This is yet another way of saying that the approach proposed here is more interested in the figural than in the figurative. I insist, now and repeatedly throughout this book, that this shift in perspective does not discard narrative in any way but looks at it differently. It is, to borrow a phrase from Andrew Murphie, a "shift away from an interest in representation to *operation*," in this case: away from narrative as representation to *narrative as an operation* (2002, 193). The key question to be answered is not How do these narratives represent the future? (Though it is answered in passing.) Instead, I examine the following questions: What kinds of aesthetic experience does the narrative loop through the future activate? What kinds of movements—of perception, of thought—does this narrative move enable or foreclose on this side, our side, of the screen?

A tentative, general answer would be to say that preemptive narratives create aesthetic experiences that make time felt as a complex and creative process. Having indicated why such a concept of time is crucial to an adequate understanding of the *technics* of serial TV fiction and their *aesthetics*, it must be noted that it can also produce a more appropriate understanding of the *politics* in question here. Many theoretical discourses on the experience of time in modernity have foregrounded the aspect of speed and acceleration. Since Alvin Toffler's seminal work from 1970, the notion of the "future shock" has been associated with the loss of permanence produced by "the roaring current of change" (3). However, the problem of change—that is, time and the future—is largely reduced to the "accelerative thrust" in sociocultural processes and the general lack of "adaptivity" among the population (4). In the recent *Futurism of the Instant*, Paul Virilio continues to argue that the extreme acceleration of life through information and communication technologies has contracted our experience of time to an "omnipresent instant"; it has "exhausted chronodiversity" and produced the "atemporeity" of experience or a "hygiene of Time" (2010, 71, 72, 102). The difficulties these concepts pose are the same as in the case of the notion of "atemporal cinema" for they evoke a lack of experiential complexity that is belied by the processes of contemporary politics. If anything, contemporary politics (and serial narratives, for that matter) operate in more complex ways than ever before, which is to say, they are fundamentally nonlinear and co-causal processes.[34] In the geopolitical situation of the twenty-first century, sociocultural and sociopolitical processes speak not only to acceleration and instantaneity but, more importantly and worryingly, to shocks induced by means of recursive loops, nonlinear causalities, and complex modulations.[35] The concepts proposed here try to account for these developments.

Chapter 3 proposes a reading of *Flashforward* that foregrounds the temporal complexity of preemption. I will show that while the series figuratively (i.e., on the level of representation) continues to adhere to discourses of prevention and choice-based politics, the figural movement of the series thwarts any resistance to institutional politics and helps enforce a general consensus. In other words, the figurative focus on discourses of acceleration and prevention in *Flashforward* covers up the powerful figural dynamic of preemption.

Ethics: Surviving Complexity

The wager of this book is that the concepts it offers, as they open up new potentials for thought, also enable new modes of action that allow individuals to respond to the changed requirements of an increasingly complex life environment and mediascape in particular. This complexity can be usefully thought through the concept of *control* as contrasted with the Foucauldian notion of discipline (Deleuze 1995, 169–82). Within a social context of control, individuals can no longer assure success by fulfilling reliable norms or following codes. While the disciplinary society imposed a mold or form that individuals can *con*form to, the control society continuously modulates or *re*forms its requirements. For individuals, this amounts to a qualitative change of how they are held to behave and perform. Instead of proving themselves against a general standard of evaluation, they are more likely to be pitted against one another, trying to outperform competitors by constantly investing in themselves in order to "get an edge." While such self-improvement may well pass through the conventional channels of education and professional training, it more and more often requires so-called soft skills and affective labor ranging from flexibility over creativity to likability.[36] Intensified self-differentiation is the coerced virtue of the control society.

Crucially, the shift toward control, whose mechanisms are closely tied to the economic principles of neoliberalism, also produces a transformation in the ways that morality and crime are considered within society. Foucault himself addresses this issue in his lectures *The Birth of Biopolitics*. American neoliberalism, he writes, promotes the "inversion of the relationships of the social to the economic" so that economy is no longer in the service of and regulated by social concerns but, instead, is given analytical primacy over all other domains of social life (Foucault 2008, 240). As a consequence, the economic model expands and generalizes into an "analytical schema or grid of intelligibility" of society as a whole in such a way that "everything . . . can be analyzed in terms of investment, capital costs, and profit" (243, 244). As Foucault shows, this model ultimately applies to criminality as well. As opposed to the anthropological criminologists of the nineteenth century who believed that one could be a "born criminal" or physiologically predisposed toward criminal behavior, "in [the neoliberal] perspective the criminal is not distinguished in any way by or interrogated on the basis of moral or anthropological traits. The criminal is nothing other than absolutely anyone whomsoever. The criminal, any person, is treated only as anyone whomsoever who invests in an action, expects a profit from it, and who accepts the risk of a loss" (253). In other words, a criminal—like Walter White—is just another *homo œconomicus*, an economic man, and crime is just another way of making a living, albeit at a higher risk. At the same time, the aim of penal policy is no longer the complete eradication of crime on moral grounds but the regulation of the market for crime. Foucault quotes economist Gary Becker's formulation of the two questions that will henceforth guide penal policy and law enforcement: "How many offences should be permitted? Second, how many offenders should go unpunished?" Note that these are quantitative questions that subordinate qualitative concerns regarding the nature and gravity of crime. To determine these quantities, neoliberals ask at what point the investments made into law enforcement and crime prevention become unprofitable—that is, at which point a higher investment no longer corresponds to a lower crime rate. Crime that persists beyond that cut-off point will be a tolerated (business) activity. In short, the mechanisms of control and those of neoliberalism are complementary in that the former dynamize social relations and open them up toward continued modulation while the latter reevaluate social activity in primarily economic terms—such as performance and profitability—and subordinate other modes of valuation, for instance through moral values. How is an individual's life affected by such a fundamental shift in a society's functional principles? What are the effects and challenges of these transformations?

Contemporary television negotiates these questions of neoliberalism and control through its many antiheroes like Walter White, Dexter, Tony Soprano, Hannibal, *True Detective*'s Rust Cohle, Annelise Keating from *How to Get Away with Murder*, or Patty Hughes from *Damages*. The problem at the core of these series is not whether a character's behavior is morally "good" or "bad." (The answer to that question is easy: bad.) The problem to be thought consists precisely in the paradox that what old-fashioned minds might consider immoral behavior has long become necessary and even advisable under conditions of control and neoliberalism. A show like *Dexter* (Showtime, 2006–13) operates on the premise that if law enforcement limits its efficiency according to the requirements of due procedure or extramoral, economic criteria, then those who seek justice and social order must themselves move outside the law. (This is also, of course, the definition of the "state of exception.") Television's corrupt and criminal cops suggest that the police apparatus is too faithful to its outdated disciplinary origins and therefore incapable of moving at the speed and in the same directions of crime. When lawful action is slow and toothless, the only efficient way to fight crime is crime—this is the mantra of many contemporary police procedurals and legal dramas, including the ones discussed here. In chapter 4, I return to *Damages* to show that the recent transformations within the genre of the legal drama are television's way of participating in the socioeconomic shift from discipline to control.

To fight crime by bypassing the law, to move like one's enemy: these, too, are characteristics of preemption (see Massumi 2015, 12). It seems to me that, for a lot of fictional TV of recent years, narrative preemption has become the launching pad for explorations of the question how one can move through such a complex social field, how one can survive the control society. In *Breaking Bad*, the pressures of control and neoliberalism lead to a game of evasion in which Walter White is always just about to get caught, a social slalom that requires an extreme agility and sensitivity to shifts in the environment.[37] Walter and more generally *Breaking Bad* deploy impressive diversionary tactics, perform virtuoso just-in-time solutions, and creatively play with laws and rules (of narrative). Saul Goodman, the lawyer who helps Walter break the law, is an important figure in this respect inasmuch as he emphatically uses and abuses the law for economic gain. The above-mentioned trickery of the pink teddy bear is an example of how the narrative itself stretches its own rules to mislead the viewer in a complex way that is just related enough to be accepted as plausible. As I explore further in chapter 4, preemptive narratives do to the viewer as their protagonists do to their own fictional surroundings.

The proposition here is to follow these movements and modulations of the image, foregrounded by the preemptive loop, in order to develop perceptual techniques for moving through and surviving the control society. *Figures of Time* is ultimately an ethico-aesthetic project to the extent that it explores how we can attune our perception to the nonlinear and shifty processes that constitute our contemporary (media) environment. The goal is not to embrace the functionings of the control society but to critically assess and inflect them toward more livable conditions. Following Deleuze and Foucault, I argue that this task necessitates a change in thinking from moral to ethical requirements.[38] Here, morality is understood as a system of judgment based on a preexisting set of transcendent and immutable values, whereas an ethics considers the continuous recomposition of relations within a given environment. In a dynamic field of relations, the ethical requirement would be to adapt one's capacities to affect and to be affected in such a way as to create mutually sustainable relations, to maintain the field's liveliness. This creates two major differences between a morality and an ethics. First, the constraints of an ethics are not immutable, transcendent values but variable, immanent criteria. And second, an ethical practice does not produce judgments but continuous *experimentation*. Experimentation within a relational field is inevitably an *ecological* practice, leading to what Isabelle Stengers calls an "ecology of practices" (2010, 37). The first thing Stengers says about ecologies of practices is, once again, that that they create their own values. These immanent criteria that are invented as various, heterogeneous beings pose the situated "question of what counts for its mode of life" (37). From this angle, an ecology is the dynamic and therefore always only metastable constellation of various modes of life that overlap and intersect in such a way as to tentatively re-create their metastable commingling for the next now. A key requirement in this respect is *attention*. To take one's place in an ecology is to be aware of how the multiple and entangled forces intersect to maintain a metastable collectivity. In a second step, attention must facilitate the invention of *techniques* understood as situated practices, however molecular they may be, that cocreate the ecology in a future-oriented, repotentializing manner.

The concept through which this book will articulate this dynamic response to control and open up its aesthetic project toward a practical media philosophy is that of the *procedure*. Drawing on the work of artist-philosophers Madeline Gins and Arakawa, chapter 4 will conceive procedures as "processes linked, no matter how briefly, to awareness" and "staged" by a concrete assemblage of conditioning elements such as materials, textures, sounds, perspectives, techniques, and so on (2002, 53). The emphasis on composing-for-procedures highlights that aesthetic experience cannot be separated out from its concrete narrative assemblage. In a way, this is the inverse of the argument so far. Until now, I have stressed that there is more to a TV show than narrative structure and concrete images, that there are suprarepresentational, directly felt movements through time. What Gins and Arakawa stress is that this excess, to be accessed or "entered wittingly" (53), must be carefully composed for. One must rigorously compose with concrete "features and elements" and give them "physical shape" to effectuate a procedure (Gins and Arakawa 2006, 115). So in the end, the ethical questions are the following: How do you build for a procedure? How can you compose for a lift-off? How do you combine concrete techniques to form a metastable aesthetic ecology? Chapter 4 answers these questions in an engagement with the legal thriller *Damages* because it rigorously composes with three specific visual and narrative techniques to create a singular sensation of futurity. To be sure, *Damages* plays with its audience in ways that are generally similar to those deployed by *Breaking Bad*. The series loops future visions into our perception to mislead, manipulate, and trick us. However, it preempts its future not to overdetermine the present but to flush the viewer's perception with potential. In this way, the viewer becomes herself a radical empiricist held to register a multiplicity of possible relations between different characters, parallel plot strands, and moments in time. So instead of making the viewer engage in a politics of fear, the preemptive narrative of *Damages* enables a procedure that fosters speculation as a generative technique, asking what else is possible, how else a situation can play out. Through this procedure, the series aligns itself with a speculative pragmatism to the extent that it firmly (radically empirically) grounds us in its perceptual ecology and at the same time asks that we perceive at each moment the various futurities that this present contains only in germ. As the viewer learns to hold this potential and navigate the image's complex figure of time, the perceptual ecology that *Damages* composes for comes to function as an aesthetic training ground for alternative modes of perception, modes of confronting and rechanneling the demands of the control society.

So when morality and ethics are opposed in the present account, it is not to suggest that an ethical practice is "nicer" or "easier" to do. Likewise, the conceptual contrast between discipline and control does not imply that one is more or less sufferable than the other. The key point is that each regime of power comes with its own requirements. While the requirements of the control society are perhaps *less strict* than those of the disciplinary society, they are for that very reason *more demanding* in their insistence that individuals continuously attend to ever-changing relations in their shared environment. However, the contention of this book is that these aspects of attention, co-composition, and movement can be procedurally articulated and inflected toward productive modes of ethico-aesthetic engagement. Any engagement with a surrounding ecology, whether considered from a technological, perceptual, political, or other viewpoint, should consider that what an ecology "wants"—its tendency—is the potentializing continuation of its process. This also holds for the ways in which academic thought enters the media ecology of contemporary television series. For this reason, this book does not provide an objective outsider's perspective to produce positive knowledge but stages encounters between (academic) thinking and (creative) doing. This is also why, for instance, the final chapter does not end in a conclusion but in an invitation. The last word is a first step toward renewed action: a set of propositions to inflect our modes of attending within the media ecology of serial TV fiction. For, if preemptive narratives spark powerful perceptual dynamics relating to new political paradigms, we need strategies for engaging with them. As the following chapters show, preemptive narratives draw on the aesthetic force of contemporary television to drop image-bombs into sensation and creatively disrupt our sense of temporal and political orientation. How can we defuse such an explosive aesthetic or, better yet, channel its force into a productive politics of futurity (instead of looping the future into a politics of fear)? The focus on the generative force of procedures adopted here is a reminder that procedural thinking and doing are *speculative* and *experimental*. One cannot know what a procedure will end up doing, where it will move thought, and that is precisely why one should follow it. *Figures of Time* is an attempt to take the arsenal of contemporary television and turn it into ethico-aesthetic sparklers.

CHAPTER 1

THE SERIAL MACHINE

Toward Figures of Time

The Machine at Work

To begin thinking about the aesthetic experience of temporal complexity through the concept of the *figural*, I would like to start with an example. What stands out, still, after more than two thousand minutes of *Damages* is the opening sequence of thirty-five seconds:

A solemn symphonic score sets in on a black screen, each musical phrase measured by the single ring of a triangle. The scene opens to a crisp Manhattan morning, the grainy image washed in a hue of pale yellow (see figure 1.1). Pedestrians cross the street, walking backward. Cut to a cab waiting at a red light. Enter smoke—wafting in reverse: instead of billowing from its source into an extended haze, it concentrates and intensifies into a dense fog returning to where it came from. Following is a shot of the star-spangled banner waving backward in time, then more smoke gathering in front of a grid of scaffolding (see figure 1.2). Cut to the entrance of an apartment building (see figure 1.3). A biker passes by, driving *forward*. Time has changed directions. Then stillness, as movement seems to have left the image. And silence almost: the score fades out into an eerie, vibrating hum. After an interval of two or three seconds measured by the triangle, cut closer to the same building entrance. Stillness again. The triangle rings: cut to a closed elevator door (see figure 1.4). There is no motion in the image yet but the ring of the triangle, which is now the bell of the elevator and signals imminent action. "Something's doing" behind the image (Massumi 2011, 1). Eventually, the elevator door opens. Adjust focus. There she is: a young woman, covered in blood, shivering, fleeing from the building we have only just entered (see figure 1.5). Follow her.

Or rewind. Go back. (Because you *can*.) What has just happened? Certainly, this opening scene establishes the setting for the story. It sets a certain mood. Its slowness creates suspense. The very absence of human action in an urban setting suggests that something is astir. However, while there is no *human* action in this opening scene, there is movement everywhere: movement *in* and *of* the image. What is at stake here from the very beginning is a set of linkages between the various (abstract and concrete) components of the image: time, perception, and media technology. These connections can be traced individually.

Consider the smoke—or any kind of foggy, gaseous accumulation. Such mist is at no two moments identical to itself. In this sequence as anywhere else, smoke continuously differs in shape, density, and opacity. Moreover, it blurs the contours of the environment it fills. Mist "betrays, completely fills the environment with potential things" (Serres 2008, 70). Here, it covers and uncovers the orderly scaffolding, makes visible and invisible. For Michel Serres, this is how "mist disturbs ontology" (70). What it foregrounds instead is onto*genesis*, or becoming. The smoke in *Damages* is a first rendering of time. It figures the continuous differentiation that lies at the heart of a concept of duration: "Duration is *what differs from itself*" (Deleuze 2004a, 37). If there is creation and novelty in the world, this is not only because things change *in* time but first and foremost because time itself "is invention or it is nothing at all" (Bergson 2007a, 341). The smoke in *Damages* confirms this: there is no precomposed body here that moves through a determinable sequence of poses. Rather, mist is generative of itself at every instant of its becoming. It is a topological figure: drawing on its potential for variation, it creates its next now by folding forth into the world. This smoky figure connects with another element of the imagescape, the grid of scaffolding. The two contrast in many ways: The grid of scaffolding is a stable, regular construct of horizontals and verticals intersecting at right angles. As a support structure, it literally allows for construction. It is order for the purpose of efficient action. But, lacking human action, it is also where nothing happens in these images. Smoke, as we have seen, is quite the opposite: it continuously self-differentiates. Its very instability allows it to happen to the orderly grid. Blurry as they are, mists edge into the world, spill over contours, and consume color. But, while blurring ontology, mists do not undo it. What we get with the fuzzy texture of fog is a sense of topology, of becoming-with our environment as we move through it. Self-variation according to one's

Figure 1.1. *Damages*: establishing shot of New York.

Figure 1.2. *Damages*: fog passing in front of and through a scaffold.

Figure 1.3. *Damages*: building entrance.

Figure 1.4. *Damages*: elevator door close-up.

Figure 1.5. *Damages*: Ellen Parsons (Rose Byrne) in elevator.

own potentials and in relation with the world is duration. This is the importance of the first performer in *Damages*, smoke. Its frayed hues of pale yellow give us a sense of time as creative becoming that is first of all relational and nonhuman—"nonhuman" because it goes beyond the human without excluding it, because it introduces the human to a world that is already becoming. In this way, *Damages* sets a first challenge to conventional notions of time.

In another linkage, this first experience of time in *Damages* is immediately captured by the temporal order of reverse motion. The simplicity of this technique should not belie its experiential complexity for a reverse sequence is not simply the mirror image of the original sequence. Smoke wafting backward is not the mere "opposite" or "inversion" of smoke wafting forward; it is *qualitatively* different.[1] The eerie, forceful beauty of *Damages*' opening scene suggests an unnatural control over time as the sequence reverses the irreversible, as it captures the smoke and contains its spillage. Note that this process of containment is different from the first linkage between smoke and grid: the movement of the smoke *within* the image is captured by the movement *of* the image itself. The technique gets hold of becoming and, in so doing, foregrounds the technological mechanism by which television articulates time: the regular (but reversible) succession of contingent frames. This does not mean that we consciously *see* the superposition of frames in time, let alone that the experience of time in audiovisual narrative is necessarily "unnatural." The important aspect here is that *technique* calls upon *technology* to feed into an experience of time. This inevitable coupling of technique and technology is a *technic*. What this technics achieves in the present case is to make *felt* the quality of technology, to make it an integral part of the experience of time that the sequence gives. This feltness or "qualitative experience of technology" is the sequence's "technicity" (Lamarre 2009, xxiii).[2] The second linkage then suggests that television as a technic can powerfully yet effortlessly and beautifully get a hold on duration. It can homogenize, linearize, and manipulate time. The concept that enables this process is one of chronological, metric, scientific time.[3] It is profoundly human. Thus, while the smoke conveys a sense of becoming in nonhuman terms and places the human *within* it, reverse motion complicates this movement by manipulating it from without. This sequence is a preview of one of the main concerns in *Damages* as well as the other TV series discussed in this book: the technics of manipulating perceptions of time.

But, on yet another level, this technical capture is also a resistance. The third linkage of *Damages* is that it is a television series that starts by going backward. It swims against television's current. Or better yet: it wants to get out of the current, get rid of it. This current has been famously described by Raymond Williams as television's "flow."[4] This term designates the various and interwoven "series of timed units" that obliterate the unit as such. These series include (1) the programs to be broadcast, (2) commercial breaks, and (3) trailers advertising subsequent programs. Williams rightly observes that the time interval for commercial breaks and trailers at the same time *interrupts* the individual program and *connects* one program to others. Ultimately, the effect of this broadcasting technic is to relegate the continuity of individual programs to the background and to foreground continuity at another level, that of a program *sequence* as "planned flow." Insisting on its never-ending presentness, network television pulls the viewer into an anesthetizing current of indeterminate and self-obliterating contents: "Television thrives on its own forgettability" (Doane 1990, 226). Television's flow, Williams concludes, is "perhaps the defining characteristic of broadcasting, simultaneously as a technology and as a cultural form," that is, as a technic.

Perhaps this is no longer the case. If one of *Damages*' main concerns is to decompose metric time, the opening scene of the show signals that this project is also one of breaking out of television's broadcasting flow. Instead of flowing carelessly ahead, each coming frame in this reverse-motion sequence folds back on its own immediate past. The image does not distend and wear out time into a shallow and continuous flow. As a technique in this sequence, reverse motion folds the moving image back on itself; it creases time and makes it dense, intense. When the image cuts to the entrance/elevator shots, time almost seems to halt—almost, because the passage of time is still felt through the jitter of the grainy image and the ring of the triangle/elevator bell. Each toll of the bell signals the completion of an interval of time that seems to be devoid of action. But as we hear the extremities of intervals and the lack of efficient action, we also sense the grainy rustle of the image. The richness of these shots lies in their foregrounding of the duration between measured points of time. What is felt is the quality of time as it slows down without thinning out. Here, time is felt as both extensive and intensive at the same time.

This opening sequence speaks to the new potentials of fictional television for going beyond plot-driven narrative, technology as a mere material support, and flow as a mode of indifferent consumption. Over the last twenty years or so, television has fundamentally changed both "as a technology and as a social practice," to use Williams's phrase. As a technology, television no longer passes through the TV set exclusively: it has incorporated recording devices like VCR, DVD, and, more recently, video-on-demand (VOD) platforms such as Hulu or Netflix; it has gone online to official homepages, episode guides, fan forums, smartphone applications, and social media. As a social practice, the television experience is no longer confined to a sequential flow of broadcasting. Experiencing television henceforth passes through practices of rewatching, blogging, tweeting, gaming, rating, speculating, and many more.[5] Part and parcel of what I call the serial machine, these practices are also techniques for resingularizing individual programs. Six years after its first airing, the opening sequence of *Damages* is *not* forgotten because digital archives create the possibility for qualitatively different ways of watching and studying TV. Finally, the numerous shifts in serial production have created a remarkable variety of narrative temporalities: speeds and slownesses, extensions and intensions, loops, intervals, anachronisms, and so forth.

It is not evident how these changes and their relatedness might best be addressed. Returning to the example of *Damages*' opening scene, so far we have three linkages that make for three potentially contradictory arguments on time depending on which components of the experience one pulls out: (1) the smoke that veils the grid and renders duration supplanting metric time; (2) the technique of reverse motion, which captures the smoke and conveys the opposite: cinematic time containing duration; and (3) the technics of this sequence, which resist television's flow as a "social form" or practice. While all these arguments address one aspect of *Damages*' opening sequence, none of them can sufficiently describe these thirty-five seconds of felt time. The reason is that none of experience's components—image content, technique, technology, social practice—can be separated out without reducing the complexity of experience. Nor can this complexity be grasped by a single conceptual pair. As we have seen, the terms of apparent oppositions—such as grid/smoke, human/nonhuman, technique/technology, technology/social practice, and percept/concept—overlap and fold into each other to create a singular sensation of time. What opposes in thought composes in experience.[6] Therefore, rather than as stand-alone oppositions, it may be more useful to think these pairs as functional linkages that are themselves connected among each other. These interconnected linkages create a dynamic constellation whose effects are transversal to the neatly separable, structural levels of, say, "content," "discursive articulation," "material support," "social relations," and so on. The opening sequence of *Damages* creates a *machinic assemblage* in a very conspicuous way, imbricating various temporalities into one another toward experiential effect. The effect that

Damages' opening sequence composes for is a sensation of time, if only in germ. Time is experienced as a heterogeneous movement of creation, inflected by a variety of processes feeding into one another. This effect is not a representation of time; it is what will be called a figure of time.

Figures of Time

In *Francis Bacon: The Logic of Sensation*, Gilles Deleuze conceives the figural as a way of going beyond the "figurative, illustrative, and narrative character" of art (2004b, 6). Going beyond is not the same as leaving behind: working *toward* the figural is to work *with* the figurative. In this sense, the figure "extracts" from the figurative (6, 10). This extracted figure is abstractly lived. Consequently, it should be read as a provocation when Deleuze writes that, in art, "it is not a matter of reproducing or inventing forms, but of capturing forces. For this reason no art is figurative" (48). Why this denial when figuration has previously been proposed as the ground from which the figure extracts? Where does Deleuze want to push thought? In *A Thousand Plateaus*, Deleuze and Guattari write: "No art is imitative, no art can be imitative or figurative. Suppose a painter 'represents' a bird; this is in fact a becoming-bird that can occur only to the extent that the bird itself is in the process of becoming something else, a pure line and pure color. Thus imitation self-destructs, since the imitator unknowingly enters into a becoming that conjugates with the unknowing becoming of that which he or she imitates. One imitates only if one fails, when one fails" (1987, 304–5). Before art represents and signifies (say, a fictional world), it operates as a productive force in this world. Art cocreates a relational field in which materials, colors, textures, painters, spectators, birds, and so forth coevolve and invent what each becomes.

This notion of art as a creative force in the world is a major consistency in the thinking of Deleuze and Guattari: in his own writing, Guattari suggests that, if we think of moving images as part of a machinic assemblage, then "we are not in the presence of a passively representative image, but of a vector of subjectivation. We are actually confronted by a non-discursive, pathic knowledge" (1995, 25). Such knowledge is not preconstituted and contained in narrative; it is first of all produced in the encounter, the "confrontation" with the image. It is this pathic or embodied mode of thought that the concept of the figure pushes us toward.

The figure is a wager for thinking through the body, through sensation. In the present context, this means that there is more to narrative than story, representation, and content. If Deleuze and Guattari repeatedly deny the figurative aspect of art, it is because they write at a time when structuralist theories and "narratology" in particular reduce narrative to the double articulation of discourse and story. They provokingly refute figuration and mediation to challenge these theories and draw our attention to the more-than of art, the immediate sensation of the encounter with art, including narrative, as a lived experience. This, then, is what the concept of the figure, defined as "the sensible form related to a sensation" without "the intermediary of the brain," attempts to grasp (Deleuze 2004b, 31). The figure is a narrative movement directly felt before reflection and without signification. It is the viscerally felt gesture of a work's relational form-taking. As such, it emerges eventfully and does not express anything but itself. It is asignifying.[7]

That the figure is "directly" or "viscerally" felt means that it falls under the purview of affect. To grasp this qualification of the concept, it is helpful to distinguish between affect and emotion. Think of an emotion as "conscious, qualified, and meaningful, a 'content' that can be attributed to an already-constituted subject" (Shaviro 2010, 3). As an immediate affective force, the figure resists conscious reflection within a fully formed subject and aims at transformative sensory effects. Remember that before being conscious subjects, we are sensing bodies in an environment sustained by a multiplicity of human and nonhuman forces. The concept of affect is a proposition to think these complex relations as productive of what we tend to perceive as preconstituted subjects and objects: "Affect is of the milieu: it . . . activates the very connectibility of experience. It is the force, the lure, through which a certain constellation comes to expression" (Manning 2013, 26). Emotion, then, is codified affect, captured by consciousness; its affect has become. Affect itself is always becoming, ontogenetic. The term of the figure addresses this relational coming-together of affective forces to compose an aesthetic experience. Indeed, the opening sequence of *Damages* shows that a figure of time is not just a collection of devices or qualities. Pale yellow hue, grainy texture, vibrant sound, and aberrant movement come together not as a collection of distinct formal traits but as intersecting formative forces. These elements collectively generate a singular aesthetic experience that foregrounds the uncountable minute stirrings, the vibratory forces that co-compose the image and reality in general. In this way, *Damages* opens with an invitation to perceive the differential speeds and slownesses of microscopic temporalities as they produce our experience of a present. This emphasis on the slightest, barely perceptible movements of the image is what attunes us to the minor forces of affect: Instead of watching for shocking moments and explosive emotions (of which *Damages* offers many), we are primed to look for small shifts and changes within the image. Our attention is furthermore attuned to a slowness that prefigures the gradual pace at which *Damages*' figural movement unfolds over the course of an entire season. The concurrent movements of foggy self-differentiation, technical reverse motion, and slow resistance to televisual flow compose for an experience of attention itself widened and attuned to the complexity of the present moment understood as that which emerges out of the confluence of various temporalities. In other words, the series allies duration to affect in a way that already operates beyond concerns for linear progression and narrative structure even before it begins to tell a story and preempt its ending. The concept of affect as distinguished from emotion makes it possible to follow the minor operations of the figural beyond or below the spectacular moments of storytelling and attend to the slow intensity of the figural rather than move at the speed of the figurative.

What counts, then, are not the discrete elements as such but how they co-compose as an operative or relational field. What counts are the relations between elements, the differentials between, say, foggy billows and reverse motion, the fixed image and the dynamic grain, the metric triangle and the resonating hum. These relations are differentials because their terms do not actually connect: triangle and hum remain two separate components of the sequence; camera movement and grain remain distinguishable. Differentially co-composing, these components "come into effect *in excess* over themselves" (Massumi 2011, 20, emphasis added). This excess is the more-than, the figure of time that lifts off from the machinic assemblage. The shifting map of forces that animates the assemblage, the relational field of creative activity, is what Deleuze calls a diagram: "The diagram is thus the *operative set of asignifying and nonrepresentative* lines and zones, line-strokes and color-patches" (2004b, 82, emphasis added). "It never functions in order to represent a persisting world but produces a new kind of reality, a new model of truth" (Deleuze 2006a, 30). In other words, this concept gives a name to the ontogenetic force of becoming activated by and feeding back into the assemblage: "it is an abstract machine" that effectuates a figure of time (30). In sum, then, and in preparation for what is to follow, we can say that the abstract machine of serial TV fiction connects heterogeneous elements in a functional ensemble or assemblage. This assemblage sustains a relational force field that diagrams figures of time into experience.

In light of the above, the figure appears as fundamentally temporal. It grows out of the image's movement of shapes, colors, textures, sounds, and cuts; out of the sustained relation between the imagescape and sensation. For Andrey Tarkovsky, the sensed "more-than" of the image is essentially time itself. The filmmaker holds that time "becomes tangible [in a shot] when you sense something significant, truthful, going on *beyond the events on the screen*; when you realise, quite consciously, that what you see in the frame is not limited to its visual depiction, but is a pointer to something stretching out beyond the frame and to infinity; a pointer to life."[8] This sensation of time is not a punctuated experience but courses through an entire film. In this sense, the figural movement is a matter of a work's "consistency" that must be carefully crafted and honed in the processes of filming and editing. Through this rigorous process of composition, the work gains the potential to create "a new awareness of the existence of . . . time, emerging as a result of the intervals, of what is cut out, carved off in the process." Tarkovsky calls this process "sculpting in time," an expression that foregrounds the *plasticity* of becoming. Consider once more the opening sequence of *Damages*: the foggy and grainy textures, the measured tolls of the bell, and the vibrant hum as well as the aberrant movement of the image are ways of sculpting a figure into feeling. Think of it as the abstract shape of rhythmic movement, precariously sustained by a set of concrete techniques.[9] The examples of such topological shapes from the following chapters include "loops" and "thickets" of timelines. Despite this variety in figural renderings of time, there is a quality of time that courses through the imagescapes of *Damages*, *Flashforward*, and *Life on Mars* alike, which is that of preemption, the creation of life looped through the future.

Here we get a first glimpse of how the conceptual prism of the figural can shed light on the questions of the political. In its own way, contemporary politics has made the move from the figurative to the figural: preemption resists the representation of a given situation and produces a new reality by inducing affective charges. The doctrine of preemption draws on the creative forces of becoming, knowing that time "put[s] the notion of truth into crisis" (Deleuze 1989, 130). Deleuze is referring not to a particular truth but to the very *notion* of truth. This is because, considered dynamically, truth can no longer be conceived as preexisting, waiting to be discovered and mediated, just like time can no longer be thought of as uniform and empty, just waiting to be filled. Truths and times are created in a continuous process of composition. This proposition may be frightening if one thinks of "created" truths as fabricated or faked. In the case of preemption, it certainly is. But to think in terms of "fabrication" is to hold on to the idea of a real, incontestable truth unless one acknowledges that *all* existence is thus "machined" into existence, that the truth is always a matter of falsification. On a more constructive note, then, the concept of the figure is a proposition to consider one's share in the production of novelty. It is an invitation to be discontented with available structures and contents, stale and stable. In the context of this book, it is more specifically a proposition to make time differently, to develop techniques that lead off the "beaten time" of modernity (Guattari 1992, 142).[10] The TV series discussed here are examples of how felt realities can be generated through complex temporal movements.

If the figural has an ethical and political potential, it may be all the more surprising that television—out of all the possible candidates—should be the medium to make the cut. Television, in Chris Marker's words, is usually "deliberately moral," prone to shallowness and judgment (1994, 83, translation modified). This remains true to a considerable extent. And yet Marker, a filmmaker who knew more about time than many others, more recently "quench[ed his] thirst for fiction at its most accomplished source: the splendid American television series" (Marker, Douhaire, and Rivoire 2003). This change of mind corresponds to a shift in the "serial machine" that has opened up spaces for ethico-aesthetic projects on television—rare, admittedly, but all the more significant for that. While television oftentimes thwarts such attempts, it also allows for differing, intensive modes of perception. In order to enter such modes, one must think across the boundaries between TV content, distribution, consumption, and other seemingly unrelated "social practices." If the viewer is ready to place herself right inside such a transversal field of relation, the abstract machine of serial TV can open toward new vectors of subjectivation. If the television series—as media ecology—co-composes collective and individual subjectivities, we need to know what it is capable of. What are the potentials of living with television as many of us do? What kinds of technics does it afford? The figural is also a proposition for watching television differently, productively, lest these spaces of potential be prematurely foreclosed, captured by more palatable and profitable modes of TV-making.

This much is clear then: figures of time "aren't just there" as constituted forms; they *emerge*. They are diagrammatic *effects*. They *extract* from concrete assemblages to be *abstractly lived*. The lift-off of a figure depends on a number of *co-composing elements*: "An event of lived abstraction is strictly speaking uncaused. Its taking effect is spontaneous: experiential self-combustion. It is uncaused, but highly conditioned: wholly dependent on the coming-together of its ingredient factors, just so" (Massumi 2011, 149).[11] Some of the elements that factor into the opening scene of *Damages* have been collected above. But this is only a figure in germ, a miniature. Let us now fast-zoom out from *Damages*' miniature figure to the television assemblage as a whole. What follows in the remainder of this chapter is a slow zoom-in to explore how the more general technical conditions of TV enable a figural aesthetic that reaches all the way into the politics of preemption.

The Serial Machine

The concept of the *serial machine* refers to the diagrammatic relations that animate the heterogeneous, co-composing elements that constitute the concrete assemblage of fictional television series. These elements or components include digital technologies, production standards, postproduction, creative workers, distribution channels, viewing habits, and many more, which collectively enable television's *technics*. As such, they co-condition the singular experience of serial fiction on TV. To understand how recent TV series construct their complex temporalities and how these enable the aesthetic experiences explored in this book, it is important to put some of these conditioning factors in place. In so doing, it will be seen that, over the last twenty or so years, the assemblage of serial TV has shifted so significantly as to modify the machinic relations animating it and to allow for qualitatively new kinds of serial storytelling on TV. That such a shift has actually occurred seems to be certain. In fact, it is by now a commonplace to state we are currently experiencing a new or third "golden age of television" (see, e.g., Pérez-Gómez 2011).[12] The expression itself is certainly a response to Robert J. Thompson's *Television's Second Golden Age*. For Thompson, this period begins roughly in the early 1980s, with critically acclaimed TV shows such as *Hill Street Blues*. Tracing this development up to ER's enormous success, Thompson never suggests that this second golden age might draw to an end. And yet, a mere fifteen years later, both TV makers and scholars seem convinced that there has been so fundamental a change that one should or must speak of yet another golden age, the third one.[13] It seems that Thompson's second golden age had revolved shortly after he suggested its existence. While the point here is not to establish or correct such periodizations (because their heuristic value is doubtful), they nonetheless speak to an awareness of change and an effort to come to terms with it. The anxiety to determine what is going on has produced admirable analyses of the industrial, technological, and aesthetic innovations of TV series (see, e.g., Booth 2011; Lotz 2007; Mittell 2006; Pérez-Gómez 2011).[14] Studies frequently highlight the intersections of these different domains. However, the side effect of such attempts at pinning down television series is that they avoid more complex spillages into and from other domains, such as theories of perception, time, and politics. Much available research is aware of this far side of economic, technological, and narrative concerns but keeps it at bay.[15]

Simply put, my contention is that the emergence of preemptive narratives as a specific aesthetic trend can be traced back to broader transformations within the serial machine. The qualitative shift of television allows for new ethico-aesthetic potentials of serial TV fiction that are not merely determined by neighboring "contexts." Rather, television series co-compose with the technological, aesthetic, and political vectors of a wider social assemblage. I further propose that one of the main concerns of television (as a creative force) within that assemblage is time. Thus, as this chapter traces its way through the serial machine and its various potentials, the focus will be on those industrial, technological, and aesthetic aspects of the assemblage that have conditioned the emergence of a qualitatively new and singular experience of time. More particularly, it will be on ways in which the shifting serial machine has allowed for the emergence of preemptive narratives.

Let's begin with the introduction of cable technology and its repercussions. Somewhat surprisingly, perhaps, a first important conditioning factor for the emergence of preemptive narratives can be found in nonfictional programming and more particularly cable news. As is well known, the introduction of analog cable systems in the 1980s led to the increase of available channels, which, in turn, had a major impact on programming strategies. This is particularly evident in the context of television journalism as practiced on twenty-four-hour cable news networks like CNN. One might expect that a channel that dedicates all its around-the-clock programming to news coverage would provide more in-depth engagement with current affairs and foster investigative journalism projects. This, however, is precisely not what happened. Instead, the twenty-four-hour news cycle helped dissolve the conventional editorial separation of the newsroom from entertainment departments (see Delli Carpini and Williams 2001). In addition to continuous provision of minor updates on the same news items and the inflationary use of the "breaking news" label, rolling news allocated more airtime to so-called soft news, or news items with a focus on celebrity, sports, (local) crime, and human interest stories (see Cushion 2012, 61–84). Most importantly for the present account, the twenty-four-hour news cycle has created a tendency toward speculative news coverage and what Richard Grusin has called premediation (2010). Short of a sufficient amount of (new or properly verified) facts to report, news programs have integrated a legion of correspondents, pundits, and specialists to comment on the same issue from all possible angles, oftentimes evaluating what something *could* mean under certain, as yet unverifiable, circumstances. The potential scenarios constructed in this way carry an affective charge that feeds back into news culture regardless of whether the supposed circumstances can be verified or not. In fact, the affective charge lingers even if the supposed circumstances are falsified. As an example, consider the news frenzy around a potential anthrax attack at the Montreal airport in 2005: when two weeks after the incident the potential "toxic substance" turned out to be flour, local newspapers and other media continued to insist that the flour incident had led to important and welcome reconsiderations of airport security measures. That neither the fear caused by the event nor the measures taken to prevent similar "attacks" were grounded in fact was secondary. As Brian Massumi remarks about this incident, "the threat-determined would-be and could-be takes public precedence due to its operating in the more compelling future-oriented and affective register" (2015, 196). A potential (past, present, or future) attack to speculate over is more salable than a verified bag of flour. It is important to note that, while ethically and politically questionable, speculative and preemptive news coverage is very effective from a network perspective: statements about the future and other potentialities, though frowned upon among journalists, make for productive content because they cannot be falsified and therefore not held to the same standards of truthfulness as events in the past; they create suspense and thus bind audiences affectively; and they combine well with opinion-based (partisan) narrow-casting. In light of this, it comes as no surprise that the wider television assemblage has integrated future orientation and speculation as general editorial strategies in news coverage. As we will see later on, many of these aspects play an important role in preemptive narratives.

Of course, the introduction of cable technology and the corollary proliferation of channels have also had more immediate effects on the production and distribution of fictional TV programs. With increasing capacities for analog and later digital transmission, networks have started "multiplexing" their channels, which means that a single network transmits several channels that share the same bandwidth. Thus, while networks proliferate in number, they also diversify their contents. This is a considerable change from the golden age of the big networks when very few channels (essentially ABC, CBS, and NBC in the US) were able to reach a maximum number of viewers; that is, they were able to *broad*cast their content to large audiences. By now, this ratio between networks and viewers has practically been inversed: more and more channels have to rely on fewer and fewer viewers per channel. Under these changed conditions, the real problem for networks consists in the fact that viewers respond to a greater variety of channels by being more selective. And even though there may still be idle viewers who aimlessly zip and zap their way through channels, the probability of them getting stuck on any given channel is too small for networks to rely on them in the same way they could at the height of the so-called network era.

Consequently, networks have devised strategies to secure viewers, one of which is commonly referred to as *narrowcasting*: instead of producing consensual programs that suit the masses, networks target very specific audiences. During the network era, programs had to be acceptable for the majority and therefore controversial aspects had to be watered down and kept to an unobjectionable minimum.[16] In the postnetwork era, political and social controversy is a means of establishing and maintaining a smaller but faithful audience. A way of doing that is to create a specific, branded identity for a network. As an example, consider the cable service Showtime, which airs shows like *Queer as Folk*, *The L Word*, and *Californication*, all known for their explicit sexual content. For a few years, Showtime sported the slogan "No Limits" to indicate that the network provides programs that conventional and consensual broadcast television cannot offer.

Interpretations of this development range from the *fragmentation* and *ghettoization* of audiences to the *diversification* and *democratization* of television programming. My interest is not in such generalizing arguments of media economy but in the potential that the shift from consensual to controversial programming creates for fictional TV series. This transformation creates a zone of indetermination within television that forgoes the moralizing—that is, judgmental, determining—tendencies of the medium and allows for singular ethico-aesthetic engagements. So, to say that the serial machine harbors a zone of indetermination is not to say that individual programs are imprecise or messy. Nor does it mean that all television series have reached new levels of aesthetic, ethical, and political investment. A smaller audience is not necessarily a "gated community" and television is not freer or more democratic because it caters to the expectations of various molecular target groups. The notion of (re)singularization is a way of avoiding such quick judgments. What the confluence of above-mentioned factors produces is first of all a productive vagueness that allows individual programs to break out of ready-made patterns of storytelling and genre typologies that have crystallized into dead, unproductive structures. These first few transformations set off a dynamic in which an overdetermined media format is jolted from its gridlock and repotentializes. Resingularization is not redetermination, then. While the latter term describes the possible paralysis of dynamic movements into "structures" or a "system," the former points to the new creative possibilities within a map of TV production that has shifted.[17]

These new conditions and potentials within the television industry may seem relatively disconnected from the logic of preemption foregrounded here, but they do in fact contribute to a strong speculative impetus of industry discourses, especially in the digital era. In his book *Production Culture*, John T. Caldwell describes how the film and television industries reach beyond the present moment to ascertain a favorable reception of their future releases: "Since in American television almost 80 percent of all new shows fail and are canceled each year (low ratings), and films fare little better (uneven box office receipts), advance rhetoric and deliberation about the significance, origins, audience prospects, stylistic approach, director's background and intentions, and use of technology typically flood the trade sphere and now the blogosphere, months before the forthcoming film or television show ever appears in public" (2008, 23). Largely to reduce financial risk, then, the industry carefully crafts the conditions of reception for its intellectual properties to encourage future economic activity around them. In Caldwell's words, industrial "self-theorizing and sense making are . . . preemptive or real-time" (22). It is worth noting that many of the strategies for doing this also operate in the affective register and by no means guarantee success. For instance, discourses of "quality TV" appeal to certain industry and audience segments that might appreciate the treatment of more "serious" themes and a "cinematic" aesthetic (high image and sound standards, sophisticated art direction and cinematography, elaborate editing).[18] Such discourses outlining a program's distinctive quality circulate long in advance of its release and serve mainly to stoke the target groups' enthusiasm for the content. Actual economic success, let alone "quality," may remain elusive. Another way of trying to ensure the favorable reception of future releases is to tie them into existing intellectual properties that already have cultural cachet. The recent trend of reviving canceled TV series is a good example of this, also because revivals of shows such as *Full House* (as *Fuller House*, Netflix, 2016–present) or *Roseanne* (ABC, 1988–2018) run on the affective dimensions of nostalgia. It is industry and audience members' nostalgic attachment to the TV content from an earlier, oftentimes formative period in their lives (childhood, adolescence, young adulthood) that draws them to resurrected

TV programs. Revivals come with a loyal audience almost by default.[19] Transmedia franchises such as the Marvel Cinematic Universe work in a similar way by mobilizing fan attachment rather than nostalgia. As a final example of industry strategies for preempting economic success, consider how the relative convergence of the film and television industries has also produced a more lively transfer of above-the-line labor between film and television, thus connecting television's serial machine to the (Hollywood) star system and its economic ramifications. While in earlier decades "doing television" could be considered a career disaster for creative workers established in the film industry, a considerable number of film actors, directors, and producers have committed to TV series in the twenty-first century.[20] In an era where networks strive to create prestige content, the involvement of (possibly award-winning) "big names" creates cultural capital and helps attract audiences. These practices—narrowcasting, discourses of "quality TV," new aesthetic standards, prominent creative teams, investing in existing IPs, and so on—are a result of and at the same time reinforce the television industry's general preemptive tendency.

In light of the above, the foretold endings discussed in this book can be read as yet another preemptive way of holding the audience's attention: they create an immediate sense of mystery and suspense but also suggest that a gratifying resolution awaits faithful viewers who stick around until the events of the story catch up with the preempted future scenario. (This does not always happen, as the example of *Breaking Bad*'s second season showed. See my introduction.) Preemptive narratives can thus be seen as an attempt to valorize the entire season of a program by introducing a clear season-long story arc at its very beginning. In this way, preemptive narratives speak to what Caldwell calls TV programmers' interest "in the interrelationships between digital media and sequential time" (2003, 142) and might even be compared to other classic programming strategies for managing audience behavior, such as "tent-poling," "hammocking," or "seamlessness" (134). The important difference is that the preemptive ending is a thoroughly textual strategy and hence orders the unfolding of the narrative itself in a way that hammocking or even the seamless transition between programs did not. In preemptive narratives, it is the thrill and uncertainty created by the glimpse into the future that discourages viewers from changing the channel or losing interest in the program altogether. Somewhat curiously, narrative *uncertainty* is meant to *ascertain* economic success or at least viability.

The present account has so far briefly highlighted a number of technological and industrial innovations from the 1980s onward to support the claim that the television industry in general tends toward future orientation, speculation, and preemption. It remains to be seen how this general preemptive tendency and the above-mentioned industrial transformations contribute to the serial aesthetic of preemption under study here. To clarify this relation, the argument will include another important factor in the development of television's aesthetic innovations, namely DVD technology.

Expressive Machines: The Season

A technological innovation does not necessarily create new aesthetic practices. It must produce a qualitative shift within the assemblage to give rise to new expressive machines, or to new technical modes of expression. Expressive machines can be sets of molecular techniques specific to one program and its aesthetic project or more general components of a technic that create new aesthetic potentials, such as the season as a narrative unit or DVD technology. To explore the proposition that some technological innovations do not produce a qualitative shift within the serial machine, consider the VCR. While it has certainly changed audiences' understandings of what passes on TV and when it does, it has not done much for the aesthetics of television series. The reasons for this are technological in the first place: VHS cassettes have various running times, most commonly between 60 and 240 minutes. This range allows for a number of different uses, for example the following: (1) private recordings of television programs to be watched at a later time; (2) "best of" boxes, containing favorite episodes from popular television series; and (3) movies on VHS. Individual recordings are a first step toward time-shifting, or the breaking out of the television flow.[21] They also allow for private collections. However, these developments take place on the level of the individual and do not spill over into the economic and creative aspects of serial production. While "best of" VHS boxes do have such an economic effect, they remain miscellaneous collections of relatively disparate episodes. This archiving method is still too loose to generate new modes of storytelling. The real potential of VHS lies in the third of the above-mentioned uses: VHS transformed cinema and the film industry by displacing movies from the theaters to the small screen (see Rodowick 2007, 26–28).[22] It created a new outlet for the market and added to the uses of the television set. In this way, VHS became an integral part of the television assemblage in general without creating new modes of expression for the serial machine.

The DVD, in contrast, creates the possibility for an *integral archive* of a program by way of its enhanced storage capacity. This continuity of archiving immediately produces an internal discontinuity or segmentation. In order to be revisited, the archive must come with techniques that lure viewers into new practices of rewatching.[23] Within these developments concerning distribution and reception initially, new modes of production as well as aesthetic concerns have coalesced around the narrative unit of the season, which is not only compatible with DVD and favorable to re- and binge-watching.[24] More importantly, it has emerged in recent years as an aesthetic complex with interesting potentials for experimentation. This aesthetic complex remains open to previous and subsequent seasons but it is more than ever conceived as an intact and relatively autonomous whole, which facilitates two temporal effects. On the one hand, seasons acquire a thematic consistency that can set it off from other seasons in remarkable ways. The prime example in this case is probably HBO's *The Wire* (2002–8), which portrays urban life in Baltimore with a particular focus on the city's drug culture. Each of the show's five seasons focuses on a different aspect of urban life: drug trade (season 1), the seaport system (s. 2), city administration (s. 3), the school system (s. 4), and local news media (s. 5). What emerges over the course of the series besides a continuous story is a complex portrayal of a city's connected subsystems. On the other hand, there is extension and complication of story arcs *within* each season (see L. Williams 2014, chapter 2). While in earlier decades, stories oftentimes resolved within an episode (think of police procedurals and legal dramas like *Columbo* and *Matlock*), these self-contained episodes have come to be replaced by or integrated with season-long story arcs.[25]

Another crucial effect of this dynamic is that seasons get shorter. While the twenty-four-episode season was the standard model up until the 1990s, many TV series now have seasons that count ten or thirteen episodes. In fact, the shorter seasons are by now established standards among cable TV shows, which are less dependent on syndication and the large back catalog of episodes it requires. While the ten- or thirteen-episode season considerably *constrains* the length of individual narratives, it also *enables* more consistent and rigorous storytelling. In the context of this book, the most important aesthetic effect of this enabling constraint consists in the activation of intervals, most obviously between episodes and seasons. The pronounced formal segmentation facilitates an interplay between continuities and discontinuities. Gaps take on specific qualities and functions within a season's movement. The first season of *The Sopranos* provides an interesting example of conjunction-through-disjunction: David Chase, the creator of the show, strove toward creating "stand-alone episodes" that could be viewed as self-contained narratives *and* installments of a longer narrative process at the same time. In addition, Chase regroups episodes to form coherent sequences within the more extended season-long arc, like a quartet within a sonnet. As a result, there are multiple rhythms with varying speeds coursing through the narrative at the same time—from the "beats" of each episode to segments of episodes and on to the "arc" of the entire season—that form a temporal complex. As these rhythms are experienced as "parallels," "contrasts," "interruptions," and so on, the season functions as an expressive machine: it is a technique around which technological, distributional, and aesthetic conditions coalesce to co-activate their respective and shared potentials (O'Sullivan 2010, 62).[26] This development is central to the transformation of the serial machine because it has foregrounded temporality as a core aspect of narrative experience: through its multiple internal temporalities, the season "disfigures" linear, metric time and gives rise to figural movements.[27]

This transformation is not a general, technology-determined development. It is dependent on a number of heterogeneous conditions coming together to produce a qualitative shift where these conditions are in place. Conditions that inform the development of shorter, more consistent seasons favorable to DVD distribution include production costs and shooting schedules, to name only two. Another factor that certainly helped popularize DVD box sets and the intensified consumption of TV series is the first sale doctrine, which allows for legally owned, copyrighted material such as DVDs, books, and CDs to be sold on or further distributed by individuals, libraries, and video stores. This drastically increased the circulation of DVDs through video stores. The importance of the first sale doctrine becomes clear now that a considerable part of media distribution has moved online and legal debates question whether the first sale doctrine should apply to digital copies. (The first sale doctrine is a limitation on copyright holders' *distribution* rights, not their *reproduction* rights. The question hinges on whether the distribution of digital copies is an actual transfer of tangible personal property or the reproduction, that is, the creation of a new copy of an original product. See "Executive Summary" n.d.) As a result, the secondary markets for copyrighted material, including TV series, are subject to much stricter control. (This obviously does not apply to informal distribution networks through which much content circulates these days.)

While a variety of factors enabled the productive connection between DVD technology and season formats, other segments of serial production were deactivated by the same developments. Consider the decline of the classic soap opera, which is partly due to its resistance to the machinic shift described above. First, the temporal layout of the soap opera is strongly rooted in the day-to-day rhythm of the working week, which it reproduces, and that of the calendar seasons, which it follows in the long run. This results in an overwhelming amount of episodes to be archived, with around 250 episodes a year. Tied to this temporal matrix, the soap opera lacks a clear notion of the season as a narrative complex. Second, the format privileges novelty value over rewatchability. Its stereotypical cliffhanger—a close-up of a character meaningfully gazing beyond the frame toward harrowing things to come—constantly pushes the story into its next installment with new discoveries. In this constant advance, re-airings (like the weekly "marathons" on Saturdays or Sundays) mainly serve as an opportunity to catch up for those who missed an episode on its initial broadcast. Returning to an episode from twelve months ago, however, would be like reading last year's newspaper. Accordingly, complete archives of soap operas on DVD do not exist. While "best of" or "how it all began" collections are available for exceptionally successful and long-running shows such as *The Bold and the Beautiful*, it is significant that, even in those cases, the format does not go beyond archiving models that VHS had already made available. From this perspective, then, the soap opera's specific temporal matrix, its lack of season formats, and its incompatibility with archiving and rewatching practices are not contingent and coincidental facts. Rather, they are related conditions that can help understand the format's waning popularity since the 1990s.

Despite their technological ability to archive an immense amount of episodes, VOD services have not been able to revive the soap opera in important ways. In 2012 Netflix included two years of the British soap opera *Coronation Street* in its online library. For lack of an immanent narrative unit, the series was arbitrarily archived by the calendar year ("2006" and "2007"). It seems that streamable online archives with enhanced storage capacity manage to collect soap operas and make them rewatchable in a long-term view. It is by virtue of these very capacities, however, that the technology can archive soap operas *without* imposing any formal, temporal, or otherwise enabling constraints. The ability of VOD to bypass these limitations indicates that the *creative* potential of this technology does not lie here.[28] If Netflix produces mainly ten- or thirteen-episode seasons for its original series, it *chooses* to do so for reasons that no longer have anything to do with its technological constraints. The *technic* of Netflix's exclusive content is composed through other conditions, among them the DVD.

In short, then, if VHS cannot shift the serial machine because its storage capacity is too limited (especially for the long seasons required by syndication), VOD cannot do so because its storage capacity is too big. While the former technology is too constraining to be enabling, the latter might be too unrestrained to activate potential. This means that the aesthetic impact of different archiving technologies is not proportional to technological prowess. Tracing serial archives from VHS to VOD, one does not observe a gradual and continuous process of aesthetic innovation that corresponds to the development of archiving technologies with ever-bigger storage capacity (VHS < DVD < VOD < . . .). In this lineage, DVD makes a qualitative difference as it co-conditions the formation of the season as an expressive machine and an aesthetic complex.

Complicated Times

One of the narrative elements to be accentuated by more rigorous season models is the ending. Even as a series integrates contending arcs, rhythms, and discontinuities, the "season finale" is kept firmly in view

Figure 1.6. *Damages*: Ellen in interrogation room.

as a node for these movements to come together. Especially the long story arcs create heightened expectations for the final episode, which hovers at the season's horizon. In some cases, the pull of the ending is harnessed as the central driving force of the narrative machine: the ending is posited at the very beginning of the series; the final disaster is preempted before the story even begins.

Go back to figure 1.5. You see Ellen Parsons (Rose Byrne), the protagonist of *Damages*. And you see her at the end of the series of events covered by the first season. *Damages* anticipates Ellen's shivering, blood-smeared body after a final attack and her interrogation by the police (see figure 1.6) only to cut this moment of foresight by means of a black screen and intertitle: "6 months earlier" (see figure 1.7). The scene then opens on Ellen applying for a job in high-stakes litigation (see figure 1.8). This is, in fact, the fourth and central linkage established in the opening sequence of the series: the ending is looped to the opening as a lead-in to the beginning. The effect is an immediate sense of movement: the foretold ending provides a vector for movement, an endpoint that the narrative is pulled toward from the very outset. This is what all preemptive narratives do in one way or another. They set a clear reference point in the future at which the season will have to wind up. Last things first! The foretold ending at the same time gives a sense of direction, con-

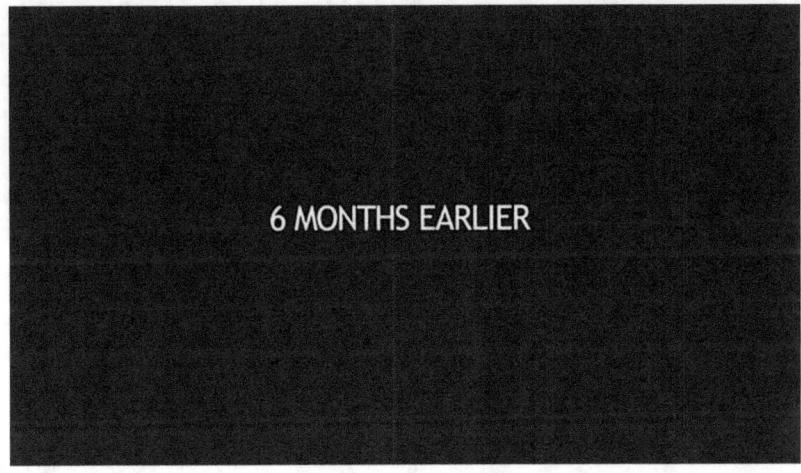

Figure 1.7. *Damages*: intertitle "6 months earlier."

Figure 1.8. *Damages*: Ellen prim and proper six months earlier.

strains the narrative's options, and imbues it with futurity. How can we start to think about this anticipation of the ending, its imposition as an inevitability?

Here is a possible line of thought. In his seminal study *The Sense of an Ending*, Frank Kermode suggests that the urge to predict the outcomes of our actions is an age-old human need to come to terms with life's unbearable provisionality: "We project ourselves—a small, humble elect, perhaps—past the End, so as to see the structure whole, a thing we cannot do from our spot of time in the middle" (2000, 7–8). Envisioned endings, Kermode suggests, appear to be safe vantage points because they allow us to look back at the present *in* the present and to see what it means. This argument may be valid for Kermode's point of departure, the biblical prophecy and its conservative moral purpose. But the opening scene of *Damages* undoes any sense of certitude and meaning: the foretold ending announces chaos and creates a sensation of instability. While Kermode holds that prediction can capture the movement of life in a reassuring way, *Damages* shows that the preempted ending triggers a movement infused with insecurity.

This stoppage of movement in thought is also at work in narrative theories of seriality, evident for instance in Umberto Eco's seminal works on serial narratives.[29] Eco argues that "serials" rely on recurrent narrative schemes. Each episode or installment of a serial repeats the same scheme with a slight variation in a dynamic that allows for the potential "infinity of the text."[30] It is important to note that Eco conceives the relation between the underlying "scheme" and its many variations as that between an ever-stable structure and its many contingent actualizations, similar to a type/token relation. He concludes that the material *excess* of serial narratives, proliferating episodes and installments as they do, belies their fundamental *stasis*: things constantly happen but nothing ever changes. And this, Eco claims, holds for *all* serial genres in *all* media, from Balzac to *Columbo*, without exception: *structuralisme oblige*. Eco calls this the "postmodern aesthetics," which also comes with an injunction for appropriate consumption: "The real problem is that what is of interest is not so much the single variations as 'variability' as a *formal principle*, the fact that one can make variations *to infinity*. . . . What must be enjoyed—suggests the postmodern aesthetics—is the fact that a series of possible variations is potentially infinite" (1994, 96, emphasis added). Let's take the above-mentioned *Coronation Street* as an example: it has been running in the UK since 1960 and each of its more than nine thousand episodes must tell the story in such a way that it can *in principle* always be continued. True, writing techniques and narrative devices to do that are certainly in place. But please do not tell me, Eco would say, that if you have been following the "same story" for the past few years, you actually take pleasure in the story's novelty. What you can and "must" enjoy about serials is certainly the *variability* of the narrative scheme. If you do not, you are "ingenuous" (95) and "naïve," a "victim" of serial narration (92).

Movement has been captured by the underlying structure. Any objections have been silenced by way of an implied allegation of naïveté. Such an argument precludes any interest in the singularity of a given serial narrative or one of its variations because scholarly value is created only when all relevant phenomena have been subsumed under the structural principle. Moreover, Eco's structuralist-descriptive mode of writing glosses over a markedly prescriptive, judgmental, and elitist reasoning. Umberto Eco is what Deleuze and Guattari would call a "state thinker" who tries to contain the potentially infinite variations across a repetitive process, to make sure that it "remain[s] identical to itself across its variations" (1987, 356, 360). He fails to appreciate variation and difference in their own right because, even though he is fascinated by what he calls "the open work," he needs it to be containable on some level, which is the level of structure, "the place where nothing ever happens," to borrow Brian Massumi's expression (2002b, 27).[31] His focus on narrative structures allows Eco to rationally halt the processual quality of narration and to see the open work as a fixed whole. The comfort of the meaningful, structural grid leads to a neglect of the movement that takes off from it, as if there were no fog around the scaffolding (see figure 1.2).

In *Breaking Bad*, *Damages*, *Flashforward*, *Life on Mars*, and many other recent series, neither the anticipated ending nor the serial movement operates in the ways Kermode and Eco suggest. One might argue that, by anticipating its ending, *Damages* creates a vantage point in the future from which the present can draw meaning, that it contains the present's provisionality and reveals its underlying wholeness. But one would still be extricating oneself from the narrative dynamic. The preempted ending does not function as a retrospective viewpoint; it is the activator of a temporal figure coming slowly into sensation. It does not stake out a "narrative scheme" but is a point of departure for movements of perception and thought that shoot off into very different directions in various preemptive narratives, posing distinct problems and providing singular solutions.[32] Now, if the anticipation of an ending is not the stoppage of movement, what kind of temporal movement does it trigger specifically?

As the foretold ending folds back onto the narrative present, it qualitatively changes it: "The backformation of a path is not only a 'retrospection.' It is a 'retroduction': a production, by feedback, of new movements. A dynamic unity has been retrospectively captured and qualitatively converted" (Massumi 2002b, 10). In the case of the TV series at hand, two impulses now determine the narrative dynamic. There is on the one hand the episodic unfolding of serial narration that foregrounds the intermittent or provisional quality of the account of events, its resistance to fixed form. On the other hand, there is the foretold ending, which seems to preimpose a fixed form but actually returns in each episode to affect each new present in new ways. The effect of these two seemingly conflicting functions—the openness of serial narration and proleptic preformation of the narrative—is a movement: a continuous loop, narrative and affective, through the future that foregrounds the interval between each present and the future.

Preemptive narratives, as in *Damages*, loop around a gap in time, continuously spiraling from future to present, back to the future and from there to the present again, slowly closing in on the time-in-between. This circling between the present and the future is also a tending toward the interval, an activation of the gap: watching these series, you feel that what matters is precisely the stretch of time that is missing, that which is no longer the present and not yet the future. A no-longer-the-present that is not-yet-the-future is a *future-past*, the interval in which the past and the future fold into each other to creatively become the present.[33] What is *never seen nor heard* in these series but constantly *felt* is this interval of becoming. To feel something that is unseen is to experience an effect that goes beyond mere content and narrative continuity. This beyond is where the figural operates as an immediate sensation of the narrative's form-taking. Time is then no longer represented as a content of narrative but experienced as the force of form. In this way, the affective loop through time invites a shift of emphasis in the experience of narrative from the figurative to the figural: You are invited to let go of a quest for reliable narrative meaning that—as you can imagine—you will only get at the very end of the season. Spend your time predicting what it all *means* and you spoil the experience by pinning the movement to one narrative trajectory. If, instead, you move with the temporal loop and attend to the interval, you are right in the middle of time-in-the-making.

Consider *Damages* once more to illustrate this point. Every episode performs the loop through time: our vision of the future returns in the exact same images. And in every episode, some kind of plot twist compels you to reconsider what you think the future, still the same, actually is; every time you see the future, you have to think the *same* images *differently*. In this movement, you do not only experience the making of meaning in time. Perception and thought mingle to make you feel how reality as a whole self-differentiates in the interval of the future-past, to become what it will have been. In other words, the interval of becoming is experienced in the linkage of thinking and feeling. As *Damages* shows, to think-feel the interval of becoming is to unknow the future, to come to know it differently all the time. This is another way of saying that the preempted endings are not techniques "to see the structure whole." *Damages* does not give us a block of metric time, a narrative trajectory entirely determined from the outset. Rather, the series extracts a "block of sensation": "a compound of percepts and affects," a complex of sensory and affective forces that give consistency to thought in motion (Deleuze and Guattari 1994, 164). An affective truth lifts off from narrative unknowing.

Future Politics

Affective truths are of political import for they indicate that, despite the best forecasting and scenario-planning techniques, our relation to the future is not only one of projective knowledge and rational calculation but also of affective qualities. Consequently, strategies of risk analysis and policies of precaution do not only "represent" future scenarios, as probable as they may be; they inject affective charges into the present. This is not to discredit techniques of prognosticating. The question of the future remains important for it asks, in pragmatic terms, what the outcomes of current geopolitical situations or industrial processes might look like. It is efficient in that it allows us to design strategies for modulating these developments or preventing certain disasters from happening. But there is more than that: an excess of efficiency that concerns the immediate present. To get to the bottom of these effects, the question of the future must be complemented with the no less pragmatic question of the present. This is in fact a radically empirical question for it acknowledges that any kind of future orientation is still an event in the now and asks in what specific ways a present that lives by a projected future is immediately changed by this temporal loop. How is our perception of Ellen Parsons's present (see figure 1.8) directly inflected by the preview of her disastrous future (see figures 1.5 and 1.6)?

Contemporary theory provides numerous accounts of this dynamic. One available line of thought passes through thinkers like Jean-Pierre Dupuy and Slavoj Žižek. What is interesting about their approaches is that they do analyze the problem of future orientation as one of uncertainty and fear, but fear as a conscious emotive state and a discursive trope. Consequently, the solutions they propose rely heavily on a rational reorientation—as if one could think away the affective impact of forecasting. Žižek takes issue with ecological movements because their most important effect is to create an "ecology of fear."[34] He argues that when environmentalists evoke global warming, nuclear disasters, and other natural catastrophes, they fuel an "ecological pessimism" that deactivates people rather than inciting them to take action: "This ecology of fear has every chance of developing into the predominant form of ideology of global capitalism, a new opium for the masses replacing declining religion." This caveat also prepares Žižek's solution because, being ideological, the above-mentioned "fear and pessimism are as a rule fake." Environmentalists' diffuse anxiety about the coming disaster is in fact a way to *avoid* facing concrete threats of the future. It is first of all a powerful discursive strategy that imposes and sustains a reactionary, conservative politics. But since, luckily, the ecology of fear is only an ideology, it comes undone once we become aware of it as a false consciousness. We will henceforth be able to look a very specific future right in the eye instead of seeing a diffuse blur of fake future fear. Drawing on Jean-Pierre Dupuy's *Pour un catastrophisme éclairé: Quand l'impossible est certain* (2004),[35] Žižek proposes this outlook as a qualitatively different mode of experiencing time.

Dupuy calls this time the "time of a project," of a closed circuit between the past and the future: the future is causally produced by our acts in the past, while the way we act is determined by our anticipation of the future and our reaction to this anticipation. This, then, is how Dupuy proposes to confront the forthcoming catastrophe: we should first perceive it as our fate, as unavoidable, and then, projecting ourselves into it, adopting its standpoint, we should retroactively insert into its past (the past of the future) counterfactual possibilities ("If we had done this and that, the catastrophe we are in now would not have occurred!") upon which we then act today. Therein resides Dupuy's paradoxical formula: we have to accept that, at the level of possibilities, our future is doomed, that the catastrophe will take place, it is our destiny and, then, against the background of this acceptance, we should mobilize ourselves to perform the act which will change destiny itself and thereby insert a new possibility into the past. (2008, 459–60)

Žižek's thinking loops back to where it came from. First, his considerable theoretical effort leads to nothing more than the most conventional principles of prevention politics.[36] The only but decisive difference in this fatalist interpretation of time is that the catastrophe is for now merely projected, hypothetical. The fact that this might also be called a false or fake disaster does not seem to concern either Žižek or Dupuy: for the former the fiction of a scientific hypothesis is better than fake fear; for the latter it is the only way to deal with the various uncertainties of our times. In this way, the authors unwittingly subscribe to the doctrine of preemption to the extent that Žižek's hypothetical conditional justifies countermeasures to threats that might never materialize.[37]

However, by far the most surprising aspect of this argument is that the problem of fear seems to have solved itself along the way. But why would this—admittedly *fatalist*—outlook into the future not be frightening? Why should this fear not be harnessed to work in the interest of those who generate it? In fact, the kind of future narrative that Žižek and Dupuy propose bears a striking resemblance to preemptive narratives: their loop through the catastrophe opens up the indeterminate interval of the future-past, which is the domain of potential and affect. The best rational roadmaps will not seal this gap and contain its ontogenetic force. Therefore there is no reason why Dupuy's "time of a project" would not be the beginning of fearful times. And this affective potential of the loop through the future is likely to feed right back into political agendas. Given the hypothetical character of the coming catastrophe itself, the *fear of* the future is the only thing that is actually real (contrary to Žižek's supposition). The hypothetical catastrophe's affective force, Massumi suggests, is its ticket into actual reality: "It will have been real because it was *felt* to be real. Whether the danger was existent or not, the menace was felt in the form of fear. What is not actually real can be felt into being. Threat does have an actual mode of existence: fear, as foreshadowing. Threat as an impending reality in the present. This actual reality is affective" (2015, 190). Now, the crucial point about this future threat and the fear it creates is that, more often than not, it will be used to actualize the threat rather than to prevent it. Consider once again as a most brief example how the logic of preemption allowed the George W. Bush administration to start a war: there could already be weapons of mass destruction (WMD) in Iraq that, if they are there, could be used to attack the US. For lack of hard evidence, it is the actual fear of potentially existent (actually nonexistent, as we later learned) WMD that created the conditions for the Bush administration to invade Iraq with the support of Congress, the Senate, and the majority of the population. "Weapons are affects and affects weapons" (Deleuze and Guattari 1987, 400).

This is the affective dynamic that Žižek and Dupuy ultimately reproduce, disregarding the reality of fear. It is also the dynamic that preemptive narratives such as *Damages* set off in their own various ways, sometimes to lay bare the ontogenetic power of fear, sometimes to employ it for their own interest.

To better grasp the politicality of these aesthetic movements, they can be thought as figures of time. The opening scene of *Damages* creates such a figure in miniature. As it prefigures the series' more complex loop through the future, its strength lies in posing the philosophical problem of time in the nonrepresentational, more-than-human, relational terms of machinic assemblages. It articulates the experience of time as a diagrammatic effect of technological, aesthetic, and political concerns. Preemption as a sociopolitical issue is entangled with the media technics in which it emerges; in return, such technics cannot be dissociated from modes of thinking and experiencing time. As we have seen, the creative coming-together of these elements co-composes more than just television series; it is connected to ecological apprehensions and actual wars based on possible futures.

To acknowledge this collective creativity "at the intersection of numerous vectors of partial subjectivation" is the first step toward the properly ethical moment of this thinking (Guattari 1995, 98). Serial TV fiction no longer functions according to the models of mass medium theory, merely reproducing dominant ideologies, articulating ready-made, conformist content. When they take up the issue of preemptive politics, these narratives enter a set of power relations to intervene in them, to shift the diagram. The ethical potential of these TV shows lies in the ways in which they insert themselves in this affective dynamic if not to disrupt then at least to disclose and derange it. From a machinic or ecological viewpoint, the key aspect is attentive participation. Instead of asking how a show already is political (in content, for instance), the viewer is invited to explore the kind of politics a series performs and how its very real figural movements can fold back into the wider assemblages of life. Attending to these complex temporal movements can prepare a collective cocreation of a next reality.

Thinking about movement, Erin Manning offers yet another concept to think machines, ecologies, and diagrams—these abstract-but-real, dynamic, relational fields that produce novelty—when she calls it a *dance of attention*: "A dance of attention is a direct feltness of the field of emergence, understood here as a quality of infinite potential with a margin of indetermination at its core. . . . A dance of attention is the holding pattern of an almost unidentifiable set of forces that modulate the event" (2013, 141). The pages that follow are a proposition for entering such a field of emergence, for becoming one of the many, almost unidentifiable but productive vectors of subjectivation. More specifically, they are an invitation to creatively participate in a collective making of time.

A proposition can fall on deaf ears. The invitation to dance the dance of attention needs to be considered.

Shall we?

VECTOR

Others delve yet deeper still. Beneath these joys and sorrows which can, at a pinch, be translated into language, they grasp something that has nothing in common with language, certain rhythms of life and breath that are closer to man than his inmost feelings, being the living law varying with each individual of his enthusiasm and despair, his hopes and regrets. By setting free and emphasizing this music, they force it upon our attention; they compel us, willy-nilly, to fall in with it, like passers-by who join in a dance. (Bergson 1911, 156–57)

CHAPTER 2

THREE REPRESENTATIONS AND A FIGURAL

Bergsonian Variations on Metric Time, the Virtual, and Creative Becoming

Lost in Representation
Time overspills any of its representations. This makes time a problem for thought: it seems it is better intuited or felt than represented.[1] This does not mean that representation, reductive though it may be, must be rejected. On the contrary, one must recognize representation itself as an ontogenetic force in the world. To say that time is always more than its representation is only to say that something gets lost in representation. The remains help build a concept that functions itself as a vector of becoming. This, of course, presupposes that a concept makes a difference in the world, that our *reflections on* the world are also *inflections of* it. As Andrew Murphie puts it, "even mimesis is never just representation" but "first and foremost a form of production." A thinking that acknowledges representation's reality-inflecting force can make the "shift away from an interest in representation to *operation*" or, as one might specify in the context of this argument, to representation-as-operation (Murphie 2002, 193). If we ignore this force more often than not, it is because we assume that the purpose of representations resolves itself in adequately reflecting a preexisting phenomenon, experience, or world *as it is*. The supposition of veracity, which is premised on the presumed correspondence or conformity between form, content, and a preexisting state of things, makes it possible to erase representation's creative force from thought.

To escape this gridlock, the series *Life on Mars* (BBC, 2006–7) proliferates representations. The show introduces three different representational logics, each of which corresponds to a different concept of time. The credit sequence of *Life on Mars* briefly introduces this ambiguity, which is also the protagonist's dilemma: "My Name is Sam Tyler. I had an accident and I woke up in 1973. Am I mad, in a coma, or back in time? Whatever's happened, it's like I've landed on a different planet. Now, maybe if I can work out the reason, I can get home" (*Life on Mars*, opening credits). Madness, coma, and time travel: each of the show's three concurring premises creates its own idea of what time might be. As these three representations contend with each other, they also indicate one another's limitations. An aspect of the experience of time that may be neglected in one rationalization of the plot becomes central in another, which in return may overlook other crucial aspects of temporal experience. *Life on Mars* makes felt the creative, reality-tweaking force of representation as the contending concepts of time falsify each other to create an affective experience of time. For what comes to the fore in the constant back-and-forth between different representational logics and their underlying concepts of time is that which gets lost in each representation, the time that lies beyond the limits of representation. What arises from the differential between the three representations is a figure of time.

The previous chapter broadly explored the conditioning factors of preemptive narratives. We have also seen how the narrative loop through the future—figurally felt—relates to the dynamics of preemption politics in general. This chapter explores a first fully fledged figure of time as it emerges in *Life on Mars* to show how an aesthetic experience of time can articulate political and ethical questions that might be obfuscated by an exclusive focus on the representational logic of narrative. To foreground the difference between the figurative and the figural, this chapter proposes a dialogue with Henri Bergson's philosophy of duration. It furthermore relies on a set of concepts around the notion of representation that will help elaborate how the operations of narrative can connect into a logic of containment and processes of rationalization and at the same time enable a figural movement of the image.

In narrative studies, the term *representation* most broadly refers to the double articulation of story and discourse. In this conception, the story—a line of events unfolding in a certain place and between a number of characters—is articulated on the discursive level in the form of, for instance, words or moving images. The discourse contains and mediates the story. The key analytical question then is *how*. With respect to temporality, a narrative discourse may, for example, reorder the line of events of the story itself. This is of course the case with preemptive narratives because they diverge from the chronological order of events in the story. It is important to note that what operates at the core of this understanding of narrative, which underlies many disciplinary studies of various kinds of "texts" (literary, filmic, televisual), is a principle of correspondence between a content and its discursive form. Inevitably, the questions that such a methodology raises reanimate this core principle, asking just how faithful or not a representation is to its content. Within this framework and again with narrative temporality in mind, one might ask whether "narration time" corresponds to the time narrated (or, as in most cases, not). And to what effect? The central question is how a narrative discourse contains its story. In this chapter, however, I consider this principle of correspondence and containment itself as the problem to be thought, and explore how the correspondence between story and discourse is ordered and reordered by the various concepts of time that *Life on Mars* introduces. The series introduces these orderings by way of *premises*, or initially postulated propositions concerning the nature of time and from which the subsequent functioning of the narrative follows. Different premises project different plotlines: If we accept the premise that Sam Tyler (John Simm) has traveled in time, then the expected solution to the story and endpoint of the narrative must surely consist in Sam's time-traveling back to the future. If, however, we follow the premise that he is in a coma, then Sam's goal is to wake up. This means that premises participate not only in the formulation of a problem; they also frame the possible solutions to the problem. Each premise and its underlying concept of time give rise to a *representational logic* that acts as an epistemic driver behind the narrative. For instance, we will shortly see that the concept of metric, calculable time animates the premise of time travel and lays out certain rules and rationales concerning the protagonist's displacement in time and the possibilities for manipulating chronology. A representational logic regulates what can or cannot happen and, indeed, what can or cannot be thought following its premise. It has a rationalizing tendency to the extent that it strives to reduce time to a knowable object that can be communicated to and grasped by a subject (instead of conceiving time as a generative process that creates the subject). By way of its principle of correspondence and its rationalizing tendency, representation can invite a practice of viewing that is in search for what "makes sense," that tries to reconstruct a coherent propositional content presumed to exist prior to its possibly disjunct formal articulation. This desire to contain formal disorder is what drives some recent approaches to so-called puzzle or mind-game films that hold that the viewer's task or unconscious cognitive activity consists in reintegrating the disorganized pieces of audiovisual material, reestablishing chronology from twisted timelines.[2] According to this view, Bergson would say, the "temporal is . . . only the confused form of the rational" (2007b, 86). The problem with such an approach is that it fails to register the effects of representation-as-operation. Of course, we can reconstruct a chronology of events in *Breaking Bad*, *Damages*, and perhaps even *Life on Mars*. But the crucial question is what has already happened by virtue of the temporal re- or disorder. How has a vision of the future already made us perceive the present differently? (As discussed in the previous chapter, the looped timeline of preemption can, for example, transduce into a real experience of fear and often does.) Such an approach is interested not only in how representation transmits content but also in how it transduces reality. The argument presented here follows the ontogenetic force of representation through the notion of the figural. For the figural, much like time, is precisely that which cannot be represented and only exists as an immediately lived, transductive effect of representation. So if the present chapter explores the various premises and representational logics of *Life on Mars*, it is not to establish how they contain and explain the events of the story but to point out their limits, to see what escapes and exceeds them, and to articulate how that excess discharges into a figure of time.

"Back in Time": Metric Time and Memories of the Future

Sam Tyler considers the possibility of being a time traveler. The collision of his body with a car may have created a rift in time that allows him to slip into 1973 unimpaired. This means, among other things, that he has retained his memory, complete with recollections of the future. Time travel folds memories of the past over into a memory of the future and, furthermore, makes it possible to change that bygone future, thereby putting at stake the supposedly dead past that the traveler came from. In popular culture, this idea is often explained through the "paradox of the grandfather": If you travel into the past and kill your grandfather when he was a child, you will never be born and thus cannot travel back in time to kill your grandfather. Which means that your grandfather will live and you will be born and can time-travel to kill your grandfather as a child, in which case you will not be born and . . . so forth.

Time travel, as any other event, modulates duration as a whole. One of its most intriguing aspects is precisely that it initially assumes a linear homogeneous timeline to logically motivate its premise—the displacement along a trajectory of time—but eventually falls back onto a notion of topological time. Even more interestingly, this shift in the underlying conceptual framework is rarely acknowledged. Time travel narratives oftentimes avoid such logical problems. Rather, they tend to stay within linear chains of (suspensefully complicated) causal connections in order to uphold an underlying schema of cause and effect, action and reaction, sensation and movement.[3] Henri Bergson calls this a sensory-motor schema, which is also the functional principle of what Gilles Deleuze calls the movement-image: a perception-image is related to an affection-image and prolonged into an adequate action-image (see Bergson 2004, 177; Deleuze 1986, 63–66 passim).

Sam Tyler himself denies that his awakening in 1973 may have changed time as a whole, that the linear schema of cause and effect may have been disrupted. He assumes that he has been displaced along a homogeneous timeline and that he can manipulate the past to prevent the accident that caused his temporal displacement. For that purpose, he uses his knowledge of the future to reshape his new present. This is the first variation in *Life on Mars* of the double problem of representation and future orientation. Sam's action plan is a concretization of "teleological retrospect": he looks back on his new present from a point of view in the future in order to make sense of it (see Currie 2007, 21). Sam thinks that his *epistemic* head start will allow him to *act* more efficiently. What he fails to acknowledge is that his displacement in time is not so much a matter of *knowing* time but of *making* it. Here as in many other places, time (travel) is construed as an epistemological problem and not, as Bergson would say, a vital problem (2004, 281, 307). Time is more about activity and creation than knowledge.

What *Life on Mars* is going to foreground in its first representation is that Sam's epistemic loop through the future is first and foremost a creative act. In return, Sam's reduction of this creative act to an epistemological problem is what produces his alienation from the present. Sam's insistence on knowing all of time before acting in time will also be his ethical stumbling block. The show uses the generic framework of the police procedural—Sam is a detective inspector of the Manchester police—to explore the stagnant, regressive, and even destructive effects of future orientation. In his quest to get back to the future, Sam will find out what it means to live metric time and what its limits are. He will learn what harm a literal "memory of the future" can do. But what else could a memory of the future be in a philosophy of duration?

Life on Mars relies on a modern concept of metric time in order to construct its first representation. In fact, time travel narratives in general seem to depend on this concept of time: they only emerge in the eighteenth century when an understanding of time as a homogeneous and measurable container medium becomes dominant.[4] It is in the wake of the scientific revolution and especially industrialization that this new concept has supplanted locally varying, affective attitudes toward time.[5] In a newly industrial, capitalist economy, time was increasingly important: factory workers must be paid *by the hour*, trains must run *on time*, and so on. The monotonous tick-tock of the factory clock measures the intervals of production. The authoritative station clock offers synchronized time and demands punctuality to guarantee the circulation of commodities: "Time is everything, man is nothing; he is no more than the carcase of time" (Marx 2008, 57).[6]

In order to fill time most profitably, it must first be conceived as a preexistent, empty, and homogeneous medium. For this purpose, it is spatialized. Moments of time may be lived as succeeding and replacing one another but are henceforth thought as units juxtaposed in space. Most human representations of time speak to this tendency: consider timelines, clock faces, calendar sheets, and so forth. In the case of the calendar sheet, for instance, time is spread out in two-dimensional space and dissected into equal units such as days and months. The result is an orderly grid with one square for each day. In this way, time can be measured decades in advance, projecting empty and homogeneous units of time into the future. It is now "abstract, chronological, measurable"

(Lim 2009, 18). The calculation and administration of time eventually supplant the unpleasant intuition by which the future is unknown and unforeseeable. To follow Deleuze and Guattari's suggestive homonym, the act of metricizing time (*métriser*) comfortingly implies that one might also be able to master time (*maîtriser le temps*) (1980, 607).

Why should this be problematic? What has happened in the intellectual spatialization of time? What are its flaws and side effects? After all, if Sam Tyler wants to impact on a point of time that lies thirty years ahead, then a concept of metric time that allows him to calculate effects and consequences of the present across vast stretches of time arguably provides the most adequate approach. Bergson argues that the philosophical and pragmatic weakness of metric time lies in that it accounts for an intensive, qualitative multiplicity in the terms of an extensive, quantitative multiplicity (2004, chapter 1).[7] Here, the term *multiplicity* stands for a complex reality; *qualitative* and *quantitative* describe two different types of relation between the elements and the ensemble. A quantitative multiplicity is that which, "in dividing, does not change in kind" (Deleuze 1988a, 41). Simply said, divide three acres of land by three and you end up with three patches of land of the same size. It is a question of numbers. Time as a *qualitative* multiplicity is different, but not because it is indivisible. As Deleuze explains, "In reality, duration divides up and does so constantly: That is why it is a *multiplicity*. But it does not divide up without changing in kind, it changes in kind in the process of dividing up. . . . There is *other* without there being *several*" (42). Add to duration or subtract from it and you change duration as a whole.[8]

But *Life on Mars* does not (yet) make time as duration. We must first consider the shortcomings of thinking time as a quantitative multiplicity. The seeming advantage of spatialized time consists in the representation of a fully rolled-out line of causally linked events. It suggests the possibility of determining change by means of a targeted correction of chronology understood as "an already worked out blueprint," a correction that will leave the rest of the design untouched (Grosz 2005, 110–11). Bergson calls this belief the mechanistic explanation of the relations between past, present, and future: "The essence of mechanical explanation, in fact, is to regard the future and the past as calculable functions of the present, and thus to claim that *all is given*. On this hypothesis, past, present and future would be open at a glance to a superhuman intellect capable of making the calculation" (2007a, 37). Sam Tyler assumes that he occupies such a privileged position, that his supernatural displacement in time allows him to calculate a desired future. After all, Sam can situate his 1973 present within Manchester's social and political developments up to 2006 and use this knowledge to his advantage.

The first episode of *Life on Mars*'s second season gives a telling example of Sam's attempts to act on his knowledge. The protagonist encounters Tony Crane (Marc Warren), a law-bending casino owner who has, as of 1973, not been convicted for any major crime. However, Sam knows that, by 2006, Tony Crane will have been responsible for several homicides. In fact, Sam investigates against Crane in 2006 and several details suggest that the suspect may have intentionally involved Sam in a car accident to obstruct his investigation. Sam's logic is simple: If Tony Crane never commits these murders in the future, then Sam will not have to investigate him and Crane will not attack Sam. And if Sam does not have the accident, he will not be displaced into the past. The rift in time will never have occurred. The ethical pitfalls of linear, homogeneous time become apparent in Sam's action plan to prevent Tony Crane from murdering. In order to "stop [Crane] becoming a killer," Sam tries to "fit him up," to put him behind bars before he can actually commit his crimes. In other words, for lack of a reliable factual basis in the present, self-preservation must be ensured by means of preemptive law enforcement. The problematic aspect here is not so much that Sam is willing to fake the evidence as his claim that the difference between fact and falsehood is no longer relevant to begin with: what is now a lie will become a fact. In Sam's worked-out blueprint, the truth is only a matter of time. His future knowledge allows and even impels him to create the circumstances under which Tony Crane can be arrested for murder.

In this way, Sam Tyler justifies the passage from crime prevention to preemption. It is this passage that helps us understand both the general problem of metric time and Sam's ethical dilemma. The main difference between a preventive and a preemptive approach is that the former "assumes an ability to assess threats empirically and identify their causes" in order "to avoid their realization" while the latter "actively produces what it fights, the better to choose the battle ground and respond with prepared tactics of choice" (Massumi 2015, 5; 2012, 1). The ethical dilemma in *Life on Mars* consists in Sam's unacknowledged slippage from one regime to the other. He pretends that he is still reacting to an objectively given preexistent reality when, in fact, he is already shaping the present to prematurely correspond to a "postexistent" reality. Because Sam refuses to acknowledge that his epistemic advantage is an ontogenetic force, he must remain incredulous to the idea that his epistemic certainty might translate into ontological—and ethical—*un*certainty. After all, Sam *knows* for a fact that Tony Crane will commit several murders in the future. And it appears that, no matter what Sam does, he will have been right in retrospect. However, it is by virtue of this very conviction that he feels entitled to falsify the present so the murderer-to-be can be preemptively arrested. Criminality is short-circuited into an a priori conviction: Tony Crane is eternally guilty of murder—whether he kills or not. And Sam Tyler will have been right.

In the fiction of *Life on Mars*, this ethical problem is foregrounded through time travel and the detective genre. It is also resolved rather easily when Sam can prove that Tony Crane has already murdered in 1973. In the contemporary reality of austerity politics, this problem is at the same time much more latent and much less easily resolved. The manageability of the future is therefore no less a preoccupation of cultural theorists and philosophers. The previous chapter introduced the work of Jean-Pierre Dupuy through a brief discussion of Slavoj Žižek's critique of an "ecology of fear" based in historical time. It is worth noting here that Dupuy himself proposes an action plan that is strikingly analogous to Sam's intention of preemptively arresting Tony Crane. In *Pour un catastrophisme éclairé* and *Economy and the Future*, Dupuy develops a metaphysics that considers the future to be *fixed* and that "consists in projecting oneself after the catastrophe and retrospectively considering it both necessary and improbable" (2004, 87; see also Dupuy 2014, 139–41). According to Dupuy, such an attitude toward the future makes it possible to *avoid* the unlikely catastrophe that *will happen*. Interestingly, Dupuy presents this as a kind of Bergsonism for our time, though fully aware of his conceptual contortions.[9] Bergson, in turn, never tires to point out that the inadequacy of such an approach resides in that it assumes the future to be given. As it assumes the "concreteness" of the future, this kind of thinking neglects the "abstract" dimensions of the present. To avoid this kind of oversight, the concrete and the abstract must be thought as different but *co-constitutive* aspects of the same reality. This conceptual distinction allows for an articulation of the world's becoming as the self-differentiation of concrete matter through the infolding of its abstract potentials. Following this line of thought, "abstraction is synonymous with an unleashing of potential" (Massumi 2002b, 33). Thinking reality in concrete terms exclusively, however, is to assign concrete entities definite positions on a linear arrow of homogeneous, immutable time; it is to thwart the potentialities of each present and to neglect the world's capacity to self-differentiate.

But, just like Sam's concrete future, Dupuy's "future considered to be fixed" merely prepares the slippage into preemptive politics. Despite Dupuy's many careful steps,[10] this is obvious in his reflections on prophecy, another mode of predicting a concrete future. The dilemma of the "efficient prophet" of doom is that, if he shares his prophecy so that people can prevent it, the catastrophe he prophesied will likely not happen: "His prophecy, as it acts in the world, by virtue of its very acting in the world, is falsified" (Dupuy 2004, 170). The prophet himself risks humiliation, disgrace. But, Dupuy suggests, we must be bold enough to take that risk; we must take measures against a catastrophe that will ideally not happen. We must learn how to use the strangely inverted performative power of prophecies of doom that, ideally producing the opposite of what they announce, operationalize the "counterfactual dependence" of the future on the present (172; see also Dupuy 2014, 26–31). We must justify our predictions as follows: "The content of my prophecy is what *would* happen *if* I did not prophecy at all" (Dupuy 2004, 170). Ethically, Dupuy may deem himself on the safe side because he mostly considers natural or ecological catastrophes, the responsibility for which is shouldered by nobody or everybody, respectively. So the question of responsibility or guilt may seem irrelevant. But what about the ethicality of the measures taken to prevent the catastrophe? In this respect, the philosopher's preemptive stroke of genius is as daunting as Sam Tyler's plan for fixing up a future murderer: the prophecy will have been *efficient* and the measures taken will have been *appropriate* if the predicted catastrophe does *not* produce itself. In other words, the *less proof* there ultimately is of an actual threat, the *more adequate* the countermeasures will have proven to be. The "false" prophecy "will always have been preemptively right" (Massumi 2015, 203).

The worrying justification of preemption in the future anterior does not belie its failings in the present. In *Life on Mars*, the neglect of potentials for becoming often leads to dangerous misjudgments of the present—not despite but *because of* Sam's prescience. When, in the third episode of season 2, his colleagues investigate a bomb threat that they believe to be IRA-related, Sam does *not* take the threat seriously, knowing for a (historical) fact that the IRA did not plant bombs in Manchester in the early 1970s. Unheedingly, he sends one of his colleagues into the danger area just when the bomb detonates. Here, Sam's future knowledge forestalls an appropriate response to a situation of great uncertainty. What Sam disregards, assuming that the "past, present and future [are] open at a glance" to him, is the contingency of the case he is investigating. Pinning time down to a metric grid, first backgridding it from 2006, then foregridding from 1973, Sam cannot take note of what slips through the meshes: he does not consider that the bomber in question might be a single individual without any ties to the IRA, which is in fact the case. Modern, metric, historical time certainly enables the production of certain kinds of knowledge. But when projected onto the future, it represents an obstacle to an adequate understanding of the present as an emergent, unforeseeable becoming. Consequently, those who rely on homogeneous and calculable time must always be stunned by this kind of becoming. It shocks them like a detonating bomb. This literalization of emergence should not be misunderstood as a metaphor. The blast of explosion *is* becoming; becoming *is* such a burst. In *Mind-Energy*, Bergson himself describes the production of novelty in the world as an "explosive action" (1920, 22). What the all-is-given view of time ignores is that the release of what Bergson calls vital energy can be effectuated by the most inconspicuous trigger. Emergence is driven by the incommensurable, uncontainable "spark which explodes a powder-magazine" (44).

In light of the above, it becomes clear that the rationalization of time in modernity, which tends to integrate the incommensurate and to dominate the contingent, has a disintegrating element of fallibility. Mary Ann Doane suggests that this double-edged tendency to dominate the contingent is common to both modern time and audiovisual representation. Just as modern time consciousness constructs a homogeneous sequence of equal units, film juxtaposes contingent, indexical images and consolidates them in a continuous "motion picture." In this way, the concurrence of cinema and modern time in what Doane calls cinematic time functions as a means to temper modernity's fear of and "obsession with contingency" insofar as it makes the contingent legible (2002, 15). For this reason, Doane considers cinema to be "a central representational form of the twentieth century": the regular flow of indexical images seems to give a reliable and temporally consolidated record of reality (19).[11] However, as we have seen, this very regularizing and homogenizing tendency is also the weakness of modern time as a "socially objectivated temporality . . .—a necessary illusion that must be exposed" (Lim 2009, 10).[12] As for cinema, Bergson has famously argued that the cinematograph's basic mechanism of representation can only produce "an impersonal movement abstract and simple" that renders concrete becoming as "abstract, uniform and invisible" (2007a, 305, 306). This means that, much like metric time, the film reel simply adds image after image in a process of linear succession. Thus, according to Bergson, the cinematograph produces an abstract form of becoming because it shows *what* happens but not *how*. By placing the present on a timeline of succeeding, uniform instants, both cinema and metric time presumably debase the now as the interval of becoming. At the same time, and quite practically, this uniformity assures the intelligibility and manipulability of past and future events.

The opening credits of *Life on Mars* seem to expose this complicity of metric time and the screen at the beginning of each episode. After Sam's remarks quoted at the beginning of this chapter, the television screen shows the partial title "Life on" followed by a countdown to the year 1973: metric time in reverse figures Sam's return to the past. The time specification disappears and is replaced by "Mars," a statement of place. Sam's "travel" to 1973 is thus clearly marked as a "temporal *displacement*" (Booth 2011). The opening credits mark the fact that the series must at least initially spatialize and homogenize time in order to make its premise work. But *Life on Mars* also marks the tacit assumptions and pitfalls of this spatialization and, consequently, of the term *temporal displacement* itself. Before the show's actual title appears, viewers see "Life on 1973" (see figure 2.1), a first hint that something about this show, which makes its protagonist "live on 1973," will ring false. Behind the title, the screen is initially split into four different images of Sam Tyler's eyes. His face expresses disorientation and an intense effort to perceive

Figure 2.1. *Life on Mars*: credit sequence with title "Life on 1973."

his surroundings. These gridded, screenlike squares subsequently proliferate and occupy the entire image space (see figure 2.2). The screen thus fragments into a multitude of contingent images that can hardly be apprehended individually. This proliferation of contingencies that are *not* integrated into one temporally unified, moving image draws attention to the fact that audiovisual discourse can not only integrate these contingencies if it "wishes" to; it can also arbitrarily break down or manipulate this integrity. It seems, then, that the opening credits picture the discursive mechanism that subtends both film and modern time and that founds their complicity.

Or one could argue something like the opposite. While the credit sequence seems to cater to Bergson's skepticism and to figure the representational mechanism underlying moving-image narratives, it also makes evident that this is precisely not how we usually perceive moving images nor how they make experiences of time. After all, the opening credits of *Life on Mars* involve a considerable aesthetic effort to make us see a mechanism that we quite effortlessly overlook otherwise. Do we not *actually* perceive the continuous unfurling of an image in time, regardless of whether we are watching analog film or digital TV, rather than perceive their (equally actual) juxtaposition in space on the film reel or, as bits and bytes, stored on a DVD? What is more, contrarily to what

Figure 2.2. *Life on Mars*: credit sequence with title "Life on Mars."

Bergson suggests, a single image can contain, create, or vectorize movement. Consider figure 2.3: the eerily blurry squares in this frame capture more than one instant of time. Or, as I see it, they capture an interval, the movement between poses.

The point is a simple one: moving images and metric time must be extricated from the mutually determining relation, which a cultural studies–oriented approach to the moving image has constructed between them. Starting from experience, it is easy to see that film, digital cinema, and television are all quite capable of creating a variety of felt temporalities. Doane's or Lim's work on the socially constructed role of film as a recording device for the contingent is an important stepping-stone toward letting go of the media determinism that consists in persistently correlating a medium and a specific temporality. This letting go acknowledges the primacy of experience over mechanisms and rationalizations. Concerning mechanisms: The technological setup of an imaging device does not determine the experience of time a film or TV show creates in me. It is the rhythm, texture, and intensive qualities of the image that create that experience, not the way in which these images are coded. As for rationalizations, let's go back to the beginning of this chapter: the determinism that accompanies the belief in cinematic time suggests once more that time poses an epistemological problem rather than an expe-

Figure 2.3. *Life on Mars*: credit sequence with motion blur.

riential one. Put in Bergsonian terms, modernity constructs time as a matter of *intelligence* rather than *intuition*. What the proponents of cinematic time—just like Sam Tyler—overlook in so doing is that metric time, though it may be an intellectual tool for humans' organized participation in the world's becoming, is not becoming. Intelligence alone will never be able to account for creative evolution. Sam refuses to acknowledge this and therefore fails to see that "homogeneous space and time" are "principles of division and of solidification introduced into the real with a view to *action* and not with a view to *knowledge*" (Bergson 2004, 281). They are action-oriented schemas that allow human beings "to divide the continuous, to fix the becoming, and to provide our activity with points to which it can be applied" (281). Intelligence is a catalyst for the sensory-motor schema; it is good enough to get us going. But that does not mean that it adequately represents the vibrancy of matter and the creativity of duration. In reverse, this means that the felt participation in becoming is anterior (logically and experientially) to the thinking of time. In order to access this creative quality of time, we must begin before or go beyond representation and its tendency toward rationalization.

For now, we have come—with Sam Tyler, Jean-Pierre Dupuy, and others—to the conceptual, ethical, and pragmatic limits of metric time.

But, as suggested, moving-image narratives are *capable* of but *not limited* to making metric time. We shall see that *Life on Mars* is a powder magazine charged with a second representation of time. (The third will be the spark that blows it all up.)

"In a Coma": Virtual Present and Actual Future

Sam Tyler had a severe car accident. Rather than having traveled through time, he might have fallen into a coma and his "awakening" in 1973 might be the dream reality of his comatose brain. Following this assumption, none of what happens in 1973 is real but only a figment of Sam's imagination.

Depending on which premise one follows, many of the show's elements undergo a shift in meaning. Consider the numerous telecommunication devices and mass media that allow for communication between 2006 and 1973. In *Life on Mars*, car radios, telephones, walkie-talkies, newspapers, and, most importantly, television itself deliver messages from the future (see figures 2.4 and 2.5). In the logic of time travel, these devices help Sam overcome the spatialized interval between 1973 and far-off 2006, in which case they are literally *tele*communication devices. If one assumes that Sam is in a coma, however, the interval that must be overcome is no longer spatial but ontological: the TV screens and telephones are ways for Sam to receive messages from the actual reality while stuck in his dream of 1973. The fact that Sam can only *receive* messages from the future and not send them himself speaks both to the coma premise and to the problem of future orientation: on the one hand, the one-way communication via mass media corresponds to a coma patient's assumed ability to perceive what is happening around them without being able to respond. On the other, it is significant that, once more, the future informs the present in *one-way* communication. Conventional mass media, and television in particular, seem to be part and parcel of a discursive dynamic that constructs a future to determine and silence the present.

This alternative between time travel and coma premises is at work in *Life on Mars* from the very first episode and creates a tension between two different ways of conceiving time. The first is the concept of metric time, discussed in the previous section. The second approaches a Bergsonian conception of time (with major modifications, as we shall see). If

Figure 2.4. *Life on Mars*: television set showing the silhouette of a man.

Figure 2.5. *Life on Mars*: Sam (John Simm) speaking on a telephone.

Life on Mars concretizes the discursive orientation toward the future, the series nonetheless insists on an aspect that the scientific or modern view of time neglects. By means of its coma premise, the show introduces the present and the future as two ontologically distinct dimensions of time. As such, Sam's present and the future emanate from the same moment in time, his life in 2006 being the actual reality, his life in 1973 a virtual reality, a mere figment of his imagination.

Such an understanding of time in terms of actuality and virtuality is a key element of philosophies of time in a Bergsonian tradition. Throughout his vast oeuvre, Bergson himself critiques modern science because it intellectually "abstracts" time from duration.[13] His own approach is based on the concrete and lived experience of time, a time that is immediately given.[14] However, even though Bergson's work is often focused on the human perception of time, his concept of *duration* also exceeds the human and the immediately given in its *virtuality*. Every moment is rich with potentialities. Some of these potentials are pulled out from the virtual to be actualized. (But, once again, the actual and the virtual are aspects of the same reality.) This ingress of the virtual into the actual is what allows for change in the world. "Evolution," Deleuze explains, "takes place from the virtual to actuals. Evolution is actualization, actualization is creation" (1988a, 98). Creation is key. The "continuous creation of unforeseeable novelty" produces a *qualitative* change of duration itself (Bergson 2007b, 73). Becoming alters duration as a whole, all the time. What follows from this is that in order for real change to occur, the future cannot be given. For Bergson, the future does not exist to the extent that it is *not yet*. It is not real (that is, neither actual nor virtual) but possible. *Life on Mars* rediscovers the conceptual distinction between the actual and the virtual but, in order to picture future orientation, it turns Bergson on his head. It is no longer an actual present that unfolds toward an unforeseeable future by actualizing virtuals. Instead, a virtual, imaginary present is subjected to a concrete, determined future. As a consequence, the "virtual present" is no longer "virtual" in the Bergsonian sense. Rather, it is a "virtual reality," a simulated environment. The difference is crucial in the present context: a virtual reality is usually understood to be a "simulation by technological means" but can also refer to "something that exists in the mind" (Jones 2005, 367). In both cases—that is, in immersive 3-D environments as well as in

Sam's coma-dream—the virtual reality is a representation. By contrast, the Bergsonian virtual is "inaccessible to the senses" and therefore cannot be represented (Massumi 2002b, 133).[15] It can, however, be *figured*. In fact, since it cannot be represented, it *must* be figured. Considering the virtual's generative force, another way of stating this difference is to oppose representation and creation. While a virtual reality fulfills its purpose by *re*presenting a simulated reality, the virtual participates in the creation of an actual, new reality.

If *Life on Mars* introduces the actual/"virtual" distinction in such a way, it does so to posit it against Sam's tendency to unify a time that is clearly out of joint. If the series capsizes the dynamic of actualizing virtuals, it is to convey the precariousness of future orientation itself. The inversion of ontological precedence between present and future has severe consequences for the temporal order constructed in the series. The concrete future weighs heavy on Sam's 1973 present. It dominates his virtual life and repeatedly breaks into the present to disturb and even disrupt it. In these moments, Sam suffers a surge of pain; his senses are stunned (see figures 2.6 and 2.7). While, for the protagonist, the intrusion of the future is a painful experience, the narrative itself is marked visually and, even more so, aurally. While the image of the virtual reality fades (see figure 2.7), the actual but precarious future of the protagonist makes itself *heard* through the sounds of the heart monitor in Sam's hospital room as well as the voices of doctors and relatives at his bedside. The audiovisual configuration of these sequences creates a tension between sound and image, each seeming to claim actuality for itself. The image, with its indexical quality, suggests that the viewer sees the accurate representation of a palpable reality. The soundtrack, however, debunks this reality as the fantastic output of a malfunctioning brain within a severely injured body. Every time Sam experiences such a "future shock," the narrative splits into the visual image of a virtual reality and the aural image of an actual reality. We begin to *see* Sam's 1973 present, but we see it as the mere reflection of a concrete, dominant future.

It is precisely because the virtual reality is merely the reflection of a concrete future that we are still far away at this point from the virtual's being-felt through a figure of time. It is worth noting, however, that the shift from time travel to coma has also produced a different kind of rela-

Figure 2.6. *Life on Mars*: Sam in a bus under future shock (color faded, desaturated).

Figure 2.7. *Life on Mars*: Sam at home under future shock (color faded, desaturated).

tion between the present and the future. In the previous section, we saw that when Sam presupposes that he has traveled in time, he also assumes that the relations between present and future are *causal*. He therefore acts in such a way as to trigger the production of a specific future across a thirty-year-long chain of causation. The coma plot, in contrast and by virtue of the inversion of actual and "virtual," foregrounds the depotentializing of the present through future orientation. The relation between the present and the future is no longer one of causality but of *correspondence and conformity*. Sam's coma life is but a mental transcript of his psychopathological state. Everything (people, events, etc.) in 1973 represents something in 2006. Consider Sam's attempt, in the sixth episode of season 1, at preventing a hostage-taker from killing his prisoners at the announced deadline of precisely 2:00 p.m. that day, which he also presumes to be the time that his doctors have set that day in 2006 for discontinuing his life-support measures unless Sam gives a sign of life. The rationale behind this plotline is something like this: Since Sam's virtual reality is but a quasi-allegorical image of his psychopathological condition, a big enough, life-saving intervention in the virtual present must, in return, force a corresponding life-saving modification in the actual future. In short, the present resembles the future.

Future orientation, from this conceptual vantage point, seems to leave ample room for maneuver. If Sam can modulate his present to force the future into correspondence, then this present has apparently regained its creative impact on what the future will be. If Sam can figure out the code to decipher his virtual reality and modify it accordingly, then alternative futures are possible. But the keywords *code*, *correspondence*, and *possibility* indicate that the apparent leeway of the present is actually the future's stranglehold on it. If Sam can modulate the future in the present, it is only because the latter has been reduced to a mere *sign* of the former. To give *meaning* to the present, he must loop through the future. This means that instead of freely creating, Sam is caught up in the worst kind of feedback loop between present and future, which is the mutually determining kind. What distinguishes Sam's virtual reality from the Bergsonian virtual is that the latter *exceeds* the actual at all times whereas the former is—once again the expression is fitting—the blueprint of a preexisting reality. *Life on Mars*'s conceptual twisting of the "virtual" into representational coextension with the actual conveys the depotentializing power of future orientation. We must therefore distinguish between the relative poverty of *possibility* and the infinite richness of the virtual's *potential*. Possible futures are projections resulting from rational operations that establish relations of causation or correspondence between the present and the future. A concrete future is always thought before it is lived. Intelligence thinks away life's boundless potential for self-differentiation.

The depotentializing power of future orientation is another effect of considering the future as a problem of knowledge and representation. If, however, we think-feel it as a matter of emergence, of creative becoming, then any concrete future becomes fundamentally unknowable. This is why, for Bergson, the concrete future is, strictly speaking, *impossible*. This does not contradict his distinction between the real (actual and virtual) on the one hand and the possible (future) on the other. What Bergson considers ontologically "possible" is *a* future. He affirms that creative evolution must "willy-nilly" produce *something* new (to use an expression dear to Bergson's early translators). But the peculiarity of true novelty consists precisely in the fact that this something new cannot be predicted or preconceived. The really new is therefore impossible before its realization. Only once it is in the realm of the real *will it have been* possible all along: *Future-past.*[16] Becoming. As an example, Bergson tells the anecdote of a journalist who interviewed him during World War I. The man, like many other journalists at the time, was interested in what impact the war would have on the arts and literature in particular. And so he asked Bergson, the renowned philosopher, how he would "conceive, for example, the great dramatic work of tomorrow." To which Bergson replied: "If I knew what was to be the great dramatic work of the future, I should be writing it." Bergson does not know because the future's indetermination is not simply a matter of "competition between possibles" that the erudite scholar can project and from which he can select the one that he considers the most probable. Such a conception of indetermination would return us to a calculable and foreseeable future inasmuch as it is already contained in the present in the form of a possibility that merely lacks actualization. This misconception suggests, first, that time moves from the past to the future as it actualizes already existing possibilities and, second, that this process consists in simply adding the status of the actuality to the preexisting possible

(Bergson 2007b, 81–86). However, as was already argued via Deleuze, creative evolution does not move from possibles to actuals but, the other way around, "from the virtual to actuals" in a process of subtraction rather than addition (Deleuze 1988a, 98). Actualization is a matter of subtracting from the virtual because the virtual is infinitely more than the real; it is the teeming reserve of potentials vying to make ingress into the actual. Indetermination, then, is not indecision between one possible trajectory and another; it is the unknowable commotion of potential that holds the future open (instead of foreclosing it by making it calculable). To paraphrase Bergson, it is the virtual share of reality that makes itself possible, and not the possible that becomes real (2007b, 85). It is precisely because the virtual exceeds the actual and is not contained in it that the future cannot be predicted. Bergson does not know the great dramatic work of tomorrow because that work is impossible to be thought in advance.

In contrast, the *will-have-been* of Sam's concrete future is first and foremost thought into being. The depotentializing feedback loop of representation deprives his present of its creative force. As Sam tries to intervene in this circuit, the back-forming intrusions of the future into the present are increasingly violent and uncontrollable. In resistance to Sam's attempts at modulating the actual future, the latter disrupts the virtual present, undoes it for the purpose of fully instating the order of a time to come. Whenever Sam incurs a future shock, his present fades. These scenes are marked not only by a doubling of the soundtrack but also by a qualitative change of the image, as if it were overexposed or washed out (see figure 2.7). In these instances, the hold of the encroaching future comes close to eradicating Sam's onscreen presence. The increasing orientation toward the future threatens to efface the here and now. The present is washed out, washed up.

Eventually, the future succeeds in visually imposing itself. Over the course of the series, Sam Tyler's virtual present is disrupted by sequences of blurred images of his hospital room (see figures 2.8–2.10). The actual future manages to temporarily reinstate itself. However, and against expectation, this "concrete" and "actual" reality is chimeric, apparitional at best. The "immediate data" from the future are corrupt, disintegrated, and unusable on top of being a practical hindrance to Sam's more palpable presence in 1973. The onslaught of the future thus manifests itself

Figure 2.8. *Life on Mars*: blurred image, double exposure of a silhouette.

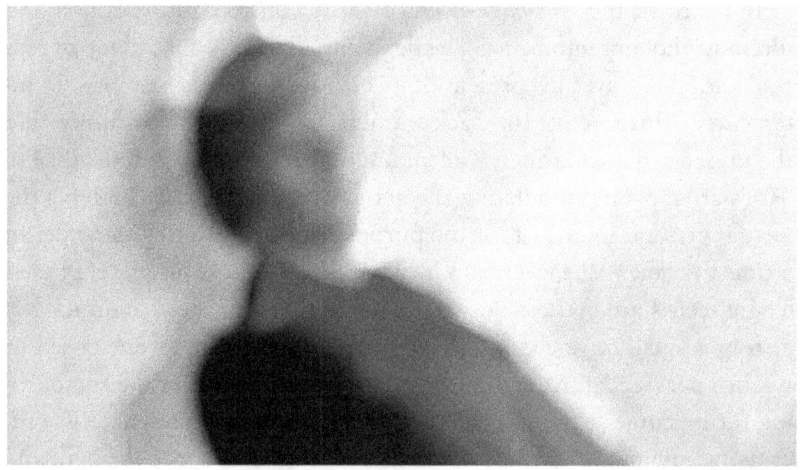

Figure 2.9. *Life on Mars*: blurred image of a male silhouette.

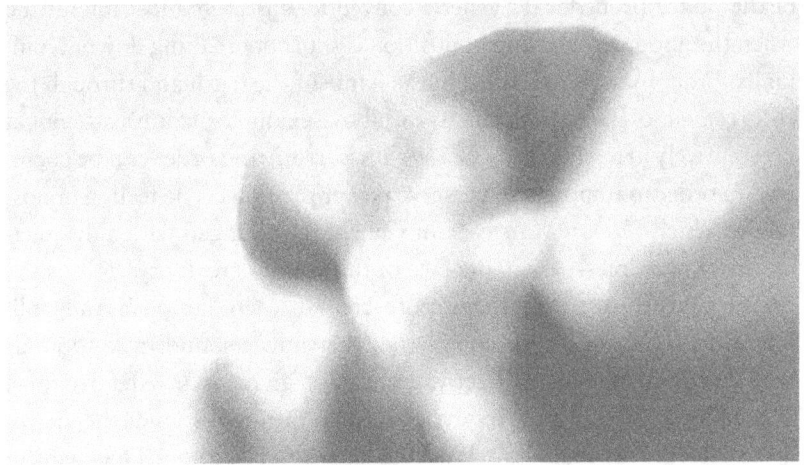

Figure 2.10. *Life on Mars*: blurred image, content unrecognizable.

as an audiovisual *and* pathological condition: it disturbs both the narrative and the protagonist.

These two premises—time travel and coma—are played through in *Life on Mars* from the very beginning, privileged in turn to various extents. From episode to episode, Sam alternately tries either to travel back to the future or, more modestly, to wake up. Accordingly, his aim is to trigger chains of causation across a three-decade interval or to impact on his actual reality by modulating his virtual reality. This back-and-forth between the two premises is certainly one of the series' driving forces throughout its first season and resonates with other rifts in the show's conceptual and aesthetic design.

Life on Mars constantly plays on the tension between Sam Tyler's "modern" and professional investigation methods and the more "hands-on" approach to law enforcement of his superior, Gene Hunt (Philip Glenister). Without giving priority to either, the show vacillates between Sam's meticulous forensic examinations, in accordance with rule of law and anticorruption codices, and Gene's hard-cop vigilantism that caters to a nostalgic longing for order. A forensic police officer upholds order in the name of (scientific) truth, says 2006. Life is rough and we may bend the truth, but we do it in the name of order, 1973 replies. This inflection of the police procedural's generic conventions is at its most interesting when the good cop/bad cop opposition is short of breaking down. Nominally, order may be sustained in the name of the truth and through the enforcement of given laws but, as the above example of Sam's attempt at preemptively arresting Tony Crane shows, truth and order can be cocreated in order to impose and preserve power relations. The feeling of nostalgia, which *Life on Mars* certainly purports, is tinged with a disquieting sense of helplessness in the face of the police's creativity.

The texture of the musical score creates a similar push and pull, bound to collapse. On the one hand, the show's soundtrack abounds with 1970s evergreens that activate the past, giving it an affective tone. Through the quality of (presynthesizer, "authentic") sound, the viewer gets a feel for the small-town working-class security in pre-Thatcher England. Consider the David Bowie song that gives *Life on Mars* its title and, appropriately, plays throughout the scenes depicting Sam's temporal displacement in the pilot episode. Its cryptic lyrics speak of loss, disillusionment, and cultural decay, culminating in the escapist imploration "Is there life on Mars?" (Because if there is, let's get out of here and now.) The show's soundtrack is the lure of the past. On the other hand, the drift into the past only increases the pull-toward-the-future that dominates the first season. Sensation's indulgence in the past is countered by a sense of belonging tied to the future, which is sounded by the opening credits' flashy cop-show theme, the digital beep of Sam's heart rate monitor, and the aseptic voices of his doctors. While the sounds of the future are much less alluring, they also give the lie to the nostalgia for a past filled with corruption and arbitrary violence.

In this way, the series suggests a double sense of alienation throughout the first season. *Life on Mars* caters to an escapist longing for the past and, at the same time, presents that past as a strange, uninhabitable place (think "Mars"). It is drawn toward a concrete future that is also a source of disturbance and destabilization. It is strained between two modes of knowing time: one consisting in calculating various instants of time as causally connected outcomes of one another; the other in casting one moment in time as the mere image of another. Depending on which premise is momentarily foregrounded, the present is reduced either to a calculable point or to a representation of the future. Regardless of which premise is foregrounded, time—in its ever-emergent inventiveness—

inevitably turns out to be more than that which either logic can account for. Time overspills into a third premise.

"Mad": Image-Event and Creative Becoming

At the beginning of its second season, *Life on Mars* insinuates a third explanation for Sam Tyler's temporal displacement, which is introduced as a doubt rather than a certainty: the protagonist could have been mad all along. This alternative explanation and its vagueness are only part of the reason why the first episode of the show's final season occupies a crucial position within the series. As a hinge between the two seasons, it hearkens back to the conceptual, ethical, and pragmatic tensions of past episodes and, at the same time, prepares a major complication within the temporal dynamics of the series as a whole. In fact, *Life on Mars*'s second season asks the viewer to review and rethink the entire first season. It rediagrams the archive. It is as if *Life on Mars* could not have known at its beginning what it was going to be about: time as invention, as creative evolution. In retrospect, it is as if *Life on Mars* had only been putting into place the conditions that allow for the emergence—right from the middle—of a figure of time.

Both of the previously discussed premises of *Life on Mars* and the corollary representations of time increasingly isolate Sam during the show's first season: since people would doubt his mental health if he voiced his apprehensions about having traveled through time or being in a dream, Sam must keep them to himself. The issue of madness takes center stage at the beginning of the second season. In an unsettling encounter, the protagonist is once more made aware of the fact that what he holds to be the truth (time travel or coma dream) is unacceptable to the world he inhabits. At the police station, Sam meets a mentally disturbed man under arrest who claims that "the world isn't what they think": "I see things. I have visions. . . . It's horrible. Because I know the truth and no one else does. . . . How do you think that makes me feel? I'm so alone."[17] Only minutes later, Sam tries to explain how he knows that Tony Crane will commit several murders in the future: "I see things. I had a vision." Sam stops short, realizing that he must sound like the madman he has just encountered. Yet Sam confronts Tony Crane with the "fact" that thirty years ahead he will have become a murderer. In a crucial scene of the series, Crane uses this information to discredit the protagonist: in an attempt to invalidate the investigation against himself, Tony Crane exposes "that DI [detective inspector] Tyler thinks he's from the future ... a time traveler" and concludes that Sam is "totally loco." Sam himself denies this charge and turns it against Crane, declaring that "it would take a seriously disturbed individual to come up with such a bizarre excuse in order to discredit the arresting officer." Sam Tyler can live by the future, he can even solve cases relying on his future knowledge, but he must not admit to this. The important thing to note here is that both of the explanations for Sam's "temporal displacement" discussed in the preceding sections are considered "insane" within the fictional world. The idea of Sam's "time travel" is enough to declare as deranged the person who voices it. But the idea that Sam's 1973 reality might be a mere "figment of his imagination" is even worse as it fundamentally questions the ontological integrity of this reality. *Life on Mars* concretizes future orientation and demonstrates that a present that posits a given and concrete future runs the risk of (onto)logically ousting itself. The entire discursive dynamic is exposed as madness.

Life on Mars, in addition to representing this dilemma, performs it as a figure of time. Its emergence is triggered at the end of the episode under discussion, from within the story: Sam receives what he initially believes to be another call from the future (see figure 2.5). Heart sounds first appear but quickly fade away. More surprisingly, Sam is able to communicate with the voice on the telephone for the first time. The interlocutor tells him: "I understand your frustration, Sam. The job's almost done. Don't blow it now! Remember, if they find out why you're really there, you'll never make it back. Once we've dealt with it all, you can come home, Sam." This enigmatic reply is soon explained: Sam has not traveled in time but in space. He has been sent to Manchester as an undercover investigator to produce evidence for the corrupt policing methods of the local force. The accident he has suffered on his way to Manchester at the beginning of the series has actually taken place in 1973 and caused amnesia; his impaired brain consolidates his undercover identity as "time travel" and produces hallucinations of the future. In subsequent episodes, evidence in support of this hypothesis proliferates. In short, then, the protagonist *does* live in 1973. It is not time that is unhinged but Sam Tyler himself.

All this not so much changes the storyline as it impacts on the status of the image as such. Take a moment to re-view figures 2.6–2.10 in order to try to *see* the exact opposite of what has been argued so far with respect to these excerpts. The third rationalization of Sam Tyler's "temporal displacement" capsizes the established logic of the narrative and, eventually, pulls the comforting rug of representation out from under the viewer. The clear distinction between a virtual present and an actual future collapses: the virtuality of Sam's 1973 reality is less and less secure; the viewer might have been unknowingly witnessing the experience of a psychosomatically affected protagonist. Yet the narrative never fully endorses any of the explanations it offers: *Life on Mars* does not simply reinvert the order of the actual and the virtual realities. It offers this inversion as one way of seeing the series, all the while maintaining the alternative explanation. Consequently, there are two coexisting but mutually exclusive ways of visually accessing the narrative: You can continue to believe that Sam is in a coma and that the main narrative represents the activity of a comatose brain; in this case, the actual image on the screen remains that of a virtual reality that corresponds to an actual but invisible reality. Alternatively, you may consider that Sam actually lives in 1973 and suffers from amnesia and hallucination; consequently, the narrative represents an actual reality that is disturbed by the virtual images or "visions" of a diseased mind. The point is, in any case, that the narrative maintains both of these incompossible views. The storyline is constructed such that the viewer must consider both possibilities at the same time.[18]

In this way, the narrative is doubly saturated with meaning and splits the act of viewing into a kind of double vision. This semantic excess of the image ultimately undercuts its own economy of stable and unifying representation. No longer only a representation, the image eventfully becomes figure. By virtue of its sustained ambiguity, the series triggers a continuous oscillation between its two logics through which the actual and the virtual realities continuously twist and fold into each other: the concurrence of the series' double logic and the duplicitous audiovisual rendition of each splits the narrative into two distinct stories and four images. Significantly, though, the proliferation of contending actual and virtual images emerges out of a single and concrete audiovisual narrative. Not unlike a topological figure, the formerly reliable narrative folds in and out on itself. The different images are distinct and can be *con-*

ceived individually but, on a *perceptual* level, they are indiscernible. The narrative of *Life on Mars* is unified and split at the same time. The act of seeing persistently doubles on itself and the viewer's eye is caught up in a "continual flicker between these two visions" (Massumi 2002b, 65). Similarly, the conceptual distinction between the present and the future is maintained within each storyline, but this distinction can no longer be unequivocally and concretely perceived by the viewer. It is impossible to settle the question of the chrono- and ontological relations between the 1973 and 2006 plot strands. Any sense of linear time has been lost. In very much the same way, it is impossible to settle the question of consciousness. Sam's consciousness must be impaired (by his coma or his hallucinations) to allow for the strange loops and inversions of *Life on Mars*; this much we know. Once more, however, the "future shocks" do not produce a simple negation of conscious perception. Rather, they make consciousness and its negation indiscernible: Sam's future shocks (figures 2.6–2.10) increase the ambiguity of the narrative. In these sequences, we see either Sam-the-madman *lose* his consciousness in 1973 or we see Sam-the-coma-patient *regain* it in 2006. While the viewer can distinguish between these two possibilities, she cannot know which of the two she sees.

This indeterminacy does not make *Life on Mars* messy. The show is not "jumping the shark" but rather putting in place one more conditioning factor to sculpt its diagrammatic movement. In fact, representation's indetermination is more appropriately thought as its incipience in the elastic relational field of storytelling: neither the discursive separation into *story* and *discourse* nor the functional distribution of narrator, narrative, and recipient is a structural given. What *Life on Mars* makes felt is that the relation between narrative and spectator cannot be settled once and for all. One continuously becomes a listener or viewer or storyteller, possibly shifting between various positions, in the relational field of storytelling. The figure lifting off from the various forces pulling at the image gives an unseen-unheard plasticity to reality in the making.

This eventful coming-into-being of the image cannot be seen or heard because it is not *in* the image; it is what constitutes the image-event and must be thought-felt. Watching *Life on Mars*, one cannot resolve the above-mentioned ambiguities and must grasp the narrative as a multiplicity of possible scenarios always only on the cusp of being fully actualized. Thus, the breakdown of the representational image and the breakout from linear narrative progression bring incompossible potentialities into immediate proximity and make them resonate eventfully in a nonlinear process. As the narrative fails to "perfectly *represent* the contingent," perceptual certainty is constantly delayed (Doane 2002, 22). But this delay, this interval, in which it is possible to experience becoming, is a zone of indetermination and, hence, a center of action. In this zone of indetermination, the received notion by which the television spectator has a fixed, passive, and privileged vantage point onto a contained image-space comes apart. One can no longer separate the message or "text" and the spectator into preexisting entities. *Life on Mars* makes clear that spectatorship—all spectatorship—is more appropriately understood as an event that lifts off from a relational field of continuous activity between images, sounds, and the senses. This means that here indeterminacy is not simply a matter of conflicting "interpretations" of a "text," a phrasing that would insist on the material anteriority of the text as object and the intellectual superiority of the viewer as the decoding, sense-making subject. In this view, the "text" would remain a stable object and the various interpretations could be reduced to subjective points of view regarding the text. What is at stake here is the very act of regarding, the very experience of viewing that is composed by what Raymond Ruyer calls a "spectacle-spectator complex." In such a complex, there is no linear cause (intention) or effect (interpretation); all elements of the field collectively compose the event of viewing in a network of multidirectional, reciprocal relations (Ruyer 1958, 205; see also Massumi 2014, 75–76). In *Life on Mars*, the indetermination of the narrative and the uncertainty of cognition, perception, and, in particular, their cofunctioning affectively involve and evolve the viewer. Affective involvement activates vision: instead of following an unambiguous narrative, the viewer experiences the continuous differentiation of several incompossible stories unfolding simultaneously. She unsees-unhears but senses and participates in the creative evolution of images, a process that continuously postpones a unifying, representational solution within and across episodes. Sam's former life in a concrete future is no longer more than one possibility among many, lingering at the edge of the image. To think-feel the interval of the image's becoming is to unknow the future. Thus, after critiquing metric time in various ways within the story, *Life on Mars* offers an immediate experience of duration as it "hinders everything from being given at once" (Bergson 2007b, 75). Time, Bergson says, "retards, or rather it is retardation. It must therefore be elaboration" (75). In a similar way, the second season of *Life on Mars*, far from representing a reliable fictional narrative, asks the viewer to continuously elaborate her own vision. As the series ceases to obey its premises that regulate how its images can be seen, its representational indeterminacy creates the sense of a nonpreempted, unforeclosed future that leaves the image and the viewer herself open to constant elaboration.

This is also the beginning of a different ethical attitude toward time. Alternatingly leaning into the various entangled possibilities of the narrative's playing-out, the viewer senses its potential for becoming. Once the viewer has unknown the future, *Life on Mars* is all about the present; it contracts toward the middle. However, this present is not that of Sam's story, which is now as indeterminate as the future. We suddenly feel ourselves to be in the midst of the narrative's very own unfolding. This attention to the now is not a conceptually blown-up version of carpe diem. If the present emerges in the middle, it must come to be in the middle of something. On the one end, the entire past billows up against the unfurling now; what furls in from the other end is futurity, a tendency toward the not-yet. An attending to the present is a *tending-toward* the future; to lean into the incompossible potentialities of the now is at the same time to lean into what is next. Importantly, it is the past that prods us into the new: "The Bergsonian revolution is clear: We do not move from the present to the past, from perception to recollection, but from the past to the present, from recollection to perception" (Deleuze 1988a, 63). This pushy past acts as what David Lapoujade calls a "memory of the future," which is also a memory *for* the future. It is "something which has been present, that has been sensed, but that has not been acted" (Lapoujade 2013, 22). It is these recollections of the unacted that contract and dilate around the present and from which the latter draws its explosive force—contraction (and dilation) of the unlived past around the present instead of its constriction by a concrete future.

By overfilling one concrete image with representational potential, *Life on Mars* creates a relational field of storytelling that makes felt the force of such a memory of/for the future as it edges into the world. Simultaneously, the series affirms the viewer's co-individuation *as viewer* by making felt her own partaking of time-in-the-making. The point is not that, in so doing, *Life on Mars* achieves something unprecedented. Rather, it is to acknowledge that such relational, co-composing becoming happens all the time despite our tendency to unthink-unfeel it. In moving toward the uncomfortable edge of representation, *Life on Mars* undercuts this tendency and emphasizes the form-taking of the representational. Yet *Life on Mars*'s ethics-in-germ is not simply a matter of self-reflectively becoming aware of what is already going on. It is an ethics of intuition. In a Bergsonian tradition of thought, intuition is precisely this "relational movement through which the present begins to coexist with its futurity, with the quality or manner of the not-yet that lurks at the edges of actual experience" (Manning 2012, 355). The figural release from the tensions between representational solutions in *Life on Mars* is a proposition to resist one's reliance on the comfortingly concrete, an invitation for flushing the present with the abstract potentials of the past. It consists in thinking-feeling the unknown as an opportunity to create (rather than as a threat) and in attending to the world's becoming with a sense of care for the not-yet. The challenge is to achieve a maximal holding of indetermination—three uncertain representations in the present case—in order to sense the world's becoming before making sense of it, to feel the openness of the future as an invitation to create.

Easily said, one might object. It is true that this is infinitely more difficult to do. In order to achieve this, one might have to radically reorient one's way of being in the world. A good way of going about it is to learn from those who already know the difficulties of inhabiting this world. It is no coincidence that the figure of time in *Life on Mars* lifts off from the linkage of two psychosomatic conditions: coma and amnesia/hallucination. The series introduces each of these conditions into its fictional world to give its protagonist a particular scope and quality of temporal experience. Within either representational logic, the protagonist's psychopathologic dysfunctionality corresponds to a specific thought-feltness of time of the protagonist. But, it should also be noted, it is only afterward, in an anxiety-driven reaction to the felt quality of time, that Sam assumes his various attitudes toward the future. In either case, Sam's lived experience of time is limited to one or several of its aspects and his attitude is unproductive. In either case, time is mediated, contained *within* representation just as, in turn, representation seems to be *in* time as a linearly unfolding container medium. This changes, however, once coma dreams, amnesia, and hallucinations are no longer confined within the representational rules of correspondence and signification. *Life on Mars* introduces its doubly psychopathological protagonist so that the viewer, by way of a figural image-event, can break out of the habitual modes of experiencing and thinking time. What leaks through the porous confines of representation into felt reality is an inkling of the "richness of ontological experimentation" that neurologically diverse conditions allow for and that is barely known to a neurotypical mind (Guattari 1995, 82).[19] The point of such an ethical reorientation can obviously not be to completely relinquish efficient action or, to take up Bergson's vocabulary, to permanently disrupt the sensory-motor schema. Rather, it is about minding the gap between perception and movement, about flushing the interval of becoming with creative potential. Guattari's words are key: We need to become sensitive to the richness of the world, an abundance that lies *beyond* concrete reality, spatiotemporal grids, and action-oriented schemata. We need not look for an absolute alternative but for a more-than in the well known. (This also means that there is no point in debunking the said concrete reference points, grids of intelligibility, and the action-oriented schemata. It means we are impelled to work around and with them.) If we acknowledge that the future is always in the making as the past contracts and dilates to creatively nudge the present into a not-yet, then we acknowledge that our activity in the world is a matter of experimentation.

Loop-Through

At the beginning of its second season, *Life on Mars* plunges into figural experimentation. The series moves to the uncomfortable edge of representation and recasts the future as the not-yet, as an attention to the present tending toward what it will have been. At the same time, *Life on Mars* reactivates the past, the series' first season, by creating an eerie sense of what this past could have been but was not at the time (madness instead of coma instead of time travel). Far from being a stable archive, the past is felt as a diagrammatic force that co-composes the future-tending now. *Life on Mars* figures topological time as it makes the audiovisual image encompass more than the presently visible, as sensation exceeds perception, as the present is experienced as a future-past. In this way, the series manages to foreground the creative becoming of the image in a mediascape that conventionally foregrounds the progression of a story. *Life on Mars* creates a productive relation between the image and the viewer, who experiences the potential of the (audiovisual) present moment as its pasts and futures fold into it, as it vibrates within a multiplicity of virtuals, to create the next now.

VECTOR

A book of philosophy should be in part a very particular species of detective novel, in part a kind of science fiction. By detective novel we mean that concepts, with their zones of presence, should intervene to resolve local situations. They themselves change along with the problems. . . . I make, remake and unmake my concepts along a moving horizon, from an always decentred centre, from an always displaced periphery which repeats and differenciates [sic] them. The task of modern philosophy is to overcome the alternatives temporal/non-temporal, historical/eternal and particular/universal. Following Nietzsche we discover, as more profound than time and eternity, the untimely: philosophy is neither a philosophy of history, nor a philosophy of the eternal, but untimely, always and only untimely—that is to say, "acting counter to our time and thereby acting on our time and, let us hope, for the benefit of a time to come." . . . We believe in a world in which individuations are impersonal, and singularities are pre-individual: the splendour of the pronoun "one"—whence the science-fiction aspect. . . . Science fiction in yet another sense, one in which the weaknesses become manifest. How else can one write but of those things which one doesn't know, or knows badly? (Deleuze 1994, xx–xxi)

CHAPTER 3

LOOP INTO LINE

The Moral Command of Preemption

Knowledge and Thought: From Detective Fiction to Science Fiction

"A book of philosophy should be in part a very particular species of detective novel, in part a kind of science fiction."[1] Inversely, detective fiction and sci-fi share characteristics of philosophical thought. As I transition from *Life on Mars* to *Flashforward*, it becomes possible to understand what detective fiction and science fiction can do for philosophy. Deleuze spells it out: "concepts," not unlike a detective, "should intervene to resolve local situations" and produce knowledge. But, he continues, these concepts change as the problem changes. We have seen in the previous chapter that *Life on Mars* repeats its problem of time three times, each repetition changing both the problem itself and the concepts put to work to resolve it. The series' movement from representation to a suprarepresentational figure of time generated an understanding of time as the creative becoming of a topological world. This chapter explores the political implications of preemptive narratives through an engagement with the science fiction series *Flashforward* (ABC, 2009–10). If science fiction lends itself to philosophical thinking, this is because it continuously confronts the unthought. This unrelenting impulse makes science fiction resonate with philosophy: "How else can one write but of those things which one doesn't know, or knows badly?"

The transition from the police procedural to science fiction is also a shift in focus from knowledge production to thought and to the limits of knowledge as the motor of thought. This relation between knowledge and thought is a complex one. For if the unknown triggers movements of thought, knowledge comes with a risk of stopping thought. In other words, this relation poses a temporal problem: the tension between thought and knowledge is that between process and product. What further complicates the matter is that knowledge especially as conceived in the scientific and idealist traditions tends to present itself as a positive fact or law once it has taken form and thus obliterates its form-taking through thought. To defend the primacy of knowledge over the unruly dynamism of thought, the dominant philosophical traditions construct it as a stable *above* and *below* of thought: a transcendental *above* to be accessed, a truth to be discovered *below* the surface of things. As such, true knowledge is reliable and secure precisely because it is atemporal.[2] Bergson elaborates this in his explanation of the "mechanistic" conception of time, according to which "all is given" (see chapter 2). Past, present, and future are equally determined; we just do not know them in equal measure. By implication, then, the future is merely a truth to be discovered, not to be created. Time is thus treated as a problem of knowledge and, indeed, the laws of Galilean and Newtonian mechanics manage to solve this problem for their areas of inquiry, namely the motion of celestial and earthly bodies. This overall argumentation prepares an ingenious twist that safeguards the stability of true and lawful knowledge. For if time is merely a matter of knowledge, knowledge cannot appear as a matter of time. It is always already there, waiting to be discovered. As time is thus twisted into a problem of human ignorance, the world becomes strangely atemporal.[3] A similar consequence is implied in Immanuel Kant's philosophy of cognition. In distinction to the *phenomena*, which are things as they appear to the sensing subject, he postulates the existence of *noumena*, that is, things in themselves, independent of and inaccessible to human cognition.[4] Because Kant has previously defined space and time as "the sensible forms of our intuition," it follows—again, strangely—that things in themselves are not in space or time.[5] How this must be understood exactly is, of course, one of the questions that has preoccupied readers of Kant for over two hundred years, and the various interpretations cannot be discussed here. Two things are worth noting, however. The first is that space and time are once again epistemic conditions for human cognition and consequently pose an epistemological problem. The second is that, outside of human intuition, the world of things in themselves is neither spatial nor temporal. These implications lead Bergson to reject theories that construe time as an epistemological problem and to reinvent it as a matter of vitality, of activity and creation. They are the reason why he says that we are "really giving up time" if we treat it as merely a problem of human understanding (Bergson 2001, 98).⁶ Or, rather, time thus conceived as a question of knowledge will feed back into our engagements with the world and modulate them. Our presumed knowledge of time "falls back into experience" (Deleuze 1994, 166). How does it fall back into experience? Kant's philosophy as well as Galilean and Newtonian physics are in keeping with what William James describes as the "ruling tradition in philosophy [, which] has always been the platonic and aristotelian belief that fixity is a nobler and worthier thing than change" (1920, 237). Assuming that change is merely an idiosyncrasy of human perception, this tradition allows one to posit "a science single and complete, embracing the whole of the real" that "is not, then, a human construction" but "prior to our intellect, independent of it, veritably the generator of Things" (Bergson 1911, 356, 321). Knowledge is a resource to be mined for, discovered, and exploited. This belief continues to influence social relation in our contemporary "knowledge societies," in which information has become a commodity to be exchanged, arguably at the expense of creative thought. Time itself is increasingly metricized, for instance, in practices of forecasting or high-frequency trading.

Beyond that, this particular relation between knowledge and time also informs moral and ethical considerations. Your conception of ethics and politics will change according to whether you argue for a deterministic world governed by the laws of nature (and in which time is merely an illusion) or for a world of becoming abounding with novelty (in which intellectual certainty is an illusion). The TV series *Flashforward* addresses this problem in popular terms: if you think "the future is unwritten," then you can change it and prevent catastrophes from happening.⁷ If you think "it's all mapped out," then the future is inevitable and your options range somewhere between defeatism and preempting the future before it can hit you unawares. Prevention *or* preemption, the science fiction of *Flashforward* suggests, are the two materially and therefore politically viable paths. However, as the narrative oscillates between these two options of a questionable alternative, its serial movement gradually crafts a figure of time that indicates a political dynamic far more disconcerting than a deterministic universe or a world of becoming full of uncertainty: a self-causing future.

Security and Identity: Be Gone, Self-Difference!

The premise of *Flashforward* is summed up at the beginning of each episode: "On October 6 [, 2009], the planet blacked out for two minutes and seventeen seconds. The whole world saw the future." Every single person on the planet loses consciousness at the same time, an event that in itself causes the death of more than 20 million people: planes and cars crash, people drown in pools or bathtubs, fall down stairs, and so forth. But the actual disaster is of a different kind: during the 137 seconds of what will be referred to as "the blackout," people see their own future exactly six months ahead. They experience roughly two minutes of their life on April 29, 2010. These "flash-forwards" will cause personal and political crises that threaten to unravel the present. Consider the protagonist, Mark Benford (Joseph Fiennes). This FBI agent investigating the causes of the blackout is also a recovered alcoholic who sees himself drinking again in the future. His wife, Olivia (Sonya Walger), sees herself in a relationship with another man, Lloyd Simcoe (Jack Davenport), a quantum physicist whose experiments at NLAP may have caused the blackout.[8] Others, like Mark's friend Aaron (Brían F. O'Byrne), have a rosier glimpse into the future: Aaron sees his daughter, who was presumed dead. Understandably, Mark and Olivia will do everything to prevent their future visions from happening whereas Aaron would reunite with his daughter sooner rather than later. To complicate matters, all these futures are linked in a global ecology of connected fates: bringing about one desirable future might drag another undesirable vision into actuality, or have further, *un*foreseen effects. Prevention or preemption, what will it be? Let the thought experiment begin.

Let's start by pointing out that people on either side of this alternative resemble each other in one major respect. What brings all the characters in *Flashforward* together—so much so that it becomes one of the series' central themes—is that they are stunned by their own self-difference. The show's generalized crisis is produced by the characters' practical insight into the nonidentity of their present and future selves. The immediate reaction is an urgent desire to reinstate self-sameness: Mark and Olivia resist change and take measures in order *not* to become what their future visions suggest (i.e., drinking and adulterous divorcées). They want to *stay* the same. In contrast, others who, like Aaron, have had a promising flash-forward will take measures to realize their future visions, in order to make their present selves identical to their future selves. In either case, it is the discrepancy between the present and the future self that triggers panic and euphoria. Viewed through the prism of a philosophy of creative becoming, the curious thing to note then about *Flashforward* is that the entire world flies into a frenzy at the prospect of self-differentiation. What causes a global turmoil is the idea of change. This suspicion of change could not be rooted more deeply in the science fiction of *Flashforward*: the horror of change is directly related to the other big threat of our time, terrorism. *Flashforward*'s villain is—literally—a time terrorist. This identification is interesting for several reasons. First, it equates terrorism and uncertainty: while it is true that terrorism acts as a force in the world by virtue of the fear caused by the unpredictable when and where of the next attack, *Flashforward* seems to suggest a kind of biunivocal correspondence by which uncertainty and incalculable change also always indicate terrorism. This is noteworthy because one could be inclined to think that the show's future visions allow for greater certainty given that they provide useful information about coming events. One might further assume with Jean-Pierre Dupuy and Slavoj Žižek that knowing the future would make it easier for individuals and collectives to both rationally consider the projected calamities and deliberate on adequate counterfactual action plans. However, the exact opposite happens in *Flashforward* because the primary effect of the future visions is not to spark the reasonable reflections of "projected time" but to activate the interval of becoming that is the domain of affect. Though the characters of *Flashforward* may know exactly what their lives are going to look like in the future, they do not know when, where, and how change will occur. It is this indeterminacy of becoming that discharges into a collective panic before rational preventive measures can even be considered. *Flashforward*'s future visions trigger the preemptive dynamic laid out in chapter 1 and whose affective charge is primary to and far exceeds the possible benefits of factual information about the future.

Second, the shocking threat of change is identified with an individual adversary, the mad scientist Dyson Frost (Michael Massee). That the figure of the mad scientist should be cast as a global terrorist further complicates *Flashforward*'s time politics. Besides the obvious implication that scientific knowledge turns into a dangerous weapon once it gets in the wrong hands, the narrative constructs its adversary as a malevolent outsider, excluded by means of a vague notion of "evil madness." We are far from Guattari's productive understanding of madness evoked in the previous chapter. Here, madness is not the enabling condition for a "richness of ontological experimentation" otherwise unavailable (Guattari 1995, 82). Instead it serves to pinpoint an individual's identity, exclude that individual from a discourse of reasonable politics, and motivate an act of terrorist violence. In a few strokes, *Flashforward* has sketched Dyson Frost, the time terrorist, as the perfect threat to national security and the blackout/flash-forward as a "violation of the self-same by an external intruder" (Manning 2007, 52). But the threat to security is not only the insane other from the outside. In addition to Dyson Frost as the terrorist other, the threat to security arises from the differences of the self to itself in time. In fact, the former threat is mainly a means of figuratively capturing and discriminating the latter. In short, then, change is constructed as a threat to national security. On the level of the individual, the problem is that there will be change. For social groups—from families to the world population—the peril consists in diverging notions of which kind of change is desirable, how fast it should occur, and so on. What becomes clear is that the main issue of political contention in *Flashforward* is time itself. It is relatively clear which strategy must subtend the reaction to such a threat: if change is the threat to national security, then security must be reinstated by preventing change, by reestablishing self-sameness.

As *Flashforward* correlates self-sameness and security on the one hand as well as self-differentiation and insecurity on the other, it also constructs an opposition between these pairs that is partly reminiscent of the above-mentioned relation between knowledge and thought. Thought, because it is in motion, carries within itself an element of risk. And because thought in motion is nonlinear, its outcome cannot be predicted. This means that to start thinking is always also to accept the possibility of failure. As long as failure is made to coincide with unproductivity, thought implies danger and incites fear. In contrast, the stability of knowledge's representational content suggests relative security. In *Neuropolitics*, William Connolly suggests that there is "a constitutive element of wildness in thinking [that is] marked by danger" (2002, 113). This dangerous wildness results from the fundamentally temporal quality of thought, which also makes it "a fragile and vulnerable activity" (98). Danger, fragility, and vulnerability: these are hard to sell to a population struggling through times of crisis. Connolly nonetheless proposes that we embrace the "compositional dimension of thinking" instead of concealing it to solidify positive knowledge, for uncertainty and risk cannot be separated out in a world of becoming (92). The idea is obviously not to discard stability, security, and knowledge for the sake of change, uncertainty, and thought in motion. Rather, the question is how the two can be brought together. *Flashforward* does bring them together, though not overtly. It appears to struggle with this alternative as a self-inflicted binary, a struggle that shows in its dual generic affiliation: it is both a detective story and science fiction. That is, the series depicts at the same time the FBI's search for those responsible for the blackout and the consequences of future orientation in macro- and micropolitical environments. This tension between the *whodunit* and the science fictional thought experiment leads into two directions: the first is Deleuze's description of philosophical thought quoted at the beginning of this chapter; the second leads to yet another differential, that between the figurative and the figural.

Imaging the Future

Flashforward's present is precariously suspended between two catastrophes, the blackout and the foreseen future. This suspension strains the present. Instead of past and futurity feeding into the present, they feed on the present, so to speak. As the unfolding narrative tends in both directions, it does, however, try to hold the two together—by looping the future through the past. While people's flash-forwards pull them into the future, they do so as *memories* of the flash-forward, or "memories of the future" (ep. 1). This is not, however, David Lapoujade's *mémoire de l'avenir* discussed in the previous chapter. Instead of activating the future potentials of the past, *Flashforward*'s memories of the future create an indeterminacy that threatens to unravel the present.[9]

The show begins with a *mise en abyme* that familiarizes the viewer with its logic. *Flashforward* opens without a slow establishing shot, an intriguing musical score, or any other televisual opening convention. It begins right in the noisy, upside-down middle of the flash-forward's aftermath (see figure 3.1): a close-up on a man's head upside down, car horns, ambulance sirens; cut to oranges rolling on the overhead ground, bits of broken glass falling up (see figure 3.2). As the man works himself into an upright position, the camera zooms out and we see that he is hanging in an overturned car. As the man inspects the surrounding chaos (and we with him), a shaky camera moves aberrantly around him, suggesting vertigo, creating disorientation. The frame takes in smoke, fire, and numerous injured people on what seems to be a massive pileup on a freeway. Abruptly, the show's title appears, accompanied by an animated lens flare (see figure 3.3). A black screen and intertitle appear: "four hours earlier" (see figure 3.4). Now we get the most conventional of openings in the form of a panoramic establishing shot on the sun rising behind the Hollywood Hills. "Good morning, Los Angeles," the radio says as the birds twitter over an easy piano tune. The image cuts to another static shot of suburban family homes, only to didactically cut in closer on one particular street, then a particular house (see figure 3.5). Finally the camera lands on a loving couple—we recognize the man hanging upside down in his car—starting their day with good-morning kisses (see figure 3.6).

Considering the conventions of broadcast television (after all, this is ABC), the contrast could not be more startling. Within two minutes, *Flashforward* has sunk its hooks into the viewer, who wants to know what it is she just saw, what it is that is going to happen. Of course, this proleptic glimpse of an imminent narrative future has become a stock technique of serial television: it creates suspense, pulls the audience in, and pushes toward the future. But what happens in perception when the future is already a memory, bound to repeat itself?

As the second opening sets out to catch up with the first one, *Flashforward* takes up speed until, just before the blackout, it offers one of its most interesting montage sequences, in which the rapid intercutting between various characters renders the interconnectedness of their social relations. The sequence begins with shots of Mark, who is caught up in a car chase, and then cuts to his daughter, who is asleep at home. Meanwhile, the daughter's babysitter sneakily makes out with her boyfriend in the downstairs living room and Olivia preps for an operation at the hospital. At the same time, Aaron, also at work, climbs an electric pole while Olivia's doctor colleague Bryce (Zachary Knighton) skips work to blow a bullet through his brain at Venice Pier, where surfers ride

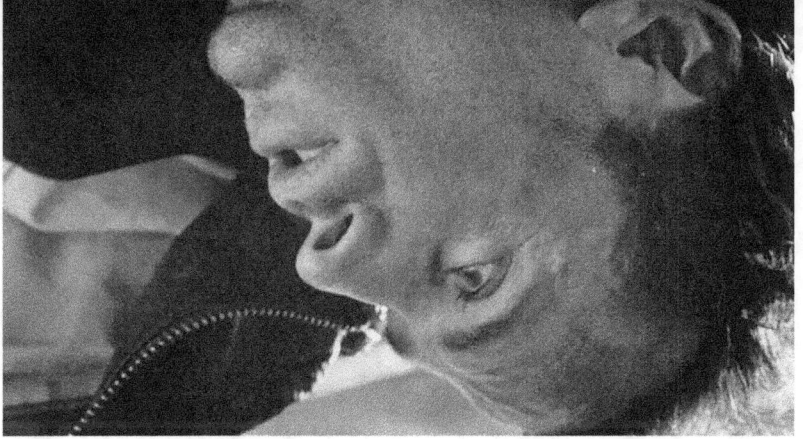

Figure. 3.1. *Flashforward*: Mark Benford (Joseph Fiennes) hanging upside down in car.

Figure. 3.2. *Flashforward*: oranges on the ground upside down.

Figure. 3.3. *Flashforward*: series title and lens flare.

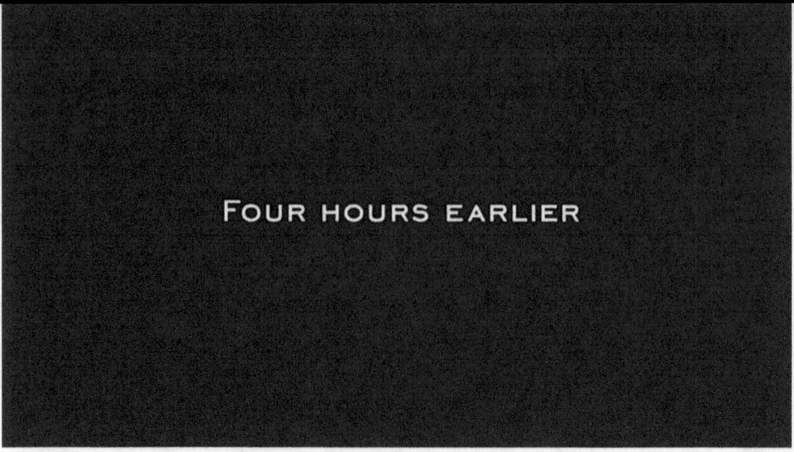

Figure. 3.4. *Flashforward*: intertitle "four hours earlier."

Figure. 3.5. *Flashforward*: exterior view of suburban home.

Figure. 3.6. *Flashforward*: Mark Benford and Olivia waking together.

the waves. In fact, the way in which this sequence holds together a complex and shifting reality is not unlike riding with a wave that forcefully pushes you into the not-yet. Just when you think that the wave might break, that the image might trip over its abundance of information, it cuts to agent Benford's iris and zooms in to a sound effect that suggests maximum acceleration (see figures 3.7–3.9). Welcome to Mark Benford's future vision. The sequence consists of blurry, shaky images of Benford in his office, investigating the blackout and drinking. In addition to numerous jump cuts between shots, the image is further saturated by double exposures, lens flares, and color filters.

This concurrence of future visions, suspended consciousness, and post-continuity editing leads Patricia Pisters to consider *Flashforward* an "interesting contemporary example of a neuro-image (with movement-image tendencies) that is told from the point of view of the future" (2011, 111). Pisters proposes her concept of the *neuro-image* as a continuation of Deleuzian film philosophy, correlating it with Deleuze's philosophy of time in *Difference and Repetition.* If the movement-image, grounded in the first synthesis of time, produces a sensory-motor present and the time-image, grounded in the second synthesis of time, activates the past, Pisters suggests, then the neuro-image can be related to the third synthesis of time, which continuously culls a next now by in- and remixing the first two syntheses.[10] In addition, the cinema of the neuro-image is "a mental cinema that differs in major ways from previous dominant modes of filming" (111).[11] Pisters detects that the preoccupation with the future in contemporary moving-image narratives correlates with a new interest in issues of consciousness, neurological processes, and madness. These observations allow Pisters to describe "a change in cinema, where we slowly but surely have moved from following characters' actions (movement-image), to seeing the world filtered through their eyes (time-image), to *experiencing directly their mental landscapes* (neuro-image)" (110, emphasis added).

While Pisters provides an adequate description of *Flashforward*, it is on the issue of direct experience, of immediacy, that the present argument parts ways with her account. It is true that *Flashforward* uses jump cuts, shaky cam, unusual camera angles, double exposures, fast editing, lens flares, and color filters to image agent Benford's brain space and to create a sense of disorientation, uncertainty, and urgency, but the expe-

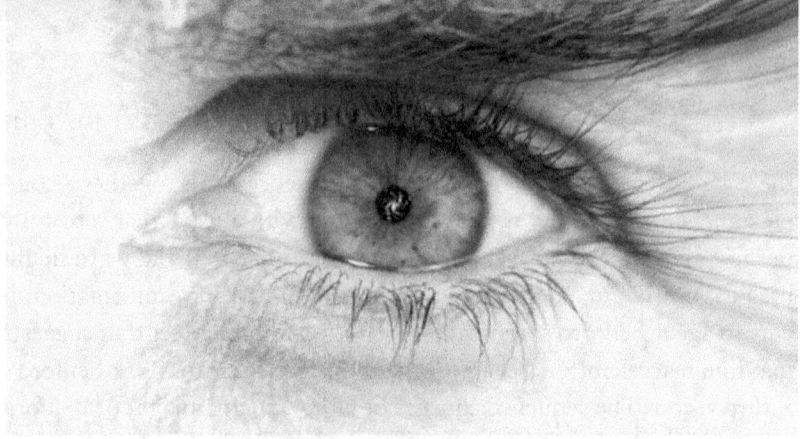

Figure. 3.7. *Flashforward*: close-up of Mark Benford's eye.

Figure. 3.8. *Flashforward*: animated zoom into pupil.

Figure. 3.9. *Flashforward*: animated zoom into pupil with spiral of light.

rience of both the future and mental landscapes remains utterly mediate (or indirect). The visions in *Flashforward* may be "images from the future" but they are first of all images *of* the future. They are not examples of Deleuze's notion that "the brain is the screen": what Benford's future vision and the many to follow give us is, once more, a screen that is an *image of* the brain, a representation of a mental landscape (Deleuze 2006b, 282–91).[12] This insistence on the figurative prevents an engagement with the figural movement in *Flashforward*. Moreover, it disregards the moral and political affiliations of the show.

If the neuro-image still confines us within the figurative, then where is it that the bubbling of a figure can be sensed? Consider once more the first eight minutes of the series' pilot episode building up to the global blackout/flash-forward. It is here, in this unmotivated temporal loop, that the conditions for a figural movement are set. The show begins, as was said, right in an uncomfortable middle. The image—possibly upside down, certainly lacking narrative framing, shaking, and noisy—is unmoored.

It is then retrospectively given a conventional, stabilizing frame (establishing shots, musical score, cut-in). But as the intertitle ("four hours earlier") introduces retrospection, it also makes us acknowledge that the previous sequence was as an instance of prospection. The orderly second opening of *Flashforward* is already infused with our memory of the future. It is therefore useless to try to decide (in narratological terms) whether we are now looking back into the past or ahead into the future. As we learn how the future-now-past comes into being, retrospection has already inevitably folded into prospection. One must speak of *our* memory of the future and *us* anticipating the future through a memory of it because this opening sequence gives us one of the shows' few unmotivated flash-forwards, one that is not mediated as the future vision of a character within the fictional world (Mark Benford et al.). The difference is crucial. Most of the series' subsequent flash-forwards—much like the conventional flash*back*—create closed circuits anchored in a future-remembering subject. Such circuits branch out from the narrative's linear progression but ultimately return to it. In fact, the extrinsic circuit of the motivated flashback/flash-forward oftentimes serves as an explanation of the (future-)remembering subject in the present: "character *x* remembers seeing incident *y* in his or her future vision and *consequently* does *z* in the present." In this sense, the flash-forward fortifies the rational connections of the plot and reconfirms linear narrative progression. This is one of the reasons why, for Deleuze, the recollection-image and the dream-image are *not yet* time-images. Quite different is the case of the black screen and the intertitle: "The black or white screen stands for the outside of all the images, when the flickerings multiply the interstices like irrational cuts . . . , when proceeding by loops effects relinkages. . . . The film does not record the filmic process in this way without projecting a cerebral process. A flickering brain, which relinks or creates loops—this is cinema" (Deleuze 1989, 215). So, instead of moving *into* someone's headspace (for instance, through agent Benford's eye), instead of accessing an image *within* the image, instead of adding to the image's "interiority" or narrative "depth" in this way, the black screen takes us outside the image, "of all the images." The before and the after are not stacked into each other by means of a dissolve or a zoom-into-eye ushering the viewer into a character's memory (of the future). They are disconnected, in juxtaposition, divided by a black screen, the outside of all images. That the images are disconnected does not mean that they do not relate. On the contrary, it is in the interstice of the outside that a relation emerges, a "relation-of-nonrelation" (Massumi 2011, 20). The relation of times takes off from outside the black screen. Prearticulated as it is, the relation must be unseen, or nonsensuously sensed as it comes into effect. Sensed by whom, this time? The viewer. What takes off from the disconnect between juxtaposed images is a relational field that involves the viewer, is in fact coeffectuated by her. This is why the future vision at the very opening of *Flashforward* is ours, the viewers', directly experienced as a differential relation of times. Following the passage from *The Time-Image* cited above, it is here—in the outside of the image, the irrational cut, the relation of nonrelation, the unmotivated rift in time—that moving images project a cerebral process. At this point, it also becomes clear why the projection of cerebral processes must come into effect outside or in between images. This is because a relation does not coincide with the elements composing it but exceeds the concrete coming-together of its elements. It could be said then that the dictum "the brain is the screen" poses the same challenge to the study of moving images as neuroscientists and philosophers of mind face concerning the relation between the brain and neural consciousness. No measurement and description of brain activity can yet explain how exactly a chunk of matter manages to create a conscious mind by means of electrical signals (see Snaprud 2018). Neural consciousness is a qualitative leap—a lift-off, an excess—beyond brain matter. It is the effect of a relation-of-nonrelation that cannot be reduced to its conditioning factors. How this effect takes off constitutes precisely the so-called hard problem or miracle of consciousness that neuroscience tries to account for (as yet without success). The point here is that just like one cannot reduce consciousness to brain matter, the cerebral processes of the screen cannot be reduced to its material and representational content. They do not coincide with the image; nor are they inside the image, in a concrete representation of "mental landscapes." They take off from the image and these take-offs must be followed in their own right. The screen is a brain long before (and already beyond) the "neuro-image."

The future vision is ours. It is worth repeating, though, that we do not see the future *as* the future. We come to know that what we saw is a future when we are already back in the present (past?). The future is unseen. Nonetheless, our retrospective return to the past is already tinged with prospection. This prospective retrospection is a first sensation of time's intensity. It can be said that this is what comes into effect in excess of the mere juxtaposition of images in a feeling of suspense. This kind of suspense does not obey a logic of revelation; it arises neither from the detective story's *What has happened?* nor the thriller's *What will happen?* but from the intensive layering of the two in a *what-will-have-happened?* Catastrophe will have struck; this much we know. Instead of pulling us toward the production of knowledge, suspense here draws us into a zone of indeterminacy. What is felt in this zone is the ubiquity of self-differentiation: "Suspense is the experience of an intensive embodiment, the body's own propensity to become other in time. Suspense thus names a technic for an attentive awareness to the minor form of difference that (re)constitutes a body in time, a feeling of futurity immediately impinging on the body's stability and reopening it to intensive relationality" (Thain 2017, 3). Sensing the will-have-been of prospective retrospection, we feel both the no-longer and the not-yet of experience in general. This felt suspension in the future-pastness of experience—possibly uncomfortable—creates an "attentive awareness to the minor form of difference." As Thain points out, such an awareness makes the future appear not as a predetermined event but as futurity, which is here understood as the forces calling forth the minimal-multiple inflections of reality that co-compose change, the topological foldings of a becoming world. It is precisely because the future is no longer conceived as a concrete state of affairs but as the not-yet in-the-making that it is not in the image. Co-composed *by* the image, the felt awareness of futurity in the opening sequence of *Flashfoward* comes into effect in excess over the image and, consequently, sense perception. It is an unseen figure of time. The ethico-political stakes of these considerations are inscribed in Thain's formulation of a "*technic* of an *attentive* awareness." A future that lies beyond the representationally determined is one whose playing-out must be relationally composed by attending to the forces at work in the production of the next now. It is worth repeating that this concept of attention is not the commonplace of "awareness" or "mindfulness" in disguise; nor is it a matter of "paying attention," of keeping your eyes and ears open. It demands a technic, previously defined as a coupling of technique and technology. Attentive awareness calls for ways of living with technology that allow us to extract an ethics from the media formats of everyday life.

At the beginning of *Flashforward*, the above-mentioned technique—juxtaposition of images, foregrounding of the interval, forceful lift-off of a figure of time, the coming-into-sensation of futurity as a co-composing of the not-yet—consists in familiarizing us with suspension in the face of catastrophe, not for the purpose of desensitizing us to the shock of calamity but, on the contrary, to resensitize us to the continuous stirrings of a complex reality full of potential. It creates an opportunity for becoming aware of those workings of the image that lie beyond representational determination but still within the relational field of living with serial moving-image narratives. It attunes us to the ways in which the evocation of a future resonates into the present and already inflects or even determines our perception of it. Developing such an awareness, we can begin to carve out a space in which an ethics of attention can take hold and lead toward a creative co-composing of the world. For instance, it can help us develop techniques for defusing the affective charge of a preempted future and maintaining the richness of futurity. Or we could learn to relay the future's affective force into less depotentializing directions. In the case of *Flashforward*, such an ethics is politically relevant also because it makes it possible to think and act beyond the false alternatives of an "all-mapped-out" and an "unwritten" future, of anything goes and determinism. These alternatives are "false" in two senses: First, the two terms of the alternative are not mutually exclusive options. They work together and, as we shall see, contribute to the effective preemption of a future vision. The second aspect of "falsehood" concerns precisely the creativity of this supposed alternative. What emerges from the mutual falsification of one by the other is an authoritative politics that justifies its world-making by insisting that "there is no alternative." We will see shortly how this works in *Flashforward*.

Let's note for now that we are on the track of another way of imaging the future, one that acts before or beyond the mere representation of false alternatives because it is immediately felt. *Flashforward* gives us a feeling of futurity at its very beginning. Earlier I have called this a mise en abyme in passing but in light of the above it could more adequately be called a *mise hors abyme*, an emergence from the gap. At the very beginning of a twenty-two-episode season, *Flashforward* plays out its larger narrative scheme in a figural miniature before that scheme can be apprehended as such. The figural and the figurative seem to work together: once we know what is at issue in *Flashforward*—concrete future visions—the figural miniature activates the six-month interval of the story arc. It prepares us to attend to what stirs between the two moments in time.

This attentive awareness is further strengthened by the way in which the series layers story time and "real time." While the events of *Flashforward* take place between October 6, 2009, and April 29, 2010, the series itself aired from September 24, 2009, to May 27, 2010. These dates do not coincide but clearly indicate an attempt to make the broadcast schedule overlap with the period of time covered in the story. This results in an eerie sense of temporal immediacy because the six months around which the series revolves are not any old one-half year; they are *this* time, my time. One may discard this as a science fiction gimmick, as simple as it is frequent. And, indeed, from the viewpoint of narrative analysis, there is not much more to state than the quasi-simultaneity of two distinct timelines. But if we think the figural as a nonlocal, immaterial connector between the figurative, fictional world and the "real world," we can conceive an affective intermingling of the two—in fact, not so linear—temporalities. The threefold technique of the *mise hors abyme* that preempts the general *loop* of the future through the past in a *layering* of temporalities effectuates a contraction of time around my present. *Flashforward*'s future visions infuse reality with a sense of urgency despite the known fact that the witnessed events are signed with the *as if* of fiction. Fictional time, figurally felt, comes into resonance with my very own experience of time because sensation disregards the dividing line between fiction and reality. This temporal layering also provides one particular answer to the general question raised in chapter 1 regarding the kinds of seriality that television's machinic capacities are able to generate. Unlike much linear narrative, *Flashforward* does not rely on a concept of ordinal seriality in which one element or episode simply follows another in orderly fashion. In fact, the complex interfolding of temporalities—present and future, figurative and figural, fictional and nonfictional—undoes ordinal serialization and instead creates the sense that each episode is being stepped out, lived out, as a next now. Similarly to what I have argued for *Life on Mars* in chapter 2, *Flashforward* initially invites the viewer to experience its image as a relational form-taking that unfolds from this complex of temporalities and whose future remains indeterminate.

At its beginning, then, *Flashforward* goes to some figurative and figural lengths to open up the interval, to make felt the potential that the future-past of becoming holds and that allows for creativity in the world. This is also the beginning of a series of experiments with attention and with techniques for making time. However, the response in *Flashforward* consists in setting off a movement that aims at closing the interval by hook or by crook.

Self-Causing Future Visions

Closing the interval of becoming has the purpose of foreclosing attention. Please do not mind the gap, for your own sense of certainty and protection! Isabelle Stengers suggests that "once it is a matter of what one calls 'development' or 'growth,'" and I would add national security here, "the injunction is above all to not pay attention." For paying attention, in the sense of attending, "requires the ability to resist the temptation to judge" (Stengers 2015, 61–62, translation modified). Inversely, not paying attention leads to hasty judgment that, in return, stops the development of an ethics of immanence. This precipitation of captures unfolds as the figurative recuperates the figural.

If the interval of uncertainty and experimentation must be closed by all means, the suspense *Flashforward* seeks to create can no longer be of the intensive kind. The figural must be in service of the figurative, which caters to the kind of suspense that follows a logic of revelation. In order to produce positive knowledge, imaging must be confined to the order of representation. This does not mean that the asignifying dimension of the image disappears but that it is subordinated to the principles of representation. While future orientation initially drives the movement of the image itself *as a movement of thought*, this dynamism is soon arrested to obey the represented content of the image. Each temporal movement—back or forth in time—is deeply and securely rooted within the story and, instead of contributing to the lift-off of a figure, remains a mere ripple on the surface of the image.

The flattening of temporal folds is at its most conspicuous in the ways in which conventional flashbacks halt the incipient movement of the image. After the initial time loop from the opening sequence, the great majority of the nonlinear temporal movements of the series will be flashforwards that are moored to one or another character within the story. Oftentimes, people will recall their future visions and start retelling them before the image shows the remembered flash-forwards in question. This kind of framing, which says "here comes the past (or future)," is well known from conventional flashbacks. On other occasions, the flashforward may not be explicitly framed, as, for example, when Mark Benford conceals the vision of his relapse into alcoholism from his wife and fragmented images of his drinking cut into his concealment efforts. Here the return of the future is psychologically motivated as a bad conscience: the seemingly unmarked intrusion of the future vision is in fact the mark of secrecy and shame. The future returns as a memory to explain the despair, surprise, and deceitfulness of the present. It can be said, then, that the anachronisms in *Flashforward* are highly conventional in that they serve to plausibly advance a linear plot. In his suspicion against an overhasty, general appraisal of the flashback, Gilles Deleuze writes that it can "indicate, by convention, a causality which is psychological, but still analogous to a sensory-motor determinism, and, despite its circuits, only confirms the progression of linear narration" (1989, 48). The same holds for the flash-*forwards* discussed here. To reformulate in Bergsonian and Deleuzian terms: while the global future visions "unravel the present," or disrupt the sensory-motor schema of action-reaction, the narrative itself imposes measures to reinstate sensory-motor determinism, or to guarantee certainty and security. This is not a performative contradiction but an ethico-aesthetic program.

Reinforcing a sensory-motor schema is an ethico-aesthetic act because it ties perception and action closely together in order to reduce that which occupies the interval between the two and which enables an ethics of attention: affect. The ability to affect and be affected is synonymous with the potential for self-differentiation in a world of becoming. To acknowledge this is to acknowledge one's involvement in a complex topology. As Connolly argues, "The more delay built into the link between perception and action . . . , the more the memories that form part of it can become recollections open to further reflection and assessment" (2002, 28). This conceptual starting point of the delay (interval, suspension) makes it both possible and necessary to think how such a topology is going to play out according to the force relations at work within it. An ethics of attention is an ethics of immanence because what it attends to and works through are immanent criteria and values: "A possibility of life is evaluated through itself in the movements it lays out and the intensities it creates on a plane of immanence" (Deleuze and Guattari 1994, 74). This means that, in contradistinction, a "possibility of life" is not evaluated with reference to transcendent—that is, preexistent and immutable—values. The distinction between an evaluation through immanent criteria on the one hand and preexistent values on the other is correlative to the distinction between an ethics and a morality.

When *Flashforward* reduces the temporal interval by making it commensurable with linear narrative progression, when it makes future visions subservient to (psycho)logical determination, when it asks us "not to pay attention" to the interval's indeterminacy and focus on efficient action, it discards an ethics of immanence in favor of moral judgment. It does so by casting the image of the future as the arbiter of the present. Firmly relying on the unambiguous content of its images, *Flashforward*'s movement between the present and the future is nothing less than a circuit of value judgment, in which the future determines the moral integrity of the present. For this to work, it is crucial that secure knowledge and judgment be closely linked to one another as well as to the representational aspect of imaging. What you see is what you get is what you deserve, *Flashforward* seems to suggest—unless you check your conduct and make the necessary choices for a serious "course correction" (ep. 19). This is what the false alternative of an all-mapped-out and an unwritten future deliberately facilitates in concurrence with prospective retrospection: a morality of command. *Be good, otherwise . . .* This conservatism is not a latent ideology of *Flashforward*; it is frequently made explicit and endearing even, for instance, in references to the character Ebenezer Scrooge from Charles Dickens's *Christmas Carol* (ep. 10). As is well known, flashbacks into Christmas Past explain how Scrooge turns into a reckless miser whereas visions of Christmas Yet to Come explain his sudden transformation into Tiny Tim's benefactor. In fact, rather than just explain it, the visit of the ghost of Christmas Yet to Come brings about this transformation by instilling regret, bad conscience, and fear. The hero of a morality tale is the rehabilitated sinner—but, mind you, "rehabilitated" only because he fears he cannot get away with egoism and cruelty. As a consequence of closing the interval of an uncertain future-past of potentiality, *Flashforward* relates the "not-yet" less and less to the notion of creative becoming and increasingly identifies it with a determinate Catastrophe Yet to Come, a future that serves the purpose of a moral instance. Moral righteousness is back-formed from fear of the future.

The efficiency of the future as moral instance increases with the apparent precision and integrity of the knowledge of that future. This is because the more complete and precise the information is, the more attention this information will draw from self-doubting sinners who seek release from the unbearable torture of not-knowing what will be. (And in the fiction of *Flashforward*, that is everyone.) Moreover, as the future is revealed in all its complexity and precision, the moral judgments that the knowledge of the future carries acquire an overwhelming evidence. The future must therefore be determined, represented, mapped—in short: mediated. *Flashforward* abounds with diagrams and illustrations of the future. Various models are called upon to suggest the future's inevitability: mechanic devices to calculate dates (see figure 3.10), lines of falling dominos (see figure 3.11), and a (rather un-Borgesian) "garden of forking paths" (see figure 3.12, from ep. 17). Consequently, a main goal of the investigating FBI agents is to determine the inevitable future in various maps, webs, and mosaics (see figures 3.13–3.15).[13] The Mosaic

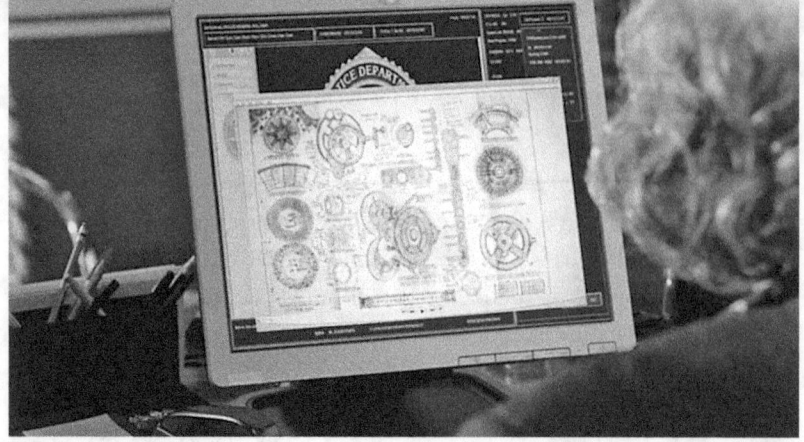

Figure. 3.10. *Flashforward*: computer screen showing the design for an ancient astronomical device.

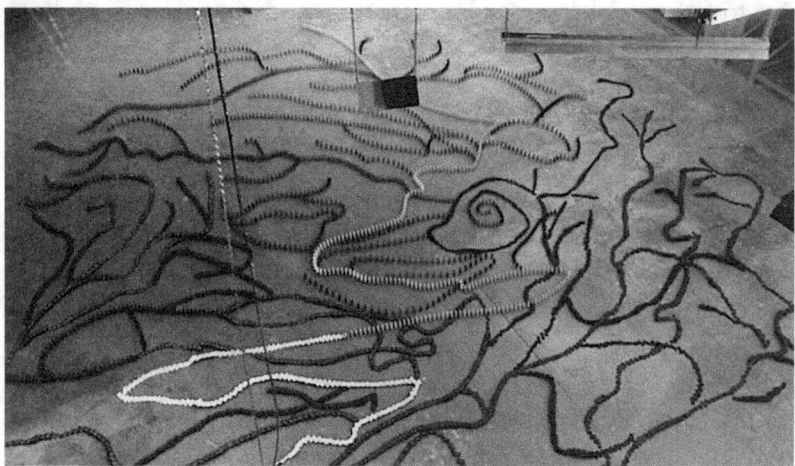

Figure. 3.11. *Flashforward*: black and white dominos on a green floor.

Figure. 3.12. *Flashforward*: colorful temporal diagram on a blackboard.

Figure. 3.13. *Flashforward*: Mark Benford in front of his crime board.

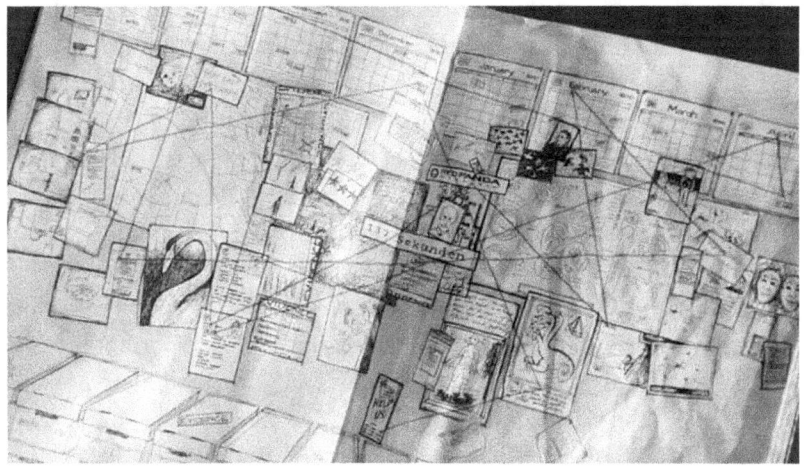

Figure. 3.14. *Flashforward*: diagram on sheet of paper.

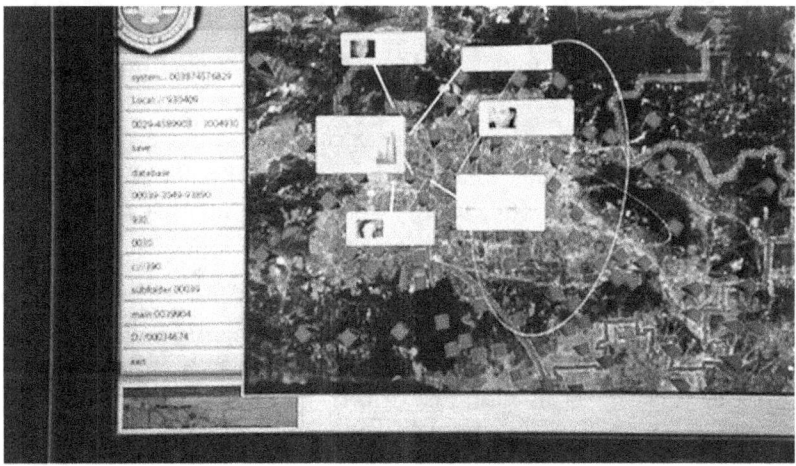

Figure. 3.15. *Flashforward*: computer screen showing map from the Mosaic Collective.

Collective, for instance, is a network database that allows individuals to register their own vision and cross-reference it to others in order to corroborate their future knowledge. *Flashforward*'s mosaic is not a Deleuzian diagram that affirms the creative aspect of immediate participation in a field of complex relations. This database is an epistemological tool for rational decision-making—for the future must be meticulously determined before it can be embraced or rejected, preempted or prevented.[14] Each experience, each sensation of the future, must be globally synchronized with all others: con-sensus. *Flashforward*'s mapping practices produce consensus in one of the etymological senses of the word: a coordinated sensing-together. Thought in this way, consensus is closely related to what Brian Massumi describes as "affective attunement" (2015, 172, 239) and what Paul Virilio calls the "Communism of Affects," the "synchronization of emotions," and "the globalization of shared emotions" (2010, 62; 2012, 30).[15] Even before taking these notions any further, they can already make us understand why the database logic must not be rashly associated with Deleuze's third synthesis of time and an "impure regime of images" in a celebration of the "neuro-image."[16] The database in *Flashforward* makes common cause with a very pure regime of orderly images and a morality of command. This is important because stating that *Flashforward*'s database "present[s] the countless possible variations of the future" is not only imprecise inasmuch as, in fact, the series *represents one consensual* global future (Pisters 2011, 112). More than that, celebrating the database disregards the politics of this kind of imaging the future.

It is these politics, not the moral conservatism of the show, that remain latent and that are concealed even more by a celebratory evocation of the neuro-image. The disempowering cruelty of *Flashforward*'s future orientation consists in occupying its characters and viewers with the false problem of knowing whether "the future is unwritten" or whether "it is all mapped out" while it slowly but steadily imposes the future it foretold. Worse: the future causes itself. This movement is first introduced as an interesting gimmick of the story. As early as in episode 2, we meet a pot-smoking, unemployed slacker who, after the blackout, applied to become an airport customs official because he saw himself working as such in his flash-forward. In another secondary plotline, window cleaner Timothy (Gil Bellows) becomes a motivational trainer and founds the religious self-improvement forum Sanctuary because that is what he saw himself doing in his vision (ep. 11). This pattern is repeated with a twist in episode 14, in which the Somalian militia leader Abdi Khalif (Owiso Odera) founds the Better Angels, an organization fighting to improve the condition of the Somalian people. The twist consists in the fact that Abdi Khalif is killed despite his promising future vision, thus "proving" that the future can be changed. At the same time, however, Khalif's death is a cause of fear for those around him, including the investigating FBI agents, because "this was not supposed to happen." Changing the future is by right possible; however, it is also considered a de facto threat by the institution charged with guaranteeing national security. One could list further examples of flash-forwards effectively and preemptively causing the predicted future, as when Mark Benford saves a hostage because his flash-forward contains the information on how he will have saved this hostage (ep. 12). But the example that probably illustrates best the self-sufficiency of the future concerns the very foundation of *Flashforward*'s plot: the main reason why the FBI team around Mark Benford is appointed chief investigator of the blackout is that, in Benford's future vision, he was chief investigator of the blackout (ep. 5). At one point, Benford's sidekick Demetri (John Cho) remarks in disbelief: "This is kind of insane. I mean we're running point on all this because he had a vision of us running point on this?" The answer is yes. The series does not simply unfold toward its ending, *an* ending. The entire story of *Flashforward* seems to have been caused by its specific, foretold ending. If there is something terrorizing about *Flashforward*'s experiments with time, it is this strange quasi-identity of cause and effect, in which the future directly imposes itself as the present. This means that the future is mediated only so that its anticipation can have an immediate self-instantiating effect in the present. If *Flashforward* emphasizes the concrete "visions" and models of mapping, it is because they are the pragmatic conditions of the future's self-creation. As mediators of billions of mutually confirming and reinforcing flash-forwards sustaining a cycle of self-causation, they are "only" the fulcrum that leverages the future *now*.[17]

It is worth pointing out the difference between this self-causing cycle and the more conventional self-fulfilling prophecies that can be found in texts as old as Sophocles's *King Oedipus* and films as recent as Rian

Johnson's *Looper* (2012). In the latter cases, the prophecy of doom will eventually come true and—in the ironic twist—this does not happen *in spite of* the hero's efforts to prevent the predicted catastrophe but *because of* everything he or she does. Such a course of events can be explained conceptually with a strong notion of destiny or, in the modern logic of time travel, by way of including the pronunciation of the prophecy within the predicted course of events. This is what time travelers or the recipients of prophecies rarely consider: that whatever the prophecy predicts is the course of events including the prediction and the time traveler's reaction to it. This is why, at the end of many a time travel narrative, the protagonist is surprised at the fact that all her efforts were to no avail and unexpectedly led straight to catastrophe. The elaborate measures taken to prevent the prophesied events from happening are precisely those that bring about these events. The case of *Flashforward* is different in that it adds a layer. There are, as was seen earlier, active struggles for and against a certain future. But there are also these self-causing cycles, in which a future is unquestioningly adopted as soon as it has been glimpsed. Mark Benford immediately starts investigating the blackout because he saw himself investigating the blackout and thereby brings about an aspect of the future, another aspect of which he tries to prevent. This uncritical, unhesitating, inattentive transposition of what will or could be into what is indicates the ontogenetic power of future orientation. It also belies an inability to conceive of a future event as the effect of a variety of co-conditioning factors. Without such a notion of nonlinear causality, Mark Benford is unable to consider, for example, that his investigation of the blackout might be one of the factors that effectuate his relapse into alcoholism. How can one disentangle such intricately entwined lines of events?[18] Answering this question would be one important step toward countereffectuating preemption's controlling force. However, since the constant debate about the mutability of the future in *Flashforward* does not go beyond the distracting and banal opposition between determinism and free will, the autogenesis of the show's ending, which combines the two terms of the opposition, easily goes unnoticed.

Going beyond this opposition requires attention. Once this overall movement of self-causation is attended to, it becomes clear that the present in *Flashforward* is entirely backformed from the characters' future visions. The eerie, overwhelming affective tone, which resonates from (but in spite of) the show's heroic fight for national security, is the result of this utterly disempowering certainty: the future no longer shows itself for humans to either submit themselves or counteract. The science fictional thought experiment points beyond these two strategies to a future that only mediates itself to instantly cause itself. The interval of the future-past has been consumed by a future-already-present. It is in this *double* function of the mediated future—as an overt instance of moral judgment and as the latent, instant creation of a new reality—that the politics of *Flashforward* are founded.

Politics: Get in Timeline!

The conclusion on future orientation to be drawn from *Flashforward* is twofold and correlative to this double function of the flash-forwards in the show. The first part of the conclusion concerns the flash-forward's moral imperative and resistance to change while the second addresses the concurrent and immediate inflection of reality produced by future scenarios.

Discussing *Flashforward*, Melissa Ames suggests that the show carries a "didactic message: changing the past/future is something to regret." Ames nonetheless detects a certain ambivalence in the way this message is conveyed: *Flashforward* "go[es] so far as suggesting that each person has the ability to control his or her own destiny" but "simultaneously urge[s] viewers to steer clear of hopes that they might fully control the future" (2012, 119–21).[19] While Ames's conclusion concerning *Flashforward*'s ambivalence is to the point, it remains too uncritical as it does nothing more than reformulate the above-mentioned false alternative between determinism and an open future. It is fair to ask for a more detailed conclusion as to the politics of such "cautionary tales" as *Flashforward*, especially when they are classified as "post-9/11 television" (114, 111). What kind of political and ethical practice are we to glean from the sad double injunction that we can "control" our future but not "fully"? Is this an ethics of a little bit of agency? "Changing the past/future is something to regret." What does that even mean in pragmatic terms if we accept that science fiction is a contemporary site for philosophical engagement? In other words, what is the relevance of such a didactic message in a world in which time travel presumably does not exist anyway?

To discern the politico-aesthetic significance of such a statement, we must rethink it outside the logic of time travel. If we fail to do so, we assume once again that the past and future preexist human and nonhuman activity and that, therefore, they are there to be modified or "changed." This confines thought within the conceptual framework of metric, calculable time. If, however, time is conceived as a creative becoming—as *change itself*—then the dictum acquires an interesting redundancy: the regrettable act would consist in changing change. This is not a meaningless play on words. For the ethics of time pursued here, to "change change" is to inflect an already self-differentiating world. Another word for the change of change is *life*. "Life is something to regret"? That cannot be right.

And yet this is the direction in which *Flashforward*'s didactic message leads, thereby challenging an ethics of time. Implying a distinction between a right and a wrong or regrettable thing, this dictum takes us right into a morality of command whose value judgment on an individual is correlative to that individual's conformism to the laid-out blueprint of time. The future in that blueprint makes its own demands and requires specific actions: the "right" thing to do is to follow the road map, to get in line, in timeline, so to speak. To avoid at all cost: hesitating before acquiescing, paying attention, intervening, and *making* time. Let's talk "post-9/11," as Melissa Ames suggests. For I would agree that *Flashforward*—and preemptive narratives more generally—can indeed be considered post-9/11 television. This is not because they literally represent the attacks on the World Trade Center in New York, nor because they are necessarily preoccupied with the theme of terrorism. (In *Breaking Bad*, *Life on Mars*, *and Damages*, the specter of terrorism appears occasionally but remains marginal or circumstantial.) Preemptive narratives are post-9/11 TV because they perform and negotiate the affective tonality of insecurity and apprehension that has been increasingly associated with an uncertain future since 9/11. Moreover, they explore the relation between this affective dynamic and changing standards of accountability and justice. In other words, they participate in a wider political ecology that is to a considerable degree governed by the doctrine of preemption, oftentimes to support it as in *Flashforward* and occasionally to dispel and undo it as in the cases of *Life on Mars* and, as we will see, *Damages*. Of course, *Flashforward* does explore this dynamic between futurity and affect in an explicit relation to terrorism.

In a now infamous speech to the US Congress and the American people held on September 20, 2001, George W. Bush laid out a clear road map for post-9/11 US policies.

> Our response involves far more than instant retaliation and isolated strikes. Americans should not expect one battle, but a lengthy campaign, unlike any other we have ever seen. It may include dramatic strikes, visible on TV, and covert operations, secret even in success. We will starve terrorists of funding, turn them one against another, drive them from place to place, until there is no refuge or no rest. And we will pursue nations that provide aid or safe haven to terrorism. Every nation, in every region, now has a decision to make. Either you are with us, or you are with the terrorists. (Bush 2001)

Either or. There is no in-between. And not just any either-or but that between just defense—which, in one big sweep, is made to include "isolated" and "dramatic strikes," a "lengthy [battle] campaign," and "covert operations"—and terrorism. There is no middle ground and therefore no reason for hesitation. *Or* . . . are you with the terrorists? We thought not. You have made the "right" choice and, incidentally, co-determined the future. The predetermination of a (rather disastrous, as we now know) decade of politics is made to correspond to a moral choice that is also a moral judgment. On the one hand, then, the dictum that "changing the past/future is something to regret" is a call for conformism, an injunction to get in timeline and stay put. Fear seems to merely reinforce this dynamic. But fear and threat are not simply added to the mix. It is *through* a massive mobilization of fear that the threat and our response to it are collectively felt into existence.

This leads into what seems to be a paradox or contradiction. If *Flashforward* tells us that "changing the past/future is something to regret" just like Bush makes it clear that whoever messes with his road map is "with the terrorists," hasn't he in the same breath created that very road map, hasn't he just effectively changed the present and future? He has—and that is the latent power of preemption politics. The imposition of a future politics—generated by really-felt fear, enforced by a morality of command, and correlative to conformism—is a creative act. We "will define our times, not be defined by them" (Bush 2001). Instead of calling this a paradox inherent in *Flashforward* and preemption politics in general, we might more productively conclude that we have reached the limits of the dictum that "changing the past/future is something to regret." Not only does it fail to explain part of what is going on in contemporary politics or in *Flashforward*, namely that those who give out this dictum respect it least. It moreover conceals this fact, which is why it is not politically innocent. What seems to be a paradox or performative contradiction is better referred to as a *duplicity*. Yes, there is only one (henceforth) immutable reality, one reliable truth. And yes, this truth has been created. Because the latter affirmation produces the former and the former conceals the latter, because, in short, they enfold one another, we can think of them as a topology.

To say this again, differently: If *Flashforward*'s visions (just like Bush's) have made one specific future entirely possible, this possibilization should be read in two ways. On the one hand, it can be understood as a creative achievement drawing on the ontogenetic force of fear, the successful crafting of *a* possible future. (After all, *others*—terrorists?—might try to "define our times" and impose their will. Executing your own creative vision can be quite a challenge.) But the possibilization of *a* future is also depotentializing to the extent to which it creates *only one* possible future. *Flashforward* makes palpable why, as was suggested in the previous chapter, possibilities are not good enough. Possible futures are prescriptive, regulating, controlling. As this aspect of preemptive politics remains latent and is therefore easily missed, the road maps drawn by Bush and *Flashforward* are easily accepted as the only "responsible" course of action. Correlatively, to say that *Flashforward* is didactic in that it suggests "changing the past/future is something to regret" cannot be an adequate response because it neglects the above-mentioned duplicity all over again, a duplicity that consists in a continuous tinkering with the future so that it is felt to be inevitable. The only productive way of engaging *Flashforward* as "post-9/11 television" is to foreground this topological duplicity of a politics that deliberately inflects reality in order to stall further, potentially contesting inflections of it, in short, to produce consent.[20] It is productive because it creates attention to the asignifying movements of the narrative that even a critical focus on didacticism is bound to ignore.

We cannot ignore this because political strategists, especially neoconservatives, understood it long ago. Yes, they might easily agree, *Flashfor-*

ward succeeds in suggesting that "changing the past/future is something to regret," in luring us into resignation, into a morality of command, and into a prescriptive politics of consent. We know the refrain: *There is no alternative!* But, creative strategists might insist, the principal question then becomes: how does the show do that? And what are techniques for depotentializing the present in one's favor? *Flashforward* does this first of all, as we have seen, by looping a mediated future through the present to directly impose a consensual road map—loop into line. The show's figural movement reinforces and disappears into its figurative subject matter. Or, to restate this in Connolly's terms used earlier, the compositional dimension of *Flashforward*'s temporal movement buttresses the series' representational content at its own expense. In this way, a politics of mediation thwarts the attention to the *immediately* political.

We can productively engage with *Flashforward* because this new focus of politics makes itself felt to the attentive in the series' overall movement and the imaging forces that animate it; to attend to the series' ways of making time is to learn how to look differently. This chapter has tried to suggest such a different way of looking at *Flashforward*. The wager is that, even if you have seen the series and not seen what was suggested here and if you go watch it (again), you cannot help but perceive the movement outlined above. In the more general context of an ethics of attention, however, the focus must be less on the techniques of foreclosing potential lest we remain in the realm of the possible, the mediate, consensus, and morality, lest the seeming certainty of knowledge stop movements of thought. We must look for techniques for harnessing the immediate potential of the present and understand it as an invitation, a challenge rather than a threat.

To understand this challenge, consider an aesthetic figure that appears at the beginning of *Flashforward* and that, not incidentally, is also a key conceptual persona for Deleuze and Guattari: the surfer. The figure is interesting because a wave, like affective politics, is topological, which is to say that it is a heterogeneous reality that self-differentiates in nonlinear and co-causal processes. Deleuze opposes surfing to the old sports that place a self-contained body in a stable Euclidian space. As an example of an "old" sport, consider a gymnast on a gymnasium floor: the task is to learn a series of deliberate and regulated movements on a flat, horizontal, and stable surface for the purpose of exact repetition in a competitive context. In a competition, the quality of a gymnast's performance is evaluated by her conformity or deviation from an ideal execution of the movement. In surfing, on the contrary, the "ground" is ever-shifting, which requires a singular energetic response from the surfer at every moment. This means that no surf ride is the same and that a surfer's performance cannot be evaluated with reference to the ideal execution by her self-contained body. The surfer, in order to stay afloat, must continuously adapt to a dynamic space-time in constant modulation. This makes her the conceptual persona of the control society (Deleuze 1995, 180).[21]

Neoconservatives have understood how to harness the dynamic potential of preemption and affect, thereby "riding the surf of 9/11" (Massumi 2015, 63). It is unlikely that a successful resistance to such politics will consist in stepping outside this new dynamic. Since there is no way of knowing how a certain "cause" will effectuate nonlinearly, we have to move with thought and affect. As Deleuze explains, "The key thing is *how* to get taken up in the motion of a big wave . . . 'to get into something' instead of being the origin of an effort" (1995, 121, emphasis added). The following chapter proposes techniques for surfing the image. The key is not control but composition.

VECTOR

Control societies are taking over from disciplinary societies. . . . Money, perhaps, best expresses the difference between the two kinds of society, since discipline was always related to molded currencies containing gold as a numerical standard, whereas control is based on floating exchange rates, modulations depending on a code setting sample percentages for various currencies. If money's old moles are the animals you get in places of confinement, then control societies have their snakes. We've gone from one animal to the other, from moles to snakes, not just in the system we live under but in the way we live and in our relations with other people too. Disciplinary man produced energy in discrete amounts, while control man undulates, moving among a continuous range of different orbits. *Surfing* has taken over from all the old *sports.* (Deleuze 1995, 178, 180)

CHAPTER 4

DAMAGES AS PROCEDURAL TELEVISION

Psychosocial Types: From Detectives to Lawyers

The previous chapter began its project by thinking through the shift from detective to science fiction. This allowed the argument to move from a quest for secure knowledge (in detective fiction in general and *Life on Mars* in particular) to the sustained confrontation with the unthought in the science fiction of *Flashforward*. Science fiction approaches the unknown and unthought in the speculative mode of *what if*. What if everyone on the planet knew their future six months ahead? We have seen that, in *Flashforward*, people's future visions attune them to an affective tonality of insecurity, anxiety, and fear. The politics of preemption take advantage of this affective tone to impose an authoritative action plan including austere security measures and armed conflict. *Flashforward* has shown that it is not in people's visions that the future is determined but in the subsequent attunement of the population to an unchallenged consensus as the only alternative to the pervasive fear of the unknown. In this way, the preemptive loop through the future leads to a morality of command that judges individuals depending on their conformism to the consensual roadmap.

But of course there *are* alternatives. This chapter explores another, more productive way of engaging with an uncertain future in the TV series *Damages* (FX/Audience Network, 2007–12). To this end, the proposition is to yet again begin by thinking through a shift, this time a shift in *psychosocial types*: we are moving from the detective (or FBI agent) to the lawyer. Unlike *Life on Mars* and *Flashforward*, *Damages* is a legal drama set in the world of civil litigation. Each of its five seasons revolves around one civil lawsuit, in which Patty Hewes (Glenn Close) and her associates try a major corporation to obtain compensation for damages incurred by their clients. Consequently, *Damages* is not predominantly concerned with a criminal act itself or with a criminal charge brought against a defendant. (In the series' first season, for instance, Hewes brings a civil class action against a corrupt CEO who has already been *acquitted* of criminal charges in a government trial.) *Damages* focuses on the area of the legal system in which justice is quantified in economic terms. The shift, then, is not simply from the police procedural to legal drama. It leads us more specifically from offenses against individuals, society, and (national) security to the financial interests of opposing private parties. Although all the preemptive narratives discussed in this book revolve around issues of crime and justice, they enable different reflections on future orientation depending, among other aspects, on their generic affiliation and dominant psychosocial type. But how is crime fiction and its detective different from a legal drama like *Damages* and its litigator? To make this question the catalyst for this chapter's argument, a short excursion into the basic framework and concepts of the US legal system is in order.

As is well known, the burden of proof in a *criminal* case lies with the investigating tribunal. Since the accused is presumed innocent until proven guilty, the investigator or prosecutor needs to produce substantial evidence that proves the defendant's culpability "beyond reasonable doubt." Only then can the defendant be convicted by the established standards of the criminal code. This strong principle for the burden of proof corresponds to the injunction to produce knowledge in crime fiction: the detective or investigator pieces together the evidence required to leave no doubt as to the culprit's identity. Though the crime cannot be undone, one can be sure that, in a police procedural, the truth will be discovered and justice will be done. This is why Raymond Chandler could say that "the detective story is a tragedy with a happy ending" (2000, 117). It is not a coincidence, then, that the police procedurals discussed here, *Life on Mars* and *Flashforward*, tend to foreground the production of secure knowledge to enforce the law, to reestablish order after a (future) shock.

The matter is quite different in civil litigation and *Damages* as, for a civil claim to be successful, one does not need to prove a defendant's guilt beyond reasonable doubt. In the context of the US, the dominant principle for the burden of proof in civil law is called "preponderance of the evidence" or "balance of probabilities," which means that it suffices for the proposition of the defendant's fault to be *more likely than* the proposition of his or her innocence. As a result (and to cut litigation costs), opposing lawyers will perform a balancing act around the mark of 50 percent likelihood, always trying to be one step ahead of their opponent. This also means that the burden of proof can shift: there "are no hard-and-fast standards governing the allocation of the burden of proof in every situation."[1] In the legal fiction of *Damages* this translates into the accepted reality that the truth itself does not matter. "What matters is whose truth plays better," Patty Hewes lectures her subordinate.[2] In addition to determining whose truth plays better, the aim of civil litigation is to establish the *degree* of damages caused by a defendant, which corresponds to the amount in monetary compensation.[3] This *gradation* of a case's financial stakes, the *ambiguity* of the standard of proof, and various other idiosyncrasies of US tort law contribute to making American civil litigation much more flexible and "business-friendly" than other tort law systems or criminal law. The result is what sociolegal scholars call "adversarial legalism," or a "uniquely aggressive and *creative*" legal style with "more *complex* bodies of legal rules" and "more legal *uncertainty* and *malleability*" (Kagan 1997, 166–67, emphasis added).

Such technicalities allow for a better understanding of the different stakes of police procedurals and legal dramas like *Damages*. As business-oriented, adversarial litigation diverges from crime prosecution, so the litigator diverges from the detective as a psychosocial type: the detective, a staple of Western literature since the nineteenth century, defends the social order, his methods being those of observation and identification (via fingerprints, DNA traces, etc.). He—in the early literary tradition, the detective is male—represents the state's executive power; he *enforces* dominant social values codified in a society's laws with the aim to arrest and punish a criminal. By way of this correlation between surveillance, knowledge production, and punishment through imprisonment, the detective can be associated with what Michel Foucault calls disciplinary societies (1995, 135–69). The civil litigator, on the other hand, has no interest in defending a social order. She—in *Damages*, the two main civil litigators are female—is interested only in defending the legal and financial interest of her private client. Patty Hewes inserts herself in the law not to uphold it but to stay ahead of her opponent, to slightly tip the scales of Lady Justice in her favor. Therefore, Patty's methods do not produce certain knowledge; they serve to create probabilities and cast doubt. And since each piece of evidence can tip the balance of probabilities in one direction or the other, persuasion must always be laboriously wrested from opposing testimonies, knowledge management, delaying tactics, and evasion strategies. In short, while the detective enforces the law, the litigator outplays it if necessary. Thus, if the detective belongs to the disciplinary society, the lawyer is a psychosocial type of what Deleuze calls control societies. Such societies "no longer operate by confining people but through continuous control and instant communication" (Deleuze 1995, 174). Instead of measuring and punishing people using a disciplinary standard (enforced in spaces of confinement such as prisons, the military, hospitals, factories, and schools), the control society pits people against one another, thereby engaging them in constant competition that enhances productivity even further. It is impossible in such an environment to figure out *one single way* to proceed because the control society sweeps its members up in a process of "*modulation*, like a self-transmuting molding continually changing from one moment to the next" (178–79). From this perspective, the litigator is to the detective as the surfer is to the gymnast (see ch. 3). Since control comes with ever-shifting and increasing requirements, the qualities valued in this new environment are performance, competitiveness, and flexibility.

Damages takes us right into the mechanisms of such a social dynamic, in which private companies—such as powerful law firms and wealthy corporations—engage in legal action for breathtaking compensation claims and in which whoever outdoes the other in a race for the more probable truth wins. Since just the slightest advantage can help gain a competitive edge, secrecy, knowledge management, and manipulation count among the litigator's most important techniques.[4] This engagement in the creation of truths produces a final important difference in *Damages* between detectives or public prosecutors and litigators. Whereas the detective figure represents the social order and the prosecutor is oftentimes cast as a mediator between the accused and the law, the civil litigator in *Damages* is immediately involved in a battle of her own. The lawyers in this series continuously run the risk of exposing themselves to their enemies, for the enormous financial stakes of each case can warrant the most destructive acts of violence against them. Civil litigation

Figure. 4.1. *Damages*: Ellen Parsons (Rose Byrne) in elevator.

in the US is "costly, complex, uncertain, and *threatening*" (Kagan 1997, 170, emphasis added).

Ellen Parsons (Rose Byrne) is the lawyer in *Damages* whose professional and private safety is constantly in danger. The precariousness of her situation is central to the series and clearly marked at the very beginning of the first season: the narrative preempts its season finale and, more specifically, Ellen's shocked, demolished body only to show us that "6 months earlier" she is a self-confident and personable law school graduate about to be hired by a law firm (see figures 4.1–4.3). As in *Flashforward*, the preempted future is catastrophic but, while *Flashforward* presents a global disaster that affects people circumstantially,[5] *Damages* is more radical in that it reduces an organized body—prim and put-together—to a shivering, blood-smeared, barely covered frame. It is significant that the series chooses a female protagonist whose body bears the marks of time and thus goes against the odd timelessness of the detective's or action-hero's (hyper)masculine body.[6] This atemporal masculinity relates to notions of reason, determination, persistence, and constancy: qualities ascribed to the law and social order themselves. The turn away from such a male body and toward a precariously "time-sensitive" female body in the context of a legal economy further under-

DAMAGES AS PROCEDURAL TELEVISION | 147

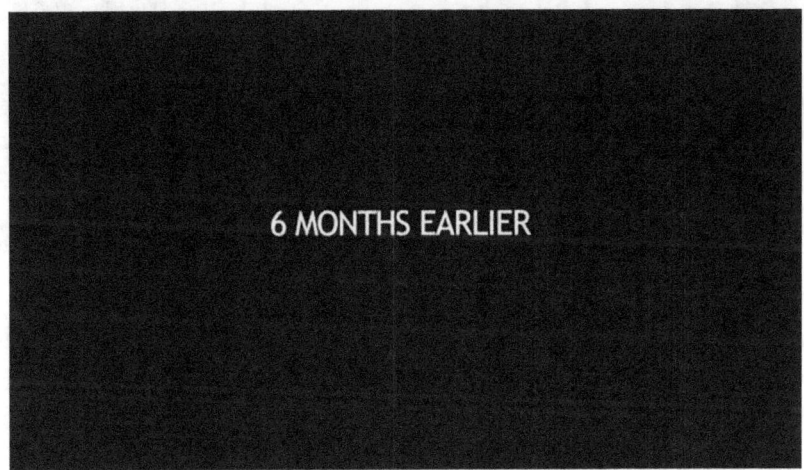

Figure. 4.2. *Damages*: intertitle "6 months earlier."

Figure. 4.3. *Damages*: Ellen prim and proper six months earlier.

scores that justice has become a matter of modulation.[7] Unlike *Flashforward*, *Damages* never asks whether the future is "unwritten" or "all mapped out": the preempted ending will have been what it was. Instead, the series' movement through time is interested in *how* one must insert oneself into a precariously metastable reality in order to modulate it in one's own favor. In other words, *Damages*' figure of time concerns *techniques* for navigating the interval of becoming.

Opening the Interval: Indeterminacy and Close-Ups

Each of *Damages*' five seasons revolves around a single case inspired by a real-life event. In season 1, Patty Hewes and Associates take on a case that is modeled on the 2001 Enron scandal and opposes her to the corrupt CEO Arthur Frobisher (Ted Danson). For ulterior motives, Patty hires Ellen Parsons, who gets caught in the line of fire between Hewes and Frobisher. The second season's defendant, the fictional corporation UNR, is based on several environmental cases and the 2000–2001 energy crisis in California due to market manipulation. While season 3 is a clear adaptation of the 2009 financial scandal around Bernie Madoff, season 4 showcases the controversies of the military-industrial complex, focusing on the private security firm High Star, a fictionalized version of Blackwater. The fifth and final season is based on the legal and ethical disputes around Julian Assange's WikiLeaks. In this way, *Damages* inscribes itself explicitly in the recent political and economic context of the United States, in which financial markets, information and communication technologies, and even energy supply and military intervention have become increasingly privatized. As a result, even basic services within a society (e.g., the provision of electricity) as well as international politics (e.g., warfare) obey the rules of private financial interest in a deregulated market. Most importantly, however, *Damages* stages the fact that the juridical system that evaluates the injustices of such an environment—that is, the damages induced and incurred between private parties—is itself a sector of competitive capitalism. The lack of an external standard by which justice is administered makes evident that a theory of morality and its immutable laws is inappropriate for thinking the mutual and ever-shifting modulation of "persons" (including, as we know, corporations) within control societies. *Damages* therefore proposes that in order to obtain "justice" in such a system, you have to enter the movement, you have to become what you fight. This is why Patty Hewes is just as corrupt as her corporate opponents, why she can be at the same time the protector of small people and the immoral violator of the law. Whether you are celebrated as a hero or convicted for fraud and obstruction of justice is a question of minor differences, a question of how well you move. What matters is whose truth plays better.

In light of the above, civil litigation (like the control society in general) appears as a "smooth space [that] is precisely the space of the smallest deviation," a field that is constantly reterritorialized by *minor* differences that can shift the *entire* spatio-temporal configuration (Deleuze and Guattari 1987, 371). And, indeed, the cinematography of *Damages* begins and repeatedly returns to the "smooth space par excellence," the sea (479). At the beginning of the series and at the end of every season, Patty Hewes can be seen standing on a pier in front of open water; in later seasons, once Ellen has abandoned the morality of the law for the constant modulations of the control society, the protégée will be at Patty's side (see figures 4.4–4.7). While the two characters may not literally be moving with the surrounding waters like the aforementioned surfer, their association with this element is telling. The aesthetic framing of the sea indicates that these litigators begin and end not so much by dealing with the hard-and-fast facts of a case but by cutting into a "vectorial, projective, or topological" field to bend the facts, make moves, play angles, and build a case (361). Trying a new case is like facing unknown, shifty waters, in which navigable routes must be explored and laid out for the first time. And the *return* to the sea in each season is crucial to understanding the modulatory field of civil litigation that *Damages* spreads around its protagonists. Each case requires that a clear line be drawn between the lawful and the unlawful so that justice may be administered. The smooth must be temporarily striated, or gridded, parsed, measured, and mastered. But the subsequent return to the smooth is just as important insofar as it enables the continuous variation that is the driving force of the control society. After their temporary striation, the "sea, then the air and the stratosphere, become smooth spaces again, but, *in the strangest of reversals, it is for the purpose of controlling striated space more completely*" (480, emphasis added). Complete control requires that every new situation come with new requirements. Minor differences and smallest deviations have no precedents.

Figure. 4.4. *Damages*: Patty Hughes (Glenn Close) in front of water, back to camera.

Figure. 4.5. *Damages*: Ellen (*face to camera*) and Patty (*back to camera*) in medium shot in front of water.

Figure. 4.6. *Damages*: Ellen and Patty in front of water; Statue of Liberty in the background.

Figure. 4.7. *Damages*: Patty in front of water, back to camera.

To say that success or failure in the control society is a question of how well you move in the topological spaces of the smooth and the striated is to say that it is ultimately a matter of process, of time. In civil litigation, *Damages* suggests, information, truth, and justice are always sensitive to re-smoothenings and re-striations or, in one word, "time-sensitive."

It is thus no coincidence if one of the most remarkable stylistic features of *Damages* is its movement through time. Each season begins in the future and preempts a final disaster associated with physical violence in the form of a shocked, immobile, or disorganized body, an accident, or a deliberate act of violence (see figures 4.8–4.11). After two or three minutes, an intertitle marks a time leap of six months into the past (see figure 4.2). This moment will henceforth be the present that slowly but gradually moves toward the foretold ending. This process of catching up with the future is regularly interspersed with additional glimpses of the future, usually at the beginning or ending of an episode. With respect to the preempted ending and the time frame of six months, the general narrative scheme of *Damages* is not unlike that of *Flashforward*. The foretold ending suggests urgency in the face of future disaster while the temporal layering of fictional and "real" time playfully engages the viewer in a similar way. The crucial difference between the two series is that, unlike *Flashforward*, *Damages* does not predominantly mediate the future through character perspective. Instead of using conventional flashbacks or flash-forwards, the different moments in time are juxtaposed directly, without any mediating device. *Damages* thus chooses the kind of temporal movement that *Flashforward* opens toward at the very beginning of its season but quickly discards in favor of a more stable mediation of the future through flash-forwards. The previous chapter argues that such an unmediated time differential in conjunction with the black screen and intertitle can open an interval from which an unseen but sensible relation of time lifts off as a figure.

In *Damages*, the direct juxtaposition of as yet unconnected moments in time has two contrasting effects. On the one hand, it disconnects each image from character perspective and, thus, from problems of sincerity, bad conscience, impaired memory, and so on, which play an important role in *Flashforward*. By emptying its narrative of mediating devices, *Damages* accords all images the same ontological status: neutral,

Figure. 4.8. *Damages*: Ellen pointing gun at camera.

Figure. 4.9. *Damages*: car accident seen from above.

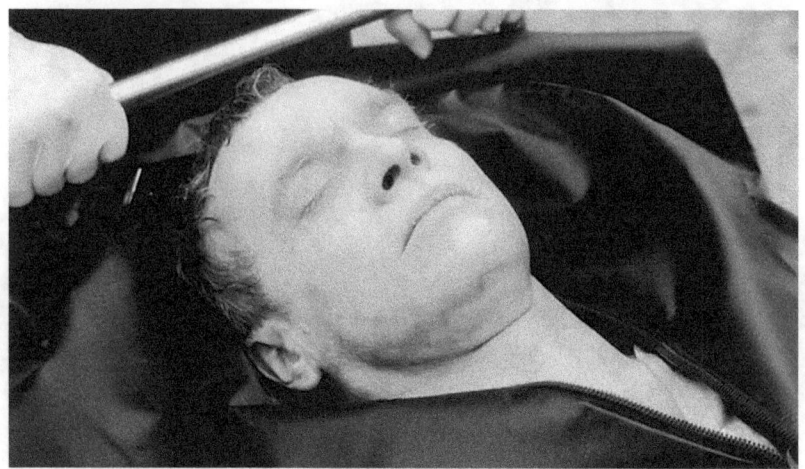

Figure. 4.10. *Damages*: close-up of dead Tom Shayes (Tate Donovan).

Figure. 4.11. *Damages*: Ellen lifeless on the floor, blood by her head.

detached, and at all times reliable. Even though *Damages* does in later seasons introduce conventional flashbacks and dream-images, these are always clearly marked and, in this sense, the image never lies. In other words, the propositional content of each image is true beyond a reasonable doubt. They are therefore "objective" and truthful images. On the other hand, the lack of mediation loosens the link between the present and future images. Although the relation between them is marked by the intertitle "6 months earlier" as one of anteriority/posteriority, it remains otherwise unqualified. As a result, the interval between the present and the will-have-been abounds with indeterminacy. There is no evidence as to *how* the two true propostions, present and future, relate to each other or how the former will evolve into the latter. In creating these two contrasting effects—the image's representational transparency and compositional opacity—*Damages* poses the question of the *how* of experience, of qualitative becoming. If every image in *Damages* is truthful and yet highly disorienting, it is because their truth is itself sensitive to time, because time puts the notion of truth into crisis.

This contrast between an impersonal image with reliable content and its inscrutability is central to the temporal movement *Damages* invites. The series makes use of a variety of tools and techniques to draw attention to this disparity and thereby further emphasizes a sense for the indeterminacy of the gap between present and future. One of the most important among these techniques is the close-up. Unlike *Flashforward*, which proposes an action-heavy detective/science fiction plot, *Damages* is a legal thriller about dissimulation and manipulation. Accordingly, the most momentous scenes in the show are conversations with numerous instances of shot/reverse shot and a conspicuously frequent and sustained use of the close-up (see figures 4.12–4.15). Interactions in *Damages* are about saving face or losing it. Not incidentally, the poker faces we see belong to some of the most recognizable actors in recent American film and television, including Glenn Close, Ted Danson, Marcia Gay Harden, John Goodman, Lily Tomlin, and many others: they stand out but say nothing. This does not mean that they are void of expression. On the contrary, it is because they try at all times to remain utterly impassive that the minutest movement in these distinctive faces can effectuate a considerable affective charge. Because a mere flicker of fear or weakness in the controlled face of Glenn Close is suggestive of exposure,

Figure. 4.12. *Damages*: Ellen in close-up.

Figure. 4.13. *Damages*: Patty in close-up.

Figure. 4.14. *Damages*: Marilyn Tobin (Lily Tomlin) in close-up.

Figure. 4.15. *Damages*: Howard T. Erickson (John Goodman) in close-up.

uncertainty, and disarray, the close-up foregrounds the character's potential to affect and be affected in an environment of secrecy. The crucial point, however, is that while the close-up in *Damages* comes with such an affective charge, it allows no immediate discharge into action or resolution. For a poker face will not let you know what might happen next. Thus, as it creates and sustains a delay within the sensory-motor schema—that is, between the perception-image and the action-image—the close-up makes felt the not-yet. A face in permanent close-up is continuously *about to* take action.

In addition, the close-up, by reducing the on-screen content to a face and out-of-focus background, creates a maximum of off-screen content. This does not mean that it cuts the face off from the out-of-field. Rather, it "*abstracts* [the face] from all spatio-temporal coordinates" and thereby releases potential (Deleuze 1986, 96, emphasis added).[8] The most evident example from *Damages* is the opening scene of the second season, in which Ellen Parsons (in persistent close-up for two minutes) speaks to another person, whose identity will only be revealed halfway through the season (see figure 4.12). Until then, this scene is repeated and continued with variations without ever making use of the standard editing technique that this conversational situation would require: the reverse shot. More than any other example, this scene uses the close-up to create indeterminacy and thereby evoke the potentialities of the situation. The viewer is invited to alternately consider all the possibilities of who might be sitting opposite Ellen Parsons. More importantly, she is invited to hold all these possibilites at the same time, to balance probabilities.

In these two senses, the close-up in *Damages* is a technique for a holding of potential. It lodges itself between perception and action and delays the switchover from the former to the latter. This stretch of the sensory-motor schema defers the linear continuation of the story and creates an intensive sensation of the potentialities that the story holds in that very moment of delay. This capacity of the close-up is the reason why, for Deleuze, it is the prime example of the affection-image, which he also describes as being "potentiality considered for itself as expressed" (1986, 98). *Damages* proliferates these delays to foreground potential, to emphasize neither what has happened nor what is going to happen but what *can* happen. The close-up achieves this because it is at the same time overdetermined (by recognizable faces and their distinctive features) and underdetermined (contextually and compositionally). As a result, the faces in *Damages* are completely exposed and utterly opaque at the same time. This very contrast within each close-up invites the viewer to examine the interval of a delayed present for its potentialities, a practice that enables perception to move through the interval.

Through the Interval: Trajectories and Plot Twists

The above-mentioned "intensive sensations of potentialities" have already—albeit briefly—been addressed in the previous chapter with reference to Alanna Thain's distinction between two logics of suspense: one that tends toward a revelation or production of knowledge, and one that creates an "attentive awareness" for the "intensive relationality" of the present. The figural movement through the interval that *Damages* proposes relies on these two logics and, more specifically, on the dynamic between them.

Thain's distinction roughly corresponds to Brian Massumi's distinction between *suspense* and *expectation*. The latter "depends on consciously positioning oneself in a line of narrative continuity" and pulls the expecting viewer along the projected timeline (Massumi 2002b, 25). Suspense, which Massumi also relates to intensity, is triggered by "nonlinear processes: resonation and feedback that momentarily suspend the linear progress of the narrative present from past to future" (26). It should be pointed out that expectation and suspense are not mutually exclusive. Rather, they are two aspects of the same moving-image narrative: "Suspense could be distinguished from and interlinked with expectation as superlinear and linear dimensions of the same image-event" (26). In light of this, the relation between expectation and suspense can be seen as a reformulation of the relation between the figurative and the figural. While the figurative encompasses the representational content of the image and drives the narrative's linear, extensive unfolding, the figural goes beyond the figurative (without abandoning it) to make felt the intensities of time. In other words, the figural and suspense do not exist without the figurative and expectation.

Damages makes a very particular use of this interrelation between the figurative and the figural, between expectation and suspense, between thinking and feeling. As we have seen, *Damages* does not break the sensory-motor schema but delays it, for instance in its conspicuous use of the close-up. But—given the direct juxtaposition of moments in time without any mediation, or ontological hierarchization of times—the general narrative scheme of the show itself can be considered a magnified version of the delayed sensory-motor schema. The viewer therefore rightly assumes that both the present and the future she views are immutable realities and part of the same continuous storyline. In this way, *Damages* insists on linear narrative progression. The viewer can *expect* that all of the show's events will lead to the foretold ending she saw at the beginning. In the first season, for instance, Ellen will go from confident, put-together young professional to the intimated, shocked, and disheveled target that the opening scene showed us. Nothing will prevent this. Remember that this was not the case in *Flashforward*, where the characters' future can be changed and their initial future visions can thus be falsified. *Damages* does precisely not allow for this kind of "actual" falsification and thereby imposes a constraint that *Flashforward* struggles against: the future has already happened. Insofar as the narrative must lead to the foretold future, a functional sensory-motor schema is the most important enabling constraint for the figural movement in *Damages*.

In this sense, the narrative is tightly constructed from movement-images that lead to the end in a linear way. But if *Damages* is one big movement-image, its sensory-motor schema is stretched out across the six months from the exposition to the final outcome. All we know is that the sensory-motor schema *will have been* functional. In the meantime of the interval, however, the preempted ending serves a quite specific purpose. The "six months later" scenes are repeated and expanded in each episode of a given season. Continuously reminding the viewer of what will have happened, these scenes pull her attention beyond the immediately next action-image into the undetermined in-between. In this way, *Damages* relentlessly catapults expectant thinking into prediction mode. And since the narrative is based on the principle of the movement-image, the viewer is right to ground her thinking in the triad of perception-affection-action and project possible narrative trajectories leading toward the end. The preempted ending in *Damages* is a technique for harnessing expectation and making the viewer trace lines through the interval. This is why the examination of both the present and the future (in close-ups, for instance) is so important. It helps sharpen one's capabilities of constructing plausible scenarios that bridge the gap between the present and the future.

This is where another technique comes into play to inflect expectation into suspense: the plot twist. In itself, the unexpected narrative turn is an established narrative device and linked to notions as old as red herrings or the MacGuffin.[9] In concurrence with the above-mentioned techniques already in place, however, the twist helps effectuate a figural movement in *Damages* precisely because it pits expectation against the unexpected. The twist falsifies the projected narrative trajectory and throws thought back into the not-yet. But expectation immediately kicks back in and asks for a new scenario to be constructed. Consequently, a new trajectory will branch off from the initially anticipated line of events. The plot twist has become a bifurcation point. The plot twist as bifurcation point is fundamentally different from the flashback as bifurcation point. Recall that, for Deleuze, Joseph L. Mankiewicz is "undoubtedly the greatest flashback author," in whose films several flashbacks fork time and create a multiplicity of recollection circuits (1989, 49). The result is "a fragmentation of all linearity, perpetual forks" (49). Thus, in the case of the flashback (or flash-forward), forks of time are first of all associated with a *decomposition* of linear narrative progression. This is not so in *Damages*: linear time is decomposed from the very beginning without, however, providing a perspective to channel (i.e., linearize) the disjunct moments in time. This is the very premise of the show's narrative scheme. Hence, linearity is not actually there to be fragmented; what is actually there is fragmentation waiting to be linearized.

Significantly, though, this alignment of past, present, and future is not immediately actualized but "merely" expected, projected, and thereby held in potential. It is this *potential* trajectory, which *could* actualize, that is forked and doubled. Thus, if the foretold ending triggers expectation to compose a possible timeline across the interval, the function of the plot twist is to recompose potential. What distinguishes the plot twist as bifurcation point from, for instance, Mankiewicz's flashback as bifurcation point is that it does not fragment the actual but recomposes potentials on the edge of actualization.

This perspective allows for a qualification of the plot twist in *Damages* and in serial TV fiction more generally with respect to a more conventional reversal of events, peripeteia, or other pivotal discovery. In, say, a feature-length film, the major plot reversal oftentimes reorders the events rather late in the narrative and produces a surprise ending. In serial television, besides occurring toward the end of a season, plot twists repeatedly intervene in the long middle, across all episodes of one season. In this position, they permanently remix the possibilities that the narrative holds and continuously reactivate expectation. In *Damages*, the proliferation of twists creates a very specific dynamic in conjunction with the foretold ending. One twist by itself forces the viewer to create a second branch as an alternative line of events leading to the preempted outcome. But as twists proliferate, so do the branches of potential trajectories. Each twist stalls linear projection, splits it, and reinfuses it with potential, leaving an ever-denser thicket of branches between the present and the future. The expectant back-and-forth through the interval becomes an intensive sensation of the interval's potential.

Now think of this thicket as what David Lapoujade calls a *memory of the future*. This concept has come up in previous chapters, first to introduce the term with respect to *Life on Mars*, then to distinguish it from *Flashforward*'s literal "memory of the future." It is *Damages*, however, that gives us a marked sensation of how the memory of the future tends into the not-yet by reactivating the past in the present. It is worth repeating that this memory is the repository for "something which has been present, that has been sensed, but that has not been acted" (Lapoujade 2013, 22). In a similar way, the plot twist in *Damages* gives a sensation of the memory of the future precisely because it draws attention to a past potential that has not been activated. This unacted past is held in reserve as a future "explosive force" until it is called upon to cocreate the next now in a singular field of emergence (95). Recall also that such a singular coming-together of heterogeneous elements that allows for novelty to emerge is not unlike a "spark which explodes a powder-magazine" (Bergson 1920, 44). The plot twist gives a sensation of the memory of the future because it *is* such a coming-together that unleashes an unacted past to open up toward a different future. It is the point of release for the explosive power of past-and-future potential. In this way, it draws the viewer feelingly into the nonlinearity of time as experience.

For this to work as a figure of time in *Damages*, it is crucial that the past not be changed. Viewers know when they are being tricked—that is, when the past is retrospectively adjusted to allow for new developments. When this is done, suspense falls flat. Therefore, the creation of a pronounced figural dimension in a serial narrative depends on a particularly rigorous method. Everything must have happened the way it did and, at the same time, allow for several diverging lines of events. If the twist is supposed to create a new potential trajectory into the future, it must first of all suggest a plausible new trajectory through the past (which, in the case of a television series, is the entire archive of previous episodes). All the different trajectories must have been there all along without being activated. This means that in order to create thickets of past and future trajectories that are only gradually perceived, *Damages* must be rigorously vague and precise at the same time—precise so that all the unacted past is effectively inscribed in the narrative; vague so that expectation does not (yet) pick up on it. As an example, consider the surprise reveal and resolution at the end of the second season that finally explains the events we saw in the season opener. As was said, the opening scene initially only shows Ellen Parsons in an extended close-up (see figure 4.12). And halfway through the season, in a long overdue reverse shot, we have already learned that Ellen is indeed talking to Patty Hewes, forcing her to admit that she ordered the hit job on Ellen in the first season. Patty is visibly shaken, seeming to regret her actions and fearing for her life (see figure 4.13). Patty appears to be close to a confession that would allow Ellen to deliver her corrupt employer to the FBI agents who are already investigating her. But as the two moments in time—advancing present and preempted ending—finally meet in the season finale, we learn that Patty's distraught appearance is not psychologically motivated at all. Just before meeting Ellen in the hotel room in order to frame her erstwhile protégée for bribing a judge (an act of revenge for working with the feds), Patty was stabbed in the side by Finn Garrity. Within the bigger picture of the second season, Garrity is a relatively small fish, involved in the illegal energy trading scheme that is the object of this season's main class action that Hewes and Associates bring against a corrupt corporation. Garrity is willing to testify against the corporation he was involved with, but Patty rebuffs him, determined to see Garrity go down with his accomplices. Now, all this is so convoluted and over the top that it might bring a smile to the viewer's (and the reader's) face. (The plot twist implies, for instance, that Patty was sitting through her twenty-minute conversation with Ellen while she was literally bleeding out.) This surprise reveal is certainly a plot twist for the plot twist's sake. But as in all of this book's analyses, the focus is not so much on more or less realistic plotlines but on the requirements of the figural movement regarding the viewer's attention. If anything, *Damages*' excessive plot twists are a testament to its playfulness, to the fact that the series really is about a perceptual game with the viewer. (Not coincidentally, the diegetic soundtrack to Ellen Parsons's extended close-up is Ray Charles's "Just for a Thrill," as if *Damages* wanted to tell its viewers at the beginning of its second season that it will take them on another temporal rollercoaster ride just for the sheer thrill of it.) True to this tricksterism, the season finale affirms a storyline that was there all along but played a minor role within the thicket of trajectories. Having figured quite prominently in the second half of season 2, Garrity's role as a free radical within the narrative—due to his desperation, opportunism, and impulsiveness—could have been predicted. The viewer could have factored him into the way the season plays out. But his storyline seemed disconnected enough from the feud between Ellen and Patty to be ignored by the viewer in her practice of constructing trajectories through the gap in time. And yet Finn Garrity is the vaguely connected circumstance that conditions the course of events in such a way as to precisely result in the season's preempted ending. One should not take this to mean that time in *Damages* is predetermined by some notion of destiny but that whatever reality will turn out to be emerges in the now of experience as a confluence of co-conditioning factors set in the past. Because *Damages* is vaguely precise and precisely vague, it falls neither into random plot adjustments nor into predictability, which is the triumph of expectation.

It falls into suspension. If *Damages* continuously takes us into the future and back into the past, it is for the main purpose of making felt the memory of the future as a present potential. For the thickets of past and future trajectories necessarily pass through the present, where they contend for ingress into actuality. They contend because even though the memory of the future traces so many lines through the past and projects them into the future, only one of these lines can be fully actualized. The remainder are further consigned to memory, where they are retained as potential. The present is a bottleneck for the virtual in this sense alone, that is, only insofar as the various contending memories of/for the future cannot be actualized at the same time. But in return, while the holding capacity of the actual is limited, the virtual dimension of the now teems with potentialities. This is what *Damages* draws attention to by means of its figure of time: the now is astir with all that could be but is not (yet), felt as so many vectors of becoming. Through this rigorous—precisely vague and vaguely precise—composition of different techniques such as the preempted ending, the close-up, and the plot twist, *Damages* folds expectation into suspension and opens up linear thinking to an intensive feeling of the interval. The show flushes the present with so many stirrings of a complex reality in order to heighten our sensitivity for potential. What emanates from the show's figural movement more specifically is a coupling of *attention* and *tentativeness*, which is also of crucial importance to the more political concerns of this legal thriller.

In *Matter and Memory*, Bergson makes an appeal to our "attention to life" (2004, 226), which, in the context of my argument, can indeed be understood as a sensitivity to the continuous stirrings of the complex reality we inhabit. Reviving this concept, David Lapoujade defines it as "a faculty for anticipation of and adaptation to the demands of the exterior world": "Adaptation, because [life] is a matter of responding to the demands of the present moment. Anticipation, because one only takes an interest in the present in view of the immediate future. To adapt is to anticipate. Attention to life submits our relation to the external world to a schema of the question/answer type" (Lapoujade 2013, 75, translation modified). In a way, Lapoujade's schema of question-and-response leads back to the importance of the sensory-motor schema in *Damages*. Every present raises a question in the form of sensation and requires a motor response. More importantly, as we have seen, *Damages*' reliance on movement-images demands that there be no response without a question that triggers it, no action without a perception that provokes it. On the one hand, then, "attention to life is determined by sensorimotor montages" insofar as it must execute question-response circuits in the present (88). But—and this is the lesson of the plot twist—the response can also come from the past. In this case, the imperative to respond "no longer emanates either from the present or from its reflection in the future; it emanates from the *past*, from the deepest past, an immemorial past which we have seen constitutes a sort of memory of the future" (88). This ingress of the past is why nonlinear temporalities can emerge from even the strictest of sensory-motor schemas. It is also why, in return, the sensory-motor or question-response schemata are irreducible to a linear model of cause and effect. Lastly, it is the reason why the composition of the future necessitates an attention to the unacted stirrings of the world, which continue to bubble below the surface of the actual. Doing justice to this complexity is a matter of tentativeness.

Tentativeness is given two different nuances here. The first is the more common usage of the word as "carefulness" or "apprehensiveness." This kind of tentativeness and attention mutually sustain each other: to attend to one's surroundings, one has to move tentatively; and to move tentatively, one has to pay attention to one's surrounding. Expectation—and future orientation more generally—can benefit from this hesitant dispersal of attention across the various heterogeneous elements in a complex relational field to probe how these elements might feed into the *how* of a process's playing-out. It can benefit because tentative attention leaves space for the creativity of the world, in the form of nonlinear processes, contingencies, and accidents. In other words, tentative attending can be a technique for expectation to include the unexpected, to be falsified in time without being foiled. *Damages* invites its viewers to develop this technique by precisely and vaguely flushing time with potential and thus triggering a tendency into the future that is projective in a way that acknowledges these potentialities. The second nuance of "tentativeness" is a specification of the first. Consulting the *Oxford English Dictionary*, one learns that it does not foreground the aspect of diffidence and apprehensiveness at all. Instead, it defines something "tentative" as being "of the nature of an experiment, trial, or attempt."[10] This is a useful reminder that tentativeness is not to be equated with procrastination, indecision, or inertia. Tentative attention moves ahead experimentally, knowing that its hypothesis may be falsified and that falsification is still a way of getting ahead, only via a detour. If one thing is certain in *Damages*, it is that the narrative will reach its preempted goal—not despite but through all the detours it has to take. In conclusion then, tentative attention does not dispense with projective planning; it allows for nonlinear plans that do not depend on us to stubbornly go straight ahead. Tentative attention creates wiggle room within the sensory-motor schema and makes it elastic. It allows us to deroute the sensory-motor without disrupting it. Someone who follows a nonlinear plan in a tentative-attentive way still has a goal but is prepared to get there in the indirect way.

That tentative attention is indeed a key concern of the control society is made clear by the resonances that *Damages* creates between its figure of time and the theme of civil litigation discussed at the beginning of this chapter. We have seen that the field of civil law is governed by the "balance of probabilities": the tiniest piece of evidence can tip the scale of justice in one direction or another, win a case or lose it. *Minor* differences can make *all* the difference. Consequently, the show is much less interested in the quest for an "objective truth" (which would be the focus of detective fiction) and instead focuses on the continuous battle of equal opponents in which minimal deflections decide about success and failure. This is why, at the beginning of the second season, Patty Hewes warns her protégée: "Oh, you have to be careful, Ellen. Everyone is looking to play an angle."[11] Everyone, that is, tries to make use of the smallest, unnoticeable deviations, "the smallest angle," to redirect the line of events as a whole (Deleuze and Guattari 1987, 361). For this reason, civil litigation requires tentative attention toward the stirrings of the world. Like the viewer attending to various incompossible potentials, the litigator must disperse attention into her surroundings to become aware of a multiplicity of contending (past and present) forces that shift and complicate the surrounding world. And like the viewer examining the close-up, she must look out for what Guattari, in his own discussion of faciality, calls "tiny territorialities" to hold on to in the smooth and modulatory space of the control society. The "derisory refuge within a smile" can be a cue to act on; a "wink of an eye" can be a vector for the future (Guattari 2011, 81). (That is also why, to make one's opponent lose grip, one must smooth one's own face.) She must furthermore insert herself in her surroundings as a force and move tentatively—that is, carefully and experimentally—to inflect the surrounding world in her favor. Finally, to resist the "closure of the future," she has to acknowledge the possibility of a response from the past; she must consider the memory of the future and "envision reverse causalities and inversions of time" (105). In the ever-shifting, modulatory field of the control society, the truth has become a matter of time. How things play out depends on immanent, or ethical, criteria. That the problem is ethical and no longer moral does not make anything any "better"; it only changes the problem's requirements. Evaluation and judgment are of little use (for, as *Damages* shows, what is morally wrong may still get the upper hand). Techniques and procedures are needed.

How It Moves: Procedural Television

An ethics is procedural and requires techniques because it is based on active and passive affects, that is, the power of acting and of being acted upon, which both animate and inanimate entities possess. An ethics therefore consists in the continuous re-creation of a metastable ecology comprising the entire set of cocreating entities. To invent and sustain the multiple relations that constitute an environment, one needs mutually sustaining techniques or what Isabelle Stengers calls an "ecology of practices" (2010, vii and 37). *Damages* not only generates an awareness of this necessity but proposes techniques—among which the preempted ending, the close-up, and the plot twist feature most prominently—that trigger and sustain a figure of time. This figure consists in a nonlinear dynamic of expectant viewing that pulls the viewer's thinking through the future *and* the past into the interval of becoming, thereby enabling a tentative attending to the stirrings of the world. As it teases, tricks, and surprises the viewer, *Damages* creates a participatory dynamism that is not merely a side effect but the main focus of the narrative practice in the first place. Since the main goal of *Damages* is this narrative procedure, one can think of it as a *procedural narrative*. Instead of "watching for the plot," for structures and devices, a procedural mode of watching television foregrounds temporal movements, abstract shapes of narrative dynamics, and figures of time. While such a shift in attention can enrich the experience of any kind of narrative—be it audiovisual or literary, serial or self-contained—it seems that recent television series are an ideal training ground for tentative attention by virtue of their slow and sustained long-arc narratives, internal rhythms, and conspicuously complex temporalities.

What is a procedure? Artists-philosophers Madeline Gins and Arakawa define procedures as "processes linked, no matter how briefly, to awareness" (2002, 53). However, their method of building for process never disregards the assemblages of concrete elements that make up an environment. On the contrary, they take them into careful consideration to examine what kinds and qualities of movements a concrete environment affords. Thus, if the focus of attention shifts to procedures in the work of Gins and Arakawa as well as in the present account of figural television, it is because of a shared interest in how embodied thinking and feeling move with an environment. As attention shifts away from identity to the productive commingling of entities in a relational field or what Gins and Arakawa call an event fabric, "agency, all agency, remains suspect" (52). For the *field effects* in a complex assemblage of human and nonhuman entities cannot be attributed to one "agent" or another. Where "propositional knowing (knowing that)" and its pinpointing of agents fails to account for the how of experience, we must develop our capacities of "procedural knowing" to better insert ourselves in our surroundings (60, 52). We must, to expand on an argument from previous chapters, move from representation to operation or composition. The requirement to deliberately construct for procedures is grounded in a double deficiency of our modes of navigating the world. On the one hand, our interactions with the surrounding world are "insufficiently procedural" and therefore inappropriate to the topological complexity of any environment (54). On the other hand, the little procedural knowing we have is oftentimes "unconscious" or "tacit" (60). The two corresponding tasks are therefore to add procedures and harness them so that they "can be entered wittingly" (53).[12] To activate a procedure, it must be given "physical shape" through the positioning of concrete "features and elements" (Gins and Arakawa 2006, 115). In other words, activation is a matter of strategically positioning constraining elements, which are not identical to but effectuate a procedural movement. Constraints "stage" procedures (Gins and Arakawa 2002, 55). In *Damages*, for instance, the preempted ending, close-ups, and plot twists do not in themselves constitute a procedure; they co-condition a procedural movement activated by the viewer and felt as a figure of time.

As a narrative, then, *Damages* is both *preemptive* and *procedural* because it "move[s] from the done to the doing, from the result to the process, or procedure," from linear narrative progression into a nonlinear figure of time (Lecercle 2006, 13). If the concept of the procedure is imported here, it is to further activate a sensibility for the figural movements of narratives through time, because the serial television narratives of the last decade demand such attentiveness by way of their complex temporalities. As was argued earlier, however, much research in film studies is constrained by a concept of "cinematic time" as linear and homogeneous, which forces it to conclude that anachronisms, discontinuities, and temporal loops take us "out of time." In television studies, the concept of "narrative complexity" has helped describe such innovations as the season-long story arc (i.e., the shift from episodic to serial narration), the resulting new *rhythms* of serial narration, as well as experiments with "real time," as in 24, for example (see Mittell 2006, 2010; Newman 2006; see also ch. 1). But while accounts of these new techniques and devices show that serial TV narratives have become more intricate and "complicated," they are not yet proof of temporal complexity understood as nonlinear and multicausal process. In fact, analyses of "narrative discourse" oftentimes stay within the paradigm of structures and linear temporality. Thus, if figures of time have been invoked throughout this book and procedures in this chapter, it has been to give traction to a different mode of thinking and feeling time in moving-image narratives in general and TV series in particular, a mode that foregrounds the abstract, temporal movements effectuated by concrete, structural elements.

The case of *Damages* suggests that these procedural movements of preemptive narratives can, once we wittingly participate in them, become the ground for "daily research" toward an ethics for surviving the control society (Gins and Arakawa 2002, 95). Looking at the modulatory reality of such societies through the prism of civil litigation, the procedural narrative of *Damages* provides a "critical edge" and takes on "transformational or reconfigurative" purpose (57). In the previous section, we have seen that the show's emphasis on attention to life and the memory of the future enables an experimental mode of adapting to and anticipating the exterior world. The term that Arakawa and Gins use for this continuous practice is *biotopological diagramming*, in which diagrams once again appear as "ongoingly organized and redistributing gatherings of all that pertains . . . , including the slightest of slight urges and what only faintly indicates itself as being operative as an organizing principle" (2006, 56). Once again, a diagrammatic practice consists in inserting oneself into a multiplicity of minor and major forces continuously pulling their topological field (aka the world) into its next singular now. *Damages* is diagrammatic because it sensitizes to the slight urges and faint indications of all that gathers and operates. As it playfully requires the viewer to see the preempted ending and still keep track of the world's complex stirrings, it trains our "capacity to know how to take direct action—keeping the end firmly in sight—through a set of indirect actions" (149). Because it takes into account notions of nonlinearity, indeterminacy, tentativeness, and the holding of potential, such diagramming is an ethical practice that attends to the environment's powers to affect and to be affected. In the context of future orientation, such an ethics, which has "foresight peering through forethought," can avoid the conservative politics and paralyzing effects of the catastrophic scenarios that our contemporary future visions oftentimes hold (Arakawa and Gins 2002, 60).

To conclude, let us trace out one more access into a procedural practice of watching serial TV fiction by following the dynamics of the "Previously on . . ." segment. This stock technique of serial narration on TV is usually understood to recapitulate past events up to the present episode. From this perspective, recap sequences summarize a TV show's archival history to keep its viewers in the picture. However, it becomes clear in recent TV series in general and in *Damages* in particular that the "Previously on . . ." sequence rarely provides a straightforward, linear, and objective recapitulation of the past. In the increasingly complex TV narratives of recent years, the "Previously on . . ." montage deliberately selects certain elements from the past to prepare a partial perception of the present. It repeats the past differently to shift certain memories into the focus of attention, make others slip into the background, or downright omit crucial information. By virtue of these shifts, slippages, and omissions, the "Previously on . . ." sequence is no longer merely an uninterested and neutral threshold into the imminent narrative. It is part and parcel of the procedural figure of time that a narrative creates. The vaguely precise narrative of *Damages* uses the recap segment to recall seemingly unimportant characters and incidents and to dissimulate other developments. Once again, it is important that everything you see in that montage sequence has effectively happened, that every image has been seen beforehand; cheating is not allowed. The past must not be changed but repeated and reconfigured in such a way as to make conceivable new trajectories into the future. In this sense, the "Previously on . . ." segment in *Damages* is not so much an aide-mémoire for the viewer as a productive remix of the past. As it pushes unacted pasts back into the present, where they create new possibilities, the recap montage acts as one more force factoring into the lift-off of *Damages*' figure of time. Once again, the show makes use of a concrete and even conventional feature of TV series to trigger a temporal movement that playfully activates the memory of the future and demands a response from the viewer: Which possible trajectories does the past hold? Which future bifurcation points does the recap montage anticipate? From the past through the future into the present: the "Previously on . . ." segment in *Damages* literally keeps the viewer in the loop.

Keeping the viewer in the procedural loop of tentative attention is a productive force that must be attributed to the recap montage in general as well as to the "Next week on . . ." sequence frequently seen at the end of broadcast episodes. Together, they feed the past and the future into expectation, contributing to its suspension in a nonlinear process. What is more, they work as powers of the false, shifting and complicating reality so as to disperse attention even further across the narrative world. In these loops through the past and the future, old potentials are reactivated and new possibilities created. Recaps and previews are meant to guide and misguide the viewer, to make the viewer tread along carefully and thoughtfully, so that television may have its procedural way. And while, conceptually, these powers of the false have little to do with lying, it occasionally happens that a preview into the next episode shows a future that will never occur.[13] Whether these are deliberate "lies" or incoherencies between early and final edits of episodes, they are idiosyncrasies of *televisual* procedures of looping past and future into an intensive sensation of time in the present, of remixing the memory of the future, suspension, and expectation in a way that few other media and genres do in so conspicuous a way.

Such is the relation between procedural television and an ecology of practices that foregrounds attention and tentativeness. As *Damages* makes time felt as a productive remix, the requirement for the viewer is to insert herself into the mix and detect the forces at work that operate as organizing principles but may only faintly indicate themselves as such. Such an attentive responsiveness to the fielded *how* of process is once again nothing else but a dance of attention, "the holding pattern of an almost unidentifiable set of forces that modulate the event" (Manning 2013, 141).

Almost unidentifiable. *Faintly* indicating. Because *abstractly* lived.

Despite the elusive quality of operating principles and holding patterns, they act as forces in the world. Because of this, we need to attune to the minor shifts and slight urges within a complex reality. The means to do this come by various names: figures of time, dances of attention, biotopological diagrams, and ecologies of practices. Each of them, however, enables and requires "a continual anticipating, self-guarding, accommodating, allowing, bypassing": ever so many techniques for surfing the wave of the control society (Gins and Arakwawa 2002, 53). Because of their intangibility, procedural constructs always come with "written instructions," which should be read as an invitation (Gins and Arakawa 2006, 151). Procedures are always named.

Directions for *Damages'* Interval-Stretching-and-Intensifying Procedure

- Accept the inevitability of the foretold ending. Rest assured that the ending will have been what you saw but will not be what you thought.
- Feel how the interval stretches between the advancing story and its foretold ending. Accept the indeterminacy of this interval.
- Consider each plot twist a bifurcation point and hold both of its possible future trajectories in potential (for they still are).
- Then reconsider bifurcation points as cues and vectors of becoming. Consequently, begin to think less in terms of trajectories than in terms of movement: know that you will not have a complete trajectory until it is all over, that is, in retrospect. Glean cues and vectors to move with the imperfect figure of time.
- To do so, look for tiny territorialities, faint indications of almost unidentifiable forces at work in the ever-shifting field of relations. Examine faces.
- Mind the responsiveness of the past! Be receptive to the past's reactivation in the present.
- Attend to the dynamic between expectation and suspense. Note that the former is continuously falsified into the latter and harness this dynamic as the creative powers of the false.
- Predict future bifurcation points, as you are invited to, *not* to deter-

mine the *outcome* of it all but for the purpose of a holding of it all. Attentively tend into becoming by considering all possible offshoots of a singular now. Have "foresight peering through forethought."
- Note that the interval encompasses *more* possibilities as it gets *smaller* (that is, as the narrative present approaches the foretold ending) and that, as a result, the at-first determinate ending is increasingly indeterminate. Think the indeterminacy of the ending as a function of the interval's elasticity, its wiggle room, its *give*, encompassing all the potentialities of your holding.

VECTOR

Deleuze's concept of the diagram and his topological aesthetics offer us a way to articulate such an experience of the twisting and folding of information into perception. Our perceptions are not of a world, but immediately part of it, in a space-time that changes as we move through it in an immanently relational configuration. The diagram is *deforming*: if the archive is a "history of forms," as Deleuze writes in his study of Foucault, it is "doubled by an evolution of forces," or the diagram. A diagram does not only map existing actualized forms nor what Deleuze terms "possibility" or what we already know can occur based on what is already there. The diagram is a topological transformation of an existing social field, engaging both with possibility and also with virtual potential, a reserve of newness and difference. Memory is one name that Deleuze gives to such potential. (Thain 2010, 53)

AFTERWORD

ANARCHIVAL TELEVISION

The figural is a concept for thinking the creativity of time. In the experience of serial TV fiction as in experience in general, time is never a stable archive. The past cannot be neatly stored away, set aside in the records of history, to make space for the next present moment to be added to the foregone ones. If reality is a topological field of creative becoming, as this book has argued through the prism of process philosophy, its singular plasticity is an effect of the past and present forces conditioning that field. One of them is the force of preemption, activated in serial television through an anticipated ending that informs the narrative as a whole. Far from constituting an epistemological problem of knowing more than the past and present yield, the foreseen future folds into the present and changes it immediately. Those who know or anticipate the future—Sam Tyler, Dyson Frost, and Ellen Parsons—move differently through time and respond to the challenges of the control society by inflecting a reality in continuous modulation. An ethics or pragmatic guide to surviving the exhausting malleability of the contemporary condition cannot consist in reaffirming the stable codes of law and morality, not least because they are themselves swept up in the dynamic of modulation. The proposition made here is to invent an ecology of practices, techniques, and procedures that are mutually sustaining and suggestive in character. The term *procedural television* itself is nothing other than an invitation to discern such ecologies in the construction of serial narratives, which pursue metastability as a continuous goal lest the show "jump the shark."

The procedural movement of serial narration makes all the past—acted and unacted—felt. It also makes our anticipated futures act in the present as abstract forces, as potential held in abeyance but ready to make ingress into actuality. This abstract activity of memories, futures, and memories of the future is what makes serial television an *anarchive*. The anarchive is not a stable repository of the past but the ongoing activity of eventfully reactivating incommensurable pasts for the creation of novelty in the present, as the present. It is a continuous remix of heterogeneous temporalities. The anarchive, Alanna Thain writes, "functions both as display of archive . . . while simultaneously making felt the emergence of newness." This means that the dynamic anarchive simultaneously "doubles and disrupts" the stable archive as it reactivates the stacked-away past (2010, 66). The series discussed in this book are such anarchives precisely because they resist stacking away information in orderly, chronological succession. Instead, they remix their future visions and recapitulations of the past to create the next now. Time's active remix occurs at all levels in these shows; it occurs *in* them and *as* them. It occurs *in Damages*, for instance, through the numerous mutual double-crossings, manipulations, and modulations discussed in the previous chapter with respect to the control society. And it occurs *as Damages* through the intricate editing, the montage of numerous loops through the future and the past, the black screens and intertitles, the tricky recap sequences, the concomitant foregrounding and backgrounding of archival material, the sudden reactivation of seemingly unimportant footage, and so forth. *Life on Mars*, in its first season, archives one story by two contending logics (time travel and coma), layering images of a dreamed present and the sound of a real future, thereby already indicating the excess of sense around the representational image. At the beginning of its second season, the series brings its anarchival qualities fully to the fore when it recasts the entire first season as a narrative of madness and subsequently oscillates between its various premises. Contrarily, *Flashforward* pretends to lead us straight to the foretold ending, determining along the way whether the future of the archive is unwritten or mapped out. And yet it became clear that preemption immediately remixes the present and that such anarchival activity concerns first and foremost the now of experience. The crucial point about these serial anarchives—the refrain of this book—is that this continuous synthesis of heterogeneous elements in-and-as time is directly felt. *Time's anarchival remix is an immediate event.*

To unfold the implications of such a proposition, let's make a last brief detour and consider the shock value that has often been attributed to cinema ever since people supposedly ran away from the *Arrival of a Train at La Ciotat* (Brothers Lumière, 1895). Walter Benjamin famously suggested that cinema reconfigured the sensory apparatus of its viewers by exposing them to the discontinuities of montage, uncommon perspectives, and speeds of film. These "shocks" are immediate effects of cinema on the nervous system. At the same time, the argument goes, people would be "vaccinated" against the surge of stimuli in a technologically advancing world.[1] Benjamin argues that film *desensitizes* its spectators for the purpose of *immunizing* them against the stressful encounters with their social environment. Film studies scholars know this argument as the "modernity hypothesis," according to which film is a phenomenon that gives expression to the sensory strains of modernity and at the same time functions as a palliative against these strains. Cinema then has a "therapeutic," or positive, effect on its public. What gets lost in this process of immunization, however, is precisely the awareness of moving-image narratives as immediate sensory events. Like so many other representational media formats, TV series focus on content and narration—that is, mediation—which often supersedes the direct sensation of the medium itself (in experience as well as in research). This dynamic is one aspect of what Jay D. Bolter and Richard Grusin call remediation, which tends to alternately foreground the medium (*hypermediacy*) or the mediated content (*immediacy*). It is telling that, in this terminology, "immediacy" should specifically refer to the immediacy of the mediated content instead of the immediate sensation of the medium itself.[2] This is decidedly not what has been suggested here. Putting to work the concepts of the figural, the procedural, and now the anarchive, this book has argued that *the process of mediation itself is immediately experienced.*

This short detour leads directly to the proposition that, in the phase of thinking television *after* the argument for a logic of remediation, we can also rethink how we experience media. Instead of focusing on the mediation of content, this project has emphasized *immediation* to explore new ways of experiencing media (Thain 2017, 11–12). Providing concepts and techniques for resensitizing us to how sensation moves with media, as the preceding chapters have done, is a crucial task for audiences and scholars alike because in some cases, like that of *Flashforward*, a narrative's stated approach to time and its actual movement can diverge significantly and in politically relevant ways. In the case of *Damages*, on the other hand, the procedural movement through time involves us in the dynamics of the control society and provides techniques for moving through a complex, modulatory reality. In this way, resensitization to immediate discursive movements can help ward off some of the "future shocks" induced by a sociopolitical order that is increasingly characterized by austerity measures and preemption.

And it becomes clear, via Benjamin, that the way to immediation is a question of measure. That the sensory effects of moving images can be both detrimental and therapeutic means that resensitization depends on dosage. Consequently, film, television, or any other moving-image media are not intrinsically "good" or "bad." Since they can be engaged with in various ways to different effects, their value is not a stable benchmark but arises from the immanent criteria of one's specific engagement. The shifting effects of such media ecologies lead right back to the continuous process of immanent valuation in the control society, to an ethics of attention. For a question of measure is a matter of attention: Benjamin is neither the first nor the last to express this idea through the image of the vaccine. In contemporary biopolitical thought, Roberto Esposito has conceptualized social contracts as a "negative [form] of protection of life," or a form of "immunization" (2008, 46). The idea is once again that the political subject comes into being only as its power for egoistic expansion is restrained. This dynamic, which consists in a simultaneous protection and negation of life, suggests that restriction must be accepted for the benefit of an ordered and satisfactory political life (*bios*) and to prevent society from falling back into what Giorgio Agamben calls "bare life" (*zoe*) (Agamben 1998).

Helpful as the concept of "immunization" may be to grasp the logic of modern theories of sovereignty, its strict distinction between "bare" and "good" life is inappropriate to the control society. It presumes an outside, "bare life," which has to be negated in order to protect political life, the inside. But the modulations of private interest and power constantly spill over the limits set by the rule of law (just like preemptive narratives continuously spill over the limits of representation and linear narrative progression). This does not mean that we can dispense with legal frameworks but, first and foremost, that our "good political life" is itself swept up in the shifting field of ubiquitous control.[3] As *Damages* suggests, contracts, codes, and laws are continuously evaded to secure an economic or political advantage. To restate this in the terms of Benjamin, Esposito, and Agamben: the immunization hypothesis assumes that everyone accepts the same vaccine dosage to stay within the boundaries of *bios*. In the global context of our times, however, someone might refuse their own dose and increase yours with poisonous intent.

The key to this dilemma lies first in resisting paranoia at the prospect of our submission to "bare life" and in asking for *alternatives* to the theoretical distinction between the inside and the outside, the good and the bare, order and disorder. As one alternative, this book has suggested making oneself comfortable in the wider, complex field of the world's multiple stirrings, in what Brian Massumi, following William James, calls "bare activity" (2011, 1). In bare activity, the above-mentioned dualities can only be temporarily extracted as points of reference and are continuously reinvented. But if everything starts from bare activity, why insist on a clear-cut separation of order and chaos? In fact, from this conceptual vantage point, chaos is *not* the opposite of order but a *surplus* of order, the immediate co-presence of several, incompossible orders. Another word for this surplus, this more-than, is *potential*. Another word for bare activity, especially with respect to the form-taking of serial narratives, is *anarchive*. The anarchive is not, then, the opposite of the archive but the abstractly lived potential from which the concrete archive is extracted (Thain 2017, 48, 236, 270). This dynamic of gradual extraction from a multiplicity of potential narrative trajectories is directly felt as a figure of time.

The paradigm of "immunization"—in both Benjamin's conception and Esposito's—sets thought in motion but only gets it so far because, in the words of Cary Wolfe, "it is unable to overcome the divisions it establishes" (2013, 39). It does not, for instance, enable us to articulate processes of mediation and immediation in a complementary and productive manner. The key dynamic it illustrates consists in the immediate sensation of the image (including sensory "shocks") self-stiflingly turning against itself. All that is left is mediation and the "immediacy" of mediated content.

It is possible to think further and go beyond film studies' modernity hypothesis by operating a slight but significant conceptual displacement from the vaccine to the *pharmakon*. Following Jacques Derrida, Isabelle Stengers describes the pharmakon as a "drug that may act as a poison *or* a remedy" (2010, 29). By virtue of this "intrinsic instability," the pharmakon distinguishes itself from the vaccine, which gains its stability because it negates and protects at the same time and thus pretends to siphon a safe inside off from a perilous outside (29). The pharmakon has no such pretensions. As Stengers points out, this uncertainty regarding its effects is the reason for our general distrust of the pharmakon: "We require a fixed point, a foundation, a guarantee. We require a stable distinction between the beneficial medicament and the harmful drug, between rational pedagogy and suggestive influence, between reason and opinion" (29). In other words, we require guidelines that do not require anything of us. The control society, however, is pharmacological in that it constantly asks us to respond to renewed circumstances and modulated conditions. To stay afloat in such a reality, one needs to attend to the duplicity of one's pharmacological surroundings and carefully put to use techniques with the aim of creating sustainable and productive relations. The concept of the pharmakon thus compels us to think and act ecologically. And indeed, for Stengers, a pharmacological attitude is part and parcel of an "ecology of practices."

Throughout this book, fictional TV series have been encountered as pharmaka. It is a (true enough) commonplace that television distracts, depotentializes, and anesthetizes (to include another, frequently used medical term). But we do not necessarily need *different*, more highbrow media as a "remedy" against disengaging TV. Nor do we need to take a step back and critique it from a more distant, macroscopic perspective. Instead, we may want to recognize the requirements of the pharmakon itself and engage it differently. The different mode of engagement proposed here foregrounds *immediation*; that is, the directly felt movements of moving images in general and time's anarchival remix in particular. *Flashforward* has been the clearest example of the TV show as pharmakon: focus on the story (the mediated content) and you are likely to fall into the trap of preemption, to fall in line, to accept the "future archive" that disavows its anarchival, bare-active coming-into-existence; but attend to the immediate movement of the image itself and the very same pharmakon makes you sense that, as preemption loops through the future to create a specific present, the anarchive and its modulation are politically contested.

The call for a heightened sensitivity to immediation and to the anarchive does not require us to reject mediation. This book does not make a case against narration because that would amount to denying narrative's inherent duplicity, denying the pharmakon's "intrinsic instability." The mediate and immediate aspects of narrative obviously work together—be it as a differential as in *Life on Mars*, in tension as in *Flashforward*, or in resonance as in *Damages*. In the same way, the anarchive of serial television can be conceptually distinguished but not disconnected from a TV show's orderly archive of episodes. Rather, the anarchive occupies the abstract dimension of the same matter. It is the activity of the past churning above and below the seemingly stable, concrete archive. *Damages* has been the exemplary case of a narrative that reconfigures its story in such a way as to foreground its anarchival activity, to give an immediately felt, abstractly lived experience of time in the making. The central concern has been to propose tools and techniques that could resensitize viewers to the duplicities of narrative, that foster and sustain an attentive practice of moving with narratives' procedural figures. Setting out from the duplicity between the figurative and the figural, the argument has moved over the actual *and* virtual in *Life on Mars*, the linearity *and* nonlinearity in *Flashforward*, the dynamic of expectation *and* suspension in *Damages*, to serial television as archive *and* anarchive in this afterword. None of the terms from these doublets can be rejected in favor of the other. This is why the argument has continuously stressed that the figural *lifts off* from the figurative and that the consideration of figural movements requires a *shift in attention* from thinking to feeling. By virtue of their conspicuously preempted endings, their vaguely and rigorously complex narratives, and many other individual techniques, recent TV series allow us to develop such an attention to intervals and a sensitivity for the movements they activate.

One last proposition toward engaging contemporary *figural*, *procedural*, and *anarchival* television: since the anarchive is an activity, a process to be entered (and not a ready-made product), it is not available for quick consumption. Though the procedural remix of the anarchive is immediately figured and directly felt, resensitization may take some time. Do not mistake the direct and immediate for the fast and easy. In time, you will feel the series' constitutive duplicity of continuity and discontinuity, linearity and nonlinearity, figurative and figural. When experimenting with *Damages*, for instance, give it one season at least. Ideally, give it a few. In any case, give it a go.

ACKNOWLEDGMENTS

Throughout this project and the ones that have grown out of it, I have found myself thinking more and more about the liveliness of life, that joyful vitality that affirms only itself and that, fortunately, traverses me every so often. Quite often, actually. One of this book's assumptions was that such experiences are always conditioned in myriad ways. So here's to the people who have allowed me to experience that joy and, more specifically, the vital import of rigorous study and philosophy, of thinking and feeling going hand in hand.

Figures of Time came into being under the mentorship of Livia Monnet at the Université de Montréal. My work certainly benefited from the many thought-provoking conversations with excellent teachers at UdeM's Department of Comparative Literature who challenged me to step out of what was then already becoming my somewhat uncomfortable academic comfort zone. I am particularly grateful to the erudite and endlessly curious Livia Monnet for pushing me toward the unexplored and the unthought. In many ways, you helped me find this project.

This book would not exist (or would be very different) if it weren't for the SenseLab, which is—without hyperbole—the most inspiring academic environment I have encountered to this day. Every conversation, every reading group, every research-creation event makes me feel the necessity and the joy of writing. I am thinking of *all* of you SenseLabbers as I write this. *Figures of Time* is clearly shaped by the work of Erin Manning and Brian Massumi. Most importantly, perhaps, you have taught me how much is at stake in philosophical thought. I deeply cherish your generosity and continued support. And thank you for the careful commentary on the various drafts of this book.

In 2014 I found a new academic home at the Department of Media Studies at the University of Amsterdam. As part of the "Television and Cross-media" team, I've been lucky to work with a group of scholars and practitioners who, besides their many other laudable qualities, are truly collegial. Working with you—Carolyn Birdsall, Sudeep Dasgupta, Joke Hermes, Jaap Kooijman, Erik Laeven, Leonie Schmidt, Judith Tromp, Markus Stauff, Jan Teurlings—is a pleasure (even in the midst of institutional frustrations). Let's keep it that way! A shout-out also to Christoph Lindner, who has moved on to new academic adventures but whose support during my first two years at UvA and afterward is much appreciated. Thanks to Markus, Sudeep, and Abe Geil for feedback on chapter drafts.

I thank Elizabeth Ault, my editor at Duke, for supporting this project from the very beginning and guiding me through all the stages of publishing a first monograph. Many thanks to Sheila McMahon for carefully copyediting this volume. I am grateful for the detailed and challenging commentaries on the manuscript provided by the anonymous reviewers (especially the person I know only as #4). You have made this a better book.

So many more people have moved and shaped this project and I would like to mention a few of them. Alanna Thain, I am always moved by your brilliance, strength, gentleness, and your deep commitment to anything you do. Ilona Hongisto, you are such a joyful and ethical thinker: your work comes out of and feeds right back into life. I cherish the memories of when the three of us put together the *Absolutely Fabulated* screening series and am grateful for all that came out of it. You two are friends, teachers, and coauthors—and I hope we'll have many occasions to come together again in all of those capacities. Eleonora Diamanti and Amine El Mourid, you two are family to me and it would take too long to explain how happy I am to have you in my life. To stay on topic, I'll just say that your close friendship during much of the writing of this book continuously gave me energy and trust in the work. Charlotte Farrell, thank you for being the kind of friend who makes you wonder about connections in a previous life and for always *wanting* to read the next draft of this. Thank you, Leslie Plumb, for appreciating my oddities as much as I appreciate yours, and for always offering a different perspective. Michael Beauvais, you are a being full of beautiful contrasts; thank you for an incredibly silly and intellectual friendship and for guiding me to certain legal references in this book.

I want to thank my parents, Birgit and Reinhard Pape, for their love and trust, and for always letting me become who I wanted to be, even though at times that may have been uncomfortable and difficult. Thank you for giving me the confidence to question the visions you had for my life. (And there is no sarcasm here but a complicated story about the end of the GDR and the various contending hopes and fears.) You taught me to define and hold on to my own values without the need for competition or comparison with others (and without the need for perfection).

I often think of my late grandmother Wilma Ziegan, a woman who lived a small but extraordinary life that spanned four very different incarnations of Germany. And even though I can't help but think of hers as a very hard life, she nonetheless filled mine with countless special moments. Among those, I remember the after-school guilty TV pleasures we shared. (Eden and Cruz!) I remember how you lined up my first job: sticking etiquettes onto can lids for the fish factory you worked at; those long, delightful summer afternoons of sticker after sticker after sticker. And I will never forget your wonderfully sharp sense of humor, which, if I'm lucky, rubbed off on me just a bit. I am forever grateful.

Last but definitely not least, my utmost gratitude goes out to Mark Vicente. Thank you for making a life together. Without you, all of this wouldn't be half as much fun.

All of you, all of you. You're giving me *life*.

NOTES

Introduction: Preemptive Narratives and Televisual Futures

1. Throughout this book, the term *loop* is not used to designate the continuous repetition of audiovisual footage, which is the established usage in media studies. By loop, I refer to the aesthetic experience of perceiving a future image, then moving back in time, only to gradually return to this future. What one might describe as a "prolepsis" in structuralist or narratological terms is—perceptually speaking—a loop through time.
2. Aside from the pilot, episodic loops occur in "The Cat's in the Bag" (s01e02), "Crazy Handful of Nothin'" (s01e06), "Grilled" (s02e02), "Breakage" (s02e05), "Box Cutter" (s04e01), "Bug" (s04e09), and "Dead Freight" (s05e05). That this is indeed a signature style of the show is also made evident in parodies of the device as can be found, for instance, in the recent pilot episode of *Lady Dynamite* (Netflix 2016). The parenthetical references are shorthand for the season and episode numbers of a given title. For instance, "s01e06" refers to season 1, episode 6 of *Breaking Bad*.
3. Following Nietzsche, one could qualify this suspenseful joy at the downfall of the hero as "tragic" (1999, 80).
4. These shots from the future, first seen in "Seven Thirty-Seven" (s02e01), return in "Down" (s02e04), "Over" (s02e10), and "ABQ" (s02e13).
5. See also Bertelsen and Murphie 2010, 139: "Refrains constitute what will always be fragile, no matter how benevolent or virulent, territories in time. These allow new forms of expression but render others inexpressible."
6. For the concepts of time implied by classical mechanics and thermodynamics, see Prigogine 1997. For the emergence of utopian and dystopian narratives set in the future, see I. Clarke 1961; Versins 1972.
7. In both their individual and collective work, Gilles Deleuze and Félix Guattari resist a conception of art that considers it as an "expression" of social concerns. This would reduce expression to the "reflection" of a preexisting reality (see, e.g., Deleuze and Guattari 1987, 89). Yet a concept of expression is central to their thought. In their thinking as in mine, expression is relational, generative, and transversal to different components of the social field. It is therefore primary to, autonomous from, and productive of subjects, objects, and content. For the example of entropy, this means that the scientific, political, and artistic contents of expression (e.g., dissipation, decline, and decadence) "*emerge*[] from expressive potential through a process of the capture of that potential" (Massumi 2002a, xx). The resulting idea that art or the aesthetic is never merely reflective of the social is further explored in this introduction as well as in chapters 1 and 2.

8. For a few examples of fictional murders involving (life) insurance, see the *Columbo* episode "Publish and Perish" (NBC, 1974); numerous episodes of *Murder She Wrote*, including "We're Off to Kill the Wizard" (CBS, 1984) and "A Quaking in Aspen" (CBS, 1995); and, more recently, *CSI*'s "Hitting for the Cycle" (CBS, 2011) as well as *CSI: NY*'s "Second Chances" (CBS, 2009).

    For a postcolonial consideration of this very real problem, see Baucom 2005 for the infamous case of the *Zong* massacre: When, in 1781, the slave ship *Zong* came into distress because of low food and water supplies, the ship's captain, Luke Collingwood, decided to drown 132 slaves in the Atlantic, reasoning that he would at the same time save the remaining crew and cargo *and secure the drowned slaves' market value fixed in the insurance policy* and for which the owners subsequently filed an insurance claim. This rationale proved Collingwood's business acumen because, due to starvation, the *actual* market value of the slaves would have been inferior to the one fixed with the insurers.
9. For the notion of "thought in motion" or "thought in the act," see Manning and Massumi 2014.
10. For an in-depth investigation into the differences between prevention, deterrence, and preemption, see Massumi 2015, 3–19.
11. For the concept of fabulation, see Hongisto and Pape 2015 as well as Bordeleau, Pape, Rose-Antoinette, and Szymanski 2017.
12. Massumi writes: "In other words, you go on the offensive to make the enemy emerge from its state of potential and take actual shape. The exercise of your power is *incitatory*. It . . . contributes to the actual emergence of the threat. In other words, since the threat is proliferative in any case, your best option is to help *make it proliferate more*—that is, hopefully, more on your own terms. The most effective way to fight an unspecified threat is to actively contribute to *producing* it" (2015, 12).
13. Slavoj Žižek, for instance, follows Jean-Pierre Dupuy in proposing a notion of "projected time" that explicitly draws from biblical prophecy (see Dupuy 2004, 166–82; 2014, 29–39, 140–45; Žižek 2008, 459–60). The positions of Dupuy and Žižek are discussed in more detail in chapters 1 and 2.
14. This controversial role of media and journalism in particular has most recently been discussed through the notion of *post-truth*. See "Art of the Lie" 2016; Davies 2016; see also Keyes 2004.
15. A comprehensive list would have to further include numerous individual episodes of TV shows like *Desperate Housewives* (ABC, 2004–12), *Modern Family* (ABC, 2009–present), *Hostages* (CBS, 2013–14), and *Atlanta* (FX, 2016). For many more examples, see TV Tropes, "How We Got Here," n.d., accessed July 23, 2018, http://tvtropes.org/pmwiki/pmwiki.php/Main/HowWeGotHere.
16. This is a selection, of course. Many other examples of narratives that preempt their ending belong to other genres, for instance the sitcom. Here too, however, the preempted ending suggests a dramatic cataclysm of events and, in this way, creates suspense (see, e.g., the *Modern Family* episode "Fizbo" [ABC, 2009]). In this sense, the present argument for a changed perception of the future and the audience's attune-

ment to an affective tone of apprehension holds, *mutatis mutandis*, for such comedic examples as well. In this book, I also bracket retrospective frame narrations such as the one in *How I Met Your Mother* (CBS, 2005–14). While this is an interesting case of temporal complexity that manages and plays with audience expectations (see Brost 2012), the primary function of the frame narration is to stabilize the overall narration through a retrospective mediation of the main story (instead of destabilizing narrative continuity through the immediate effects of prospection). The popular Twitter meme "*record scratch* *freeze frame* you may be wondering how I got here," though equally related and inspired by the conventions of moving image narratives, is equally past-oriented as it comically indicates a lack of comprehension as to how a particular (and oftentimes awkward) situation came about.

17. On the autonomy of affect, see Massumi 2002b, 23–45.
18. For instance, Umberto Eco wrote as early as 1962 that "the aspect of television that would seem most interesting and fruitful to our research is also its most characteristic, unique to the medium: namely, live broadcasts" (1989, 107). Liveness constitutes "the very particular 'time' of television, so often identifiable with real time" (106). According to Raymond Williams, the "defining characteristic" of broadcast television consists in the organization of programming into "a continuous flow" that supplants programs, commercials, and announcements to keep viewers in its thrall ([1974] 2003, 86, 95). Williams famously based his conception of flow on his confusing experience of American broadcast television: "I can still not be sure what I took from that whole flow. I believe I registered some incidents as happening in the wrong film, and some characters in the commercials as involved in the film episodes, in what came to seem—for all the occasional bizarre disparities—a single irresponsible flow of images and feelings" (92).
19. A similar argument can be made for the role that the concept of *cinematic time* plays in film studies. In her critical cultural history of the concept, Mary Ann Doane proposes that if cinema was "a central representational form of the twentieth century" (2002, 19), this is because film rationalizes time into a homogeneous succession of discontinuous, equivalent instants as it splits movement into a sequence of contingent, indexical images. This gives cinema "the capacity to perfectly represent the contingent, to provide the pure record of time" (22). Here, the functioning of the cinematograph determines the temporality of film in general. Even though Doane critically assesses this concept and its discursive power, it has remained the starting point for many subsequent explorations of the relation between audiovisual media and time. See, for instance, McGowan 2011; Mulvey 2006; Stewart 2007.
20. While more research begins to do work I call for here, the term *aesthetics* is often developed in the traditions of art theory (Cardwell 2013, 2014) or narrative studies (Mittell 2015), neither of which properly address matters of perception and experience.
21. The inseparability of notions of "machinism" and the temporality of becoming is also evident in D. N. Rodowick's chapter on cinema's "Ethics of Time" (2007, 73–87).

22. In my understanding of *technics*, I follow Murphie (2008, 2) and Lamarre (2009, 13). See also Parikka 2010, xxx. For the notion of *expressive machine*, see Lamarre 2009, xxx.
23. Of course, the relative dominance of distribution in the context of television—and thus its influence on programming—is well established. In his seminal study *Television: Technology and Cultural Form*, Raymond Williams states that, in broadcasting (as opposed to cinema), "the major investment was in the means of distribution, and was devoted to production only so far as to make the distribution technically possible and then attractive" (2003, 18). My interest here, however, is in the ways in which *specific* modes of production and distribution—as parts of a machinic media assemblage—coevolve and produce *singular* aesthetic experiences. For a recent and thorough reading of Williams in the context of media ecologies, see Lamarre 2018.
24. Interestingly, these five *c*'s are missing in the conclusion to the second edition of the book. For related arguments, see Uricchio 2004 as well as Newman and Levine 2011, 129–52.
25. In his book *Foucault*, Deleuze concisely elaborates the cornerstones of Foucault's concept of power and shows how it refutes the postulates of property, localization, subordination, essence or attribute, modality, and legality (2006a, 22–26).
26. Interestingly, the exact relation between space and time is an issue of contention in the sciences now as it was in 1905 when Albert Einstein introduced the notion of "space-time." This is due to the fact that the central theories in use—general relativity and quantum mechanics—articulate the relation between space and time in very different ways. Recent theoretical investigations tend to consider time and space as "interwoven" and "emergent" rather than universal or fundamental (Ananthaswamy 2013, 37).
27. Film scholars like Linda Williams (1991) and Vivian Sobchack (2004) have addressed the embodied experience of moving-image narratives through phenomenology. While indebted to these predecessors, this account tries to rearticulate aesthetic experience through theories of affect and media ecologies.
28. Such an understanding of aesthetics has the advantage of reminding us of the original Greek meaning of the term, which is "perception" or "sensation" (*Oxford English Dictionary*, s.v. "aesthetic"). As the above remark indicates, perception is thought less in terms of distinct sensory channels (visual, auditory, proprioceptive, etc.) than in terms of *amodality*, or a fusion of the senses in experience (Massumi 2002b, 169–71). Research on perception in psychology and the neurosciences supports this view: "[The sensorimotor system] has multimodal capacities to receive input from the other modalities (hearing, vision, and touch), which are then integrated with the original sensory and motor functions. Thus there is no need for a 'Cartesian theater' . . . , a sort of 'third place' (e.g. 'association area') in the brain where the information from the separate modules is replayed and integrated. Instead, this integration occurs in the sensorimotor system. . . . In any event, a dynamic representation of all stimuli is the primary and fundamental layer of experience" (Stern 2010, 49).

29. I use Massumi's expression of the "lift-off" to underscore that the figure of time is an *effect* of the machinically composed, concrete narrative.
30. In *The Logic of Sense*, Deleuze stresses that there are *"always only effects"* (1990, 8).
31. This functionalism is another mark of radical empiricism's influence on this project. William James, who never adopted the term himself, and the self-declared functionalists who followed him shifted the focus of study in psychology from questions of structure and content, for example of the mind, toward an enquiry into the function—the what for and how—of certain processes within a given environment, for instance the function of consciousness (understood as multiple processes) in the lived experience of animals. In this perspective, the world appears not as a collection of objects to be described but as an interplay of forces to be felt, a network of processes to be entered and followed. In the present account of television aesthetics, this functionalist angle of inquiry does not dismiss structures and narrative content. Rather, it works with and goes beyond them to find out what narrative—understood as a process, an operation—enables that is not already in its content or form.
32. The notion of *affective attunement* is Massumi's (2015, 172, 239), who derives it from Daniel Stern's concept of "affect attunement," developed in *The Interpersonal World of the Infant* (2000).
33. I am aware that the term *immediacy* is central to Jay David Bolter and Richard Grusin's conception of remediation as well as Grusin's concept of premediation. The crucial point is, however, that Bolter and Grusin use the term to refer to the immediacy of the mediated content (Bolter and Grusin 1999, 5–6; Grusin 2010, 2) whereas I use the term to refer to the immediate experience of the medium itself. I return to this divergence in the afterword.
34. For this understanding of complexity, see Massumi 2015, 174.
35. I discuss Virilio's work and what I consider to be its conceptual limitations in chapter 3.
36. For the notion of affective labor, see Hardt 1999 as well as Hardt and Negri 2000, 289–94.
37. It must be noted that the antihero's capacity to (criminally) slalom her way through the control society in many cases also relies on her whiteness. Most of the abovementioned antiheroes maintain the illusion of a white, (upper) middle-class existence, which oftentimes allows them to become imperceptible to law enforcement. A noteworthy counterexample to this tendency is *How to Get Away with Murder* (ABC, 2014–present).
38. See Deleuze (1988b, 17–29) on the difference between morality and ethics, and Foucault (1990, 49) on the recent disappearance of "morality as obedience to a code of rules."

Chapter 1: The Serial Machine

1. In an elegant essay, Maya Deren suggests that reverse motion "does not convey so much a sense of a backward movement spatially, but rather an undoing of time" (1960, 158).
2. Another major contemporary theorist of technics is, of course, Bernard Stiegler. If I do not follow Stiegler in my conception of technics, this is because I am trying to articulate a machinic or ecological—that is, more-than-human—conception of technics whereas Stiegler's thinking describes a technogenesis of humans. It seems to me that, despite his claims to the contrary, Stiegler's analysis begins with (human) subjects and (technical) objects. Consequently, when it comes to theorizing the relation between humans and technology, he toggles between the two attitudes toward technical objects that Simondon himself wanted to go beyond (2017, 17): Stiegler alternatively considers industrial machines as prostheses, or tools and instruments that ultimately strip humans of their own retentional capacities (2011, 4), or as beings endowed with a quasi-intentionality that humans merely execute (1998, 67). The combination of these two attitudes produces a fierce critique of the industrial age and contemporary media, which occasionally points to the "pharmacological" potential of its object but fails to explore it in detail. This is particularly evident in Stiegler's invective against television, *La télécratie contre la démocratie*, in which technology and television in particular are blamed for the destruction of audiences' capacity for attention and eventually the liquidation of "the public" itself (2008, xvii, 24). New media are briefly evoked as a *pharmakon* but without further elaboration (xii). For a partial translation of the book, see Stiegler 2010.
3. The conceptual distinction between metric and topological time is fully developed in the following chapter. It is inspired by Deleuze and Guattari's distinction between the smooth and the striated (1987, 474–500). They associate the striated with the metric and the smooth with the "vectorial, projective, topological" (361–62). While Deleuze and Guattari develop these concepts mostly with respect to spatial configurations, it becomes clear that topological space must be thought as a dynamic space-time.
4. All Williams quotations in this paragraph are from *Television* ([1974] 2003, 86–88).
5. For scholarly assessments of these transformations, see Gillan 2011; Lotz 2007; Murphy 2011; Uricchio 2004.
6. This is my shorthand for a core argument of radical empiricism developed by William James in *A Pluralistic Universe*: "The concrete pulses of experience appear pent in by no such definite limits as our conceptual substitutes for them are confined by. They run into one another continuously and seem to interpenetrate. What in them is relation and what is matter related is hard to discern" (1920, 282).
7. This is a major resonance with Jean-François Lyotard's conceptualization of the figural in language: for him, the figural is a way of thinking beyond representation and signification in a time when structuralist conceptions of discourse tend to reduce language to codified signification. This "oversight with regard to the sensory," Lyotard argues, produces a "flattening" of perception in thought that simply does not cor-

respond to the "thickness" of a text in lived experience (2011, 6, 4, 5). Lyotard calls this thickness an "absolute excess of sense" over signification and representation that creates a "zone of eventness" (6, translation modified, and 130). When David Rodowick later rephrases that the "figural is unrepresentable, beneath or behind representation," this is another way of addressing the more-than of language (2001, 8). For further resonances and differences between Lyotard's and Deleuze's conceptions of the figural, see Bamford 2013. Bamford 2012 introduces Lyotard's concept of the figural into performance studies.

8. All Tarkovsky quotations in this paragraph are from *Sculpting in Time* (1987, 116–21). The emphasis in this quotation has been added.

9. Daniel Stern speaks of "temporal feeling shapes" and "forms of vitality": "The dynamic forms of vitality . . . are psychological, subjective phenomena that emerge from the encounter with dynamic events. . . . They are not motivational states. They are not pure perceptions. They are not sensation in the strict sense, as they have no modality. They are not direct cognitions in any usual sense. They are not acts, as they have no goal state and no specific means. They fall in between all the cracks. They are the felt experience of force—in movement—with a temporal contour, and a sense of aliveness, of going somewhere" (2010, 7–8, and 17 for the reference to "temporal feeling shapes").

10. All translations in this book are mine unless indicated otherwise.

11. These remarks allow for yet another conceptual lineage. In *Feeling and Form*, Susanne Langer also addresses the "more-than" of art: "What is 'created' in a work of art? More than people generally realize when they speak of 'being creative,' or refer to the characters in a novel as the author's 'creations.' More than a delightful combination of sensory elements; far more than any reflection or 'interpretation' of objects, people, events" (1953, 46). She conceives a work of art as an assemblage—which she calls an "arrangement"—that effectuates a "feeling": "A work of art, on the other hand, is more than an 'arrangement' of given things—even qualitative things. Something emerges from the arrangement of tones or colors, which was not there before, and this, rather than the arranged material, is the symbol of sentience" (40). In this sense, art is a matter of "abstraction" (47). Consequently, what I call a *figure of time* is close to what Langer calls the "abstracted expressive form" or "semblance" of a work of art (1953, 54, 48). Brian Massumi (2011) develops his concept of semblance drawing, among others, on Langer.

12. The phrase is so conspicuous that television itself mocks it (see the *30 Rock* episode "Operation"). The edited volume *Cable Visions* (Banet-Weiser, Chris, and Freitas 2007) suggests that cable television has brought us to the "Platinum Age of Television" (vi). For the use of the phrase *Golden Age*, see also Thompson 1996, 12. Lynn Spigel, in her introduction to the volume *Television after TV*, foregrounds the uncertainty of what television is becoming (Spigel and Olson 2004). For an early evaluation of what this development means for TV studies, see Spigel 2005.

13. For this break, consider the two issues of *Cahiers du cinema* dedicated to American television series: no. 581 (2003), titled "L'âge d'or de la série américaine," covers

many of the series from Thompson's "second golden age," whereas no. 658 (2010), titled "Séries: Une passion américaine," discusses more recent series that would presumably belong to the "third golden age of television." While the earlier issue stresses a growing variety of genres and the flourishing industry of fictional television (*Cahiers du cinema*, no. 581: 13–14), the more recent issue presents the new aesthetic quality of serial TV fiction as an established fact (see esp. Jean-Philippe Tessé's reference to no. 581 in *Cahiers du cinema*, no. 658: 7).

14. See Expósito Barea 2011 for a detailed analysis of *Flashforward* according to Thompson's list of TV's new marks of quality.

15. Consider the subtle but momentous double edges of the following projects: TV scholar Jason Mittell explores the "nexus" of "historical forces" or "contexts that enabled the emergence of narrative complexity" and supposes that this emergence has "broader cultural implications" (2006, 30; see also Mittell 2015, 5). In a similar vein, Amanda Lotz insists that television has been "fundamentally redefined" by a "confluence of multiple industrial, technological, and cultural shifts" and supposes that "ideas appearing in multiple shows . . . might indicate concerns relevant to the broader society" (2014, 10, 42). More recently, Paul Booth agrees that "many factors influence [the] increase in contemporary temporal complexity" and intends to explore "the way these complex narratives are symptomatic of larger cultural issues" (2011, 371–72). While there is a lot to be learned from these writings, the above citations show how this research puts television in a creative deadlock on two sides. On the one hand, it is "redefined" or determined by its various contexts. Thus, when it comes to explaining recent innovations of the medium, television does not count as a force itself. Instead of one context among many, it turns into a determinable object, output. On the other hand, the new formats and complexities of fictional TV series "indicate" or "are symptomatic of" general concerns of contemporary society; that is, they seem to be a mere means of expressing or representing a preexisting social reality. Moreover, one hardly ever learns what these social "concerns," cultural "implications," or "issues" might be. In short, television—though more complex and original than ever—remains oddly sterile. In none of the above-mentioned accounts is television creative in the proper sense of the word: the new aesthetic standards of TV series, while beautiful, do not seem to make much of a difference beyond television itself.

16. For the LOP (Least Objectionable Programming) theory, see Lotz 2014, 24; Thompson 1996, 38–39.

17. On a recent and compatible account of singularity, see Lamarre 2018, 71–75.

18. On discourses of quality TV as a regulatory mechanism, see Dasgupta 2012.

19. For research on the recent trend of TV revivals, see Loock 2018 and Pape forthcoming. See also French 2017.

20. Among the actors who have turned to TV are Glenn Close, Nicole Kidman, Laura Linney, Jeremy Irons, Steve Buscemi, Laura Dern, Anjelica Huston, and many more. As for directors-cum-producers, consider, for instance, Martin Scorsese's involvement in *Boardwalk Empire* (HBO, 2010–11) or Steven Spielberg, who, in 2011 and

2012 alone, had executive producing credits on three TV shows: *Terra Nova* (Fox, 2011), *The River* (ABC, 2012), and *Smash* (NBC, 2012). David Fincher directed the first two episodes of *House of Cards* (Netflix, 2013).

21. For recent accounts of time-shifting, see Lotz 2014, 54; Uricchio 2010. In the context of media studies, the concept was originally proposed by Sean Cubitt (1991).

22. The VCR contributes to the fact that, "ever since 1987, the majority of film revenues are earned in ancillary markets, not at the box office" (E. Nelson 2014, 62).

23. The obvious precursor to more recent practices of rewatching are broadcast reruns, which already complicate the aesthetic experience of time as they disconnect narrative from a logic of revelation (Murphy 2011, 96–98; J. Nelson 1990). However, the conventional rerun has been in decline (Mittell 2010, 94). Unlike Jenny Nelson, however, I do not think that an interest in repetition necessarily indicates a compulsion à la *fort/da*. As I will argue below, repetition—both as a narrative device and in rewatching—creates an aesthetic movement that makes time felt as an intensity.

24. For the relation between the DVD box set and complex narrative units, see Mittell 2015, 40. On binge-watching, see Jenner 2015; Tryon 2015.

25. For these developments, see Creeber 2004, 9; Gillan 2011, 135–44; Newman 2006.

26. Sean O'Sullivan describes the thirteen-episode season as a "sonnet-season" (2010, 69). Besides the approximation in formal segmentation—the thirteen episodes roughly corresponding to the sonnet's fourteen lines—this format resembles the sonnet in that it has an equally "clear but flexible shape that both hews to established protocols and breaks those protocols when necessary" (61).

27. The notion of de- or disfiguration is central to most conceptions of the figural and is explored more fully in subsequent chapters (see also Lyotard 2011, 235–36; Rodowick 2001, 101–6; Vancheri 2011, 20). Deleuze more often uses the terms *deformation* and *decomposition*. The important point is that the figurative image is deformed or decomposed only to recompose a figure through it (Deleuze 2004b, 48–54).

28. As of July 2018, Netflix had taken *Coronation Street* off its online library. It should also be noted at the end of this digression that while the soap opera may have declined in popularity as a format, its generic characteristics have migrated into primetime formats. The most recent example, noteworthy for its remarkable success, is ABC's *Revenge* (2011–15).

29. The most important publications in this context are Eco 1972 and his 1985 article that was republished in 1994 and 2005.

30. All Eco quotations in this paragraph are from "Interpreting Serials" (1994, 87–96).

31. See also Kovács 2010 for a reference point to the argument presented in this paragraph.

32. Following William James, one might call the preempted ending a "terminus," that is, an experiential quality that makes felt from the beginning what "the concept 'had in mind'" (2003, 30–32). See also Manning 2013, 144–45: "Terminus as that which gets the action underway, as that which in-forms the event without preempting an outcome. Terminus as that which captivates the process and propels a dephasing that results in the nowness of this or that occasion. Terminus as that which activates the

distributed relational movement of the event in its concrescence. That which propels a transduction. . . . The terminus that activates a procedure does not create a pre-composed map, it potentializes the map."

33. Although he does not use the expression himself, Henri Bergson formulates the future-past in a lucid and beautiful passage of *Mind-Energy*: "To retain what no longer is, to anticipate what as yet is not, these are the primary functions of consciousness. For consciousness, there is no present, if the present be a mathematical instant. An instant is the purely theoretical limit which separates the past from the future. It may, in the strict sense, be conceived, it is never perceived. When we think we have seized hold of it, it is already far away. What we actually perceive is a certain span of duration composed of two parts our immediate past and our imminent future. We lean on the past, we bend forward on the future: leaning and bending forward is the characteristic attitude of a conscious being. Consciousness is then, as it were, the hyphen which joins what has been to what will be, the bridge which spans the past and the future" (1920, 8–9).

34. All Žižek quotations in this paragraph are from *In Defense of Lost Causes* (2008, 438–39).

35. The original French publication has not been translated into English. However, Dupuy also gives a detailed account of his concept of projected time—what Žižek translates as the "time of a project"—in his book *Economy and the Future: A Crisis of Faith* (2014, esp. 110, 140–41).

36. Dupuy himself relies heavily on Hans Jonas's *The Imperative of Responsibility* (2000).

37. For the conditional logic of the doctrine of preemption, see my introduction.

Chapter 2: Three Representations and a Figural

1. Consider Saint Augustine's notorious formulation of the problem: "What then is time? Provided that no one asks me, I know. If I want to explain to an inquirer, I do not know" (1991, 230).
2. For a critical overview of such approaches, see Elsaesser 2009, esp. 21.
3. There are exceptions that address and follow through the paradoxes of time travel. The film series *Back to the Future*, by virtue of its comedic character, takes on every facet of time travel and turns it into a practical joke. In fact, it is interesting to see how the topology of time is at work not only in the series' individual movies but across installments. Strictly speaking, *Back to the Future II* does not *continue* the story of its prequel. It folds back onto the first movie to replay and double its story, complete with two Marty McFlys. It intensifies time instead of extending it. Another, more serious film that takes on the quandaries of time travel to give a sensation of what it would feel like to be displaced in time is Shane Caruth's *Primer* (2004).
4. Take the telling case of utopian narratives: Thomas More's *Utopia* was published in 1516 and established the genre. Note that More's utopian society lives on a *far-away* island that is contemporaneous to More's society. There is no travel through time

here, only voyage through space. After the publication of this genre-founding text, it took an astonishing 250 years for the first *temporal* utopia to be written: in 1771 Louis-Sébastien Mercier published *L'An 2440, rêve s'il en fut jamais*. After this date, however, texts proliferate that situate a utopian society in the future (Hausmann 2009). It seems, then, that the idea of time travel required the development of a new concept of spatialized, homogeneous time in the eighteenth century. Note furthermore that the temporal displacement in Mercier's novel—as in many early time-travel narratives—is made plausible through a dream: much like the protagonist of *Life on Mars*, Mercier's hero has to be in a state of *unconsciousness* to travel through time. This indicates a fundamental ontological problem about time travel and its underlying concept of time. I return to this problem in the following section of this chapter.

5. Diverging genealogies exist: Jacques Le Goff traces the emergence of what he calls "merchant's time" back to the Middle Ages and contrasts it with then dominant theological time: "For the merchant, the technological environment superimposed a new and *measurable* time, in other words, an *oriented* and *predictable* time, on that of the natural environment, which was a time both eternally *renewed* and perpetually *unpredictable*" (1980, 35; emphasis added). Le Goff's sociohistorical viewpoint gives a first indication of the cultural implications of "merchant's time" evidenced by the attributes "measurable," "oriented," and "predictable." However, Le Goff acknowledges that the new understanding of time would only be naturalized in modernity.

6. In the "Working Day" chapter of *Capital*, Marx gives an impressive account of factory owners' tricks and schemes to "snatch[] a few minutes," for instance by "nibbling and cribbling at meal times" or by manipulating the factory clock during the day (1976, 352). But Marx never tires of reminding us that even if the capitalist ran his business with the best of intentions, even if he were morally steadfast and refused to cheat, the capitalist economy would nonetheless systematically exploit laborers by virtue of its interest in surplus value produced by the purchase and use of labor power (see "The Production of Absolute and Relative Surplus Value" in Marx 1976, 643–654).

7. In *Bergsonism*, Deleuze explains that Bergson's critique of Einstein consists in saying that the latter misrepresents space-time as an "actual . . . numerical and discontinuous" multiplicity instead of what it actually is: a "virtual . . . continuous and qualitative" multiplicity (1988a, 80). Deleuze further explains: "[Einstein] is criticized [by Bergson], therefore, for having confused the two types of multiplicity, virtual and actual" (85).

8. In this respect, the concept of *qualitative multiplicity* resonates with that of *assemblage* (see ch. 1).

9. "The era [*temps*] of catastrophes is to a certain extent an inversion of this [Bergsonian] temporality" (Dupuy 2004, 13). On another occasion, Dupuy calls his own metaphysics an "antidote" to Bergson's (165). Instances of Dupuy's argument contrasting with Bergson's thought can be found on 9–14, 86, and 175–97.

10. Jean-Pierre Dupuy goes much further than Sam Tyler when he affirms that the kind

of prediction he conceives does *not* "model itself on the causal sequencing of phenomena" in historical time (2004, 193). In his conception, prediction must be "conscious of its effect on the future, which predicts the future as if it were fixed and at the same time caused, at least in part, by the effect of the prediction" (193). But, as we shall see, this step toward topological time, in which "the past and the future mutually determine each other," is also the step toward preemption (191).

11. Doane writes further that the "significance of the cinema, in this context, lies in its apparent capacity to perfectly *represent* the contingent, to provide the pure record of time" (2002, 22).

12. While Doane and Lim express their apprehensions by repeatedly stressing that cinema's ability to contain the contingent is an *apparent* capacity, other scholars explicitly or implicitly base their arguments on the power of the *stilled, discrete* image (Mulvey 2006; Stewart 2007). Interestingly, contingency is alternately the mainstay of the frame-by-frame film reel (Stewart) or the digit-by-digit CGI (Mulvey). Depending on the argument, it is either the photographic still or the digital screenshot that becomes the "emblem of time's conceptual dismemberment into moments, into discrete and arbitrarily segmented units of temporality" (Stewart 2007, 69). This, as I have pointed out in the introduction, leads to a number of false problems around the experiential quality of moving-image narratives.

13. See the previous section; and see *Time and Free Will* for one of Bergson's earliest formulations of this argument (2001, esp. 98 and 101). A terminological clarification may be in order: "Abstraction" for Bergson is not the same as for Massumi. For Bergson, the abstraction of time is its spatialization through the faculty of intelligence. Massumi refers to the abstract as to the potential-harboring dimension of reality. Thus, while "abstraction" (as an intellectual operation) stands for the flattening-out and depotentializing of reality for Bergson, it is the opposite for Massumi: it is, to repeat a passage quoted above, "synonymous with an unleashing of potential" (Massumi 2002b, 33). Massumi also speaks of *lived* abstraction, which Bergson's is precisely not. I continue to use the terms *abstract* and *concrete* as established in the previous section, following Massumi.

14. For Bergson, the *immediate* experience of duration is opposed to the *mediation* of time through its representation as a linear, homogeneous medium. The subtitle of *Time and Free Will* indicates the importance of immediacy: *An Essay on the Immediate Data of Consciousness.*

15. On the issue of "virtual vision," see also Massumi 2011, 18.

16. For the notion of the future-past, see ch. 1.

17. All subsequent quotes from *Life on Mars* are from the first episode of the second season.

18. I speak of two rather than three incompossible premises here for the sake of clarity and because the third "time travel" premise plays a somewhat secondary role in the second season of *Life on Mars*. It nonetheless remains operational as a premise and driving force of the narrative.

19. Deleuze makes a very similar point with respect to cinema in *Cinema 2: The Time-*

Image when, in an explicit reference to Bergson, he says that "attentive recognition informs us to a much greater degree when it fails than when it succeeds" (1989, 54). Interestingly, the examples of such failures that Deleuze gives include amnesia, hallucination, and madness (55). More recently, this shift in perspective, which considers the *potential* of neurodiversity, can also be observed in autism activism and research (see, for instance, Manning 2009, 213–28; 2013, 124–32, 149–71 passim; Mottron 2011).

Chapter 3: Loop into Line

1. All Deleuze quotations in this paragraph are from *Difference and Repetition* (1994, xx–xxi).
2. Recall also that, in turn, "time has always put the notion of truth into crisis" (Deleuze 1989, 130). This crisis of the very notion of truth is what idealist philosophies attempt to avoid.
3. Cf. this passage from *Creative Evolution*: "As physics retained of time only what could as well be spread out all at once in space, the metaphysics that chose the same direction had necessarily to proceed *as if time created and annihilated nothing, as if duration had no efficacy*. Bound, like the physics of the moderns and the metaphysics of the ancients, to the cinematographical method, it ended with the conclusion, implicitly admitted at the start and immanent in the method itself: *All is given*" (Bergson 2007a, 345, emphasis added).
4. Whether "noumena" and "things in themselves" are indeed synonymous is another contentious question of Kant scholarship. Since this question is not relevant to the argument that follows, I will not further address it here.
5. For the distinction between phenomena and noumena, see Kant 1998, 354–65 (A235–60); see 426 (A 369) for the reference to "sensible forms of our intuition."
6. Bergson discusses these aspects of Kant's philosophy in 2007a, 203–6, 356–64.
7. Both citations are from *Flashforward*, season 1, episode 7. Since this show ran for one season only, hereafter I cite episode numbers only in the main text. In *Flashforward*, the proposition that the "future is unwritten" is taken to mean that the present contains a margin of indetermination that allows for creative intervention in the set of relatively determinable chains of causation that lead into the future. It could alternatively be understood to indicate the future as a radically open-ended contingency. However, prevention politics cannot work on the basis of this assumption: in order to counteract or prevent a certain line of events, one has to assume a predictable line of cause and effect leading from the present into the future. This implies a certain amount of determination (derived from the past) without excluding the possibility of willful intervention and accidental or contingent interference.
8. National Linear Accelerator Project (NLAP) is a fictionalized, Americanized version of CERN's Large Hydron Collider (LHC) situated near Geneva, Switzerland. *Flashforward* is based on a 1999 novel of the same title by science fiction author Robert J. Sawyer. The novel is actually set in Switzerland; the story revolves around an experiment at the LHC. Another interesting change that occurred in the adaptation from

novel to TV show concerns the temporal distance of the flash-forward. In Sawyer's novel, people have a vision of their lives *twenty years* in the future. The reduction of this interval to six months suggests urgency and asks for immediate personal and political reactions. The implications of this are further explored in the body of this chapter.

9. This dynamic is therefore occasionally referred to as a *traumatic* experience. In episode 11, an FBI therapist states: "For the past twelve years my job has been to help people cope by helping them explore their past. But since the blackout that's all changed. The majority of people who are coming to see me are dealing with traumas from their future."

10. Deleuze conceives time as a process that is continuously reproduced by the three passive syntheses of time, the first concerning habit and the perception of the present, the second concerning the in-folding of the past as memory, and the third concerning the out-folding into the future (1994, 70–128). The main point to keep in mind here is that time qua process is not given but *com-posed* ("*syn-thesized*") out of three co-creating dynamics: the first synthesis, which contracts a present through habit; the second, which continuously adds the past to the mix; and the third, which pulls the processual mix into the future. In one of his lectures, Deleuze repeatedly formulates a synthesis as a "mise en rapport" (putting in relation) (1978).

11. For her development of the three syntheses of time and their corresponding images, see Pisters 2011, 102–6; 2012, 137–40.

12. In my view, one of the limitations of Pister's theory of the neuro-image consists in the fact that she is ready to accept the mere representation of "mental landscapes" or quasi-synaptic connections as instances of the neuro-image.

13. Here it becomes evident why *Flashforward*'s garden of forking paths is not the same as the one Jorge Luis Borges describes. *Flashforward*'s version maps *many* individuals' determined and intersecting trajectories in *one* map of the future. Contrarily, Borges suggests that *one* individual can have *many* different (incompossible) futures and thereby emphasizes the indetermination and potentiality of each present. See Borges 1962, 98–100.

14. In *An Aesthesia of Networks*, Anna Munster distinguishes between two conceptions of the mosaic. In the first, the mosaic "conjures up a worn and scuffed kind of patterning" and assigns a precise position to each of its pieces according to the overall form. This conception is close to *Flashforward*'s mosaic as it predicts and determines the relation of the part to the whole. Munster proposes a second, alternative conception: "In the radical empiricism of William James, mosaics are less images than modes of moving thought and life along. . . . Mosaics emerge processually as a bringing-into-relation that traces and delimits the outer edge of the event, conjoining/differentiating it from the inner edge of the next. It is the edge that is the mosaic's force and that drives its patterning, not the pattern or mosaic 'bed' determining where the pieces should sit" (2013, 32). If I do not draw further on Munster's interesting proposition for rethinking the mosaic, it is because *Flashforward*'s mosaic lacks the liveliness and creativity she evokes.

15. And as in *Flashforward*, for Virilio this constant surveillance, even of the future, through the database is not unrelated to the LHC (the fictionalized NLAP in the series): "Just like the elementary particle at the heart of Geneva's Great Accelerator—the Large Hadron Collidor—we will not only be 'filed,' but tracked" (2010, 13).
16. On the impure regime of images, see Pisters 2011, 98; see 109 on databases and their logic.
17. Paul Virilio calls this the "futurism of the instant . . . the imposture of immediacy, which excludes all expanse just as it does all true duration" (2010, 25). This harsh indictment is an appealing criticism of contemporary politics. But it comes with two theoretical disadvantages: (1) It associates the futurism of the instant with a lack of chronodiversity (Virilio 2010, 71; 2012, 88–90) and an increasing monochronicity (Virilio 1997, 28). It can therefore not account for the temporal *complexity* of preemption. (2) As a consequence, it must describe the "instant" and "immediacy" as inherently detrimental to chronodiversity. I prefer to reactivate these concepts, in particular that of the immediate, in a less critical and more productive way (see introduction).
18. To complement the notion of self-causation, one might say that *Flashforward* fails to account for the *quasi-cause* of its preemptive movement. In *The Logic of Sense*, Deleuze defines a quasi-cause as "incorporeal," that is, immaterial, nonlocal, eventful. It is "the kind of causality which [an event] gathers and makes resonate in the production of its own actualization " (1990, 144). In other words, a quasi-cause is the differential force of consistency that the coming-together of enabling conditions compounds and that brings the event to expression. *The Logic of Sense* makes a strong case for the consideration of quasi-causalities and their relations, or the way in which events not only express themselves but "communicate" to bring one another to expression (169). Consider this beautiful passage: "What makes an event compatible or incompatible with another? We cannot appeal to causality, since it is a question of a relation of effects among themselves. What brings destiny about at the level of events, what brings an event to repeat another in spite of all its difference, what makes it possible that a life is composed of one and the same Event, despite the variety of what might happen, that it be traversed by a single and same fissure, that it play one and the same air over all possible tunes and all possible words—all these are not due to relations between cause and effect; it is rather an aggregate of noncausal correspondences which form a system of echoes, of resumptions and resonances, a system of signs—in short, an expressive quasi-causality, and not at all a necessitating causality" (170).
19. In her chapter, Ames also studies the TV shows *Heroes* and *Fringe*. I quote from her conclusion on all three shows.
20. In Virilio's terms, one might say that the "hygiene of Time" covers up a "war of time" (2010, 102).
21. Besides the "Postscript on Control Societies," the conceptual persona of the surfer also appears in "Mediators" (Deleuze 1995, 121–34) and *What Is Philosophy?* (Deleuze and Guattari 1994, 71).

Chapter 4: *Damages* as Procedural Television

1. Keyes v. School District No. 1, 413 U.S. 189 (1973). Argued October 12, 1972. Decided June 21, 1973. For a brief summary of the matter, see "Burden of Proof" n.d.: "In a criminal trial the burden of proof required of the prosecutor is to prove the guilt of the accused 'beyond a reasonable doubt.' In a civil trial, the plaintiff must prove their case by a preponderance of the evidence, which translates to a 51% likelihood that all the facts necessary to win a judgment as presented are probably true." See also Posner 2011, 826: "The burden of persuasion rests on the plaintiff for the main claim but the defendant for affirmative defenses . . . , and the burdens of production are allocated accordingly." For the balancing effects on litigation costs, see Kobayashi and Parker 1999, 5–6: "Both litigants expend resources to alter the probability of prevailing," which leads to "equilibrium amounts of litigation expenditures [which] depend upon the relative stakes of the parties, and upon the relative merits of the case."
2. "Failure Is Failure," *Damages* (s05e03).
3. Interestingly, this happens in relative disconnection from the strict epistemic requirement to establish someone's criminal fault within the binary options of "guilty" and "not guilty." In fact, although defendants may have been exonerated of criminal charges (as is the case in the series' first season), they can still be subject to claims for damages in a civil lawsuit. The disconnection is relative because the verdict in a criminal case obviously has an impact on the civil lawsuit: a criminal conviction will make claims for damages almost inevitable. However, and this is my point, an acquittal does not guarantee immunity from civil claims.
4. Deleuze's understanding of the control society resonates strongly with Robert Kagan's account of US adversarial legalism, which is "expensive and hard-to-control" (1997, 165), "more party-influenced, less hierarchically-controlled" (167), more "open[] to new ideas" (168), "so costly [that] lawsuits can be used as purely strategic weapons" (169), and—as referenced above—infused with "more legal uncertainty and malleability" than other national systems (167).
5. In *Flashforward*, people's lives are changed in the future inasmuch as they find themselves living in unexpected *circumstances*: Olivia is with another man, and Aaron's bemoaned daughter is alive.
6. The atemporality of the male hero can be observed in various genres. Consider the sober professionalism of detectives from Sherlock Holmes to Columbo, whose dedication to the profession forecloses any personal development or private obligation. The *James Bond* film series requires a new actor every three or four films to warrant an eternally middle-aged secret agent. In the superhero genre, which is equally related to questions of social order and justice, the hypermasculine body of Superman is forever thirtysomething years old. On these issues, see Atkinson 2008; Eco 1972, 1982, 1994.
7. "You Want to End This Once and For All?," *Damages* (s05e01).
8. On the relation between abstraction and potential, see chapter 2. I recall briefly that, following Massumi, "abstraction" is taken to be "synonymous with an unleashing of potential" (2002b, 33).

9. The term *MacGuffin* was popularized by Alfred Hitchcock and refers to an object, person, or place that is the driving force of a narrative but ultimately turns to be of little value or consequence. The standard example of a MacGuffin is the supposedly precious statue of the Maltese falcon that various parties chase after in John Huston's film *The Maltese Falcon* (1941). When Humphrey Bogart's character finally manages to obtain the statue, he realizes that it is a fake and that the entire quest was for naught.
10. *Merriam-Webster's Third New International Dictionary Unabridged* accounts for both meanings: (1a) experimental and (2) hesitant.
11. *Damages*, s02e02.
12. The architectural procedures of Gins and Arakawa can be wittingly entered in their built surrounds, such as the Reversible Destiny Lofts in Mitaka, Japan, or the Bioscleave House in East Hampton, US.
13. As a recent example, consider a preview from the first season of *Smash* (NBC, 2012–13): at the end of episode 11, we get a preview in which Uma Thurman's character utters a few (shocking) lines that never occur in the following episode.

Afterword: Anarchival Television

1. All Benjamin quotations in this paragraph are from "Das Kunstwerk im Zeitalter seiner technischen Reproduzierbarkeit" (1989, 377). The quoted passages are not included in the (better-known) first and third versions of Benjamin's famous essay "The Work of Art in the Age of Mechanical Reproduction." They can be found in the essay's second version, first published in German in 1989.
2. See Bolter and Grusin 1999, 5–6: "In all these cases, the logic of immediacy dictates that the medium itself should disappear and leave us in the presence of the thing represented."
3. To rephrase this in the words of Cary Wolfe (who takes the expression from Jacques Derrida and develops it): power as well as politics take place *before the law* "in the sense of that which is ontologically and/or logically antecedent to the law, which exists prior to the moment when the law, in all its contingency and immanence, enacts its originary violence, installs its frame for who's in and who's out" (2013, 8–9; see also 31–42 for Wolfe's discussion of Esposito's paradigm of immunization).

WORKS CITED

Agamben, Giorgio. 1998. *Homo Sacer: Sovereign Power and Bare Life*. Translated by Daniel Heller-Roazen. Stanford, CA: Stanford University Press.
Ames, Melissa. 2012. "The Fear of the Future and the Pain of the Past: The Quest to Cheat Time in *Heroes*, *Flashforward*, and *Fringe*." In *Time in Television Narrative: Exploring Temporality in Twenty-First-Century Programming*, edited by Melissa Ames, 110–24. Jackson: University of Mississippi Press.
Ananthaswamy, Anil. 2013. "Space against Time: Is Space the Warp and Weft of Reality, or Time—Or Both, or Neither?" *New Scientist* 218, no. 2921: 34–37.
"Art of the Lie." 2016. *The Economist*, September 10. http://www.economist.com/new/leaders/21706525-politicians-have-always-lied-does-it-matter-if-they-leave-truth-behind-entirely-art?fsrc=scn/tw/te/pe/ed/artofthelie.
Atkinson, Paul. 2008. "The Time of Heroes: Narrative, Progress, and Eternity in *Miracleman*." In *The Contemporary Comic Book Superhero*, edited by Angela Ndalianis, 44–62. New York: Routledge.
Augustine. 1991. *Confessions*. Translated by Henry Chadwick. Oxford: Oxford University Press.
Bamford, Kiff. 2012. *Lyotard and the Figural in Performance, Art, and Writing*. New York: Continuum.
Bamford, Kiff. 2013. "Desire, Absence, and Art in Deleuze and Lyotard." *Parrhesia* 16:48–60.
Banet-Weiser, Sarah, Cynthia Chris, and Anthony Freitas, eds. 2007. *Cable Visions: Television beyond Broadcasting*. New York: New York University Press.
Baucom, Ian. 2005. *Specters of the Atlantic: Finance Capital, Slavery, and the Philosophy of History*. Durham, NC: Duke University Press.
Bellamy, Robert V., and James Robert Walker. 1996. *Television and the Remote Control: Grazing on a Vast Wasteland*. New York: Guilford Press.
Benjamin, Walter. 1989. "Das Kunstwerk im Zeitalter seiner technischen Reproduzierbarkeit: Zweite Fassung." In *Gesammelte Schriften*, vol. 7.1, edited by Rolf Tiedemann and Hermann Schweppenhäuser, 350–84. Frankfurt am Main: Suhrkamp.
Berardi, Franco. 2011. *After the Future*. Oakland, CA: AK Press.
Bergson, Henri. 1911. *Laughter: An Essay on the Meaning of the Comic*. London: Macmillan.
Bergson, Henri. 1920. *Mind-Energy: Essays and Lectures*. New York: Holt.
Bergson, Henri. 2001. *Time and Free Will: An Essay on the Immediate Data of Consciousness*. Mineola, NY: Dover.

Bergson, Henri. 2004. *Matter and Memory*. Mineola, NY: Dover.
Bergson, Henri. 2007a. *Creative Evolution*. Mineola, NY: Dover.
Bergson, Henri. 2007b. *The Creative Mind*. Mineola, NY: Dover.
Bertelsen, Lone, and Andrew Murphie. 2010. "An Ethics of Everyday Infinities and Powers: Félix Guattari on Affect and the Refrain." In *The Affect Theory Reader*, edited by Melissa Gregg and Gregory J. Seigworth, 138–57. Durham, NC: Duke University Press.
Bolter, Jay David, and Richard Grusin. 1999. *Remediation: Understanding New Media*. Cambridge, MA: MIT Press.
Booth, Paul. 2011. "Memories, Temporalities, Fictions: Temporal Displacement in Contemporary Television." *Television and New Media* 12, no. 4: 370–88.
Bordeleau, Érik, Toni Pape, Ronald Rose-Antoinette, and Adam Szymanski. 2017. *Nocturnal Fabulations: Ecology, Vitality and Opacity in the Cinema of Apichatpong Weerasethakul*. London: Open Humanities Press.
Borges, Jorge Luis. 1962. *Ficciones*. Translated by Anthony Kerrigan. New York: Grove.
Brost, Molly. 2012. "Change the Structure, Change the Story: 'How I Met Your Mother' and the Reformulation of the Television Romance." In *Time in Television Narrative: Exploring Temporality in Twenty-First-Century Programming*, edited by Melissa Ames, 232–44. Jackson: University of Mississippi Press.
"Burden of Proof and Legal Definition." n.d. *USLegal.com*. Accessed July 30, 2018. http://definitions.uslegal.com/b/burden-of-proof/.
Bush, George W. 2001. "Address to a Joint Session of Congress and the American People." *The White House: President George W. Bush*, September 20. http://georgewbush-whitehouse.archives.gov/news/releases/2001/09/20010920-8.html.
Bush, George W. 2003. "President Says Saddam Hussein Must Leave Iraq within 48 Hours." *The White House: President George W. Bush*, March 17. http://georgewbush-whitehouse.archives.gov/news/releases/2003/03/20030317-7.html.
Butler, Jeremy G. 2010. *Television Style*. New York: Routledge.
Caldwell, John Thornton. 1995. *Televisuality: Style, Crisis, and Authority in American Television*. New Brunswick, NJ: Rutgers University Press.
Caldwell, John Thornton. 2003. "Second-Shift Media Aesthetics: Programming, Interactivity, and User Flows." In *New Media: Theories and Practices of Digitextuality*, edited by Anna Everett and John T. Caldwell, 127–44. London: Routledge.
Caldwell, John Thornton. 2008. *Production Culture: Industrial Reflexivity and Critical Practice in Film and Television*. Durham, NC: Duke University Press.
Cardwell, Sarah. 2013. "Television Aesthetics: Stylistic Analysis and Beyond." In *Television Aesthetics and Style*, edited by Jason Jacobs and Steven Peacock, 23–44. New York: Bloomsbury.
Cardwell, Sarah. 2014. "Television amongst Friends: Medium, Art, Media." *Critical Studies in Television* 9, no. 3: 6–21.
Chandler, Raymond. 2000. *The Raymond Chandler Papers: Selected Letters and Nonfiction, 1909–1959*. Edited by Tom Hiney and Frank MacShane. London: Hamish Hamilton.

Clarke, Ignatius F. 1961. *The Tale of the Future*. London: Library Associations.
Connelly, Neil. 2015. "What Writers Can Learn from *Breaking Bad*: The Risks and Rewards of Deliberate Disorientation." In *The Methods of "Breaking Bad": Essays on Narrative, Character and Ethics*, edited by Jacob Blevins and Dafydd Wood, 47–61. Jefferson, NC: McFarland.
Connolly, William E. 2002. *Neuropolitics: Thinking, Culture, Speed*. Minneapolis: University of Minnesota Press.
Creeber, Glen. 2004. *Serial Television: Big Drama on the Small Screen*. London: BFI.
Cubitt, Sean. 1991. *Timeshift: On Video Culture*. New York: Routledge.
Currie, Mark. 2007. *About Time: Narrative, Fiction and the Philosophy of Time*. Edinburgh: Edinburgh University Press.
Cushion, Stephen. 2012. *Television Journalism*. London: SAGE.
Dasgupta, Sudeep. 2012. "Policing the People: Television Studies and the Problem of 'Quality.'" *NECSUS: European Journal of Media Studies* 1, no. 1: 35–53.
Davies, William. 2016. "The Age of Post-Truth Politics." *New York Times*, August 24, 2016.
Deleuze, Gilles. 1986. *Cinema 1: The Movement-Image*. Translated by Hugh Tomlinson and Barbara Habberjam. Minneapolis: University of Minnesota Press.
Deleuze, Gilles. 1988a. *Bergsonism*. Translated by Hugh Tomlinson and Barbara Habberjam. New York: Zone Books.
Deleuze, Gilles. 1988b. *Spinoza: Practical Philosophy*. Translated by Robert Hurley. San Francisco: City Lights Books.
Deleuze, Gilles. 1989. *Cinema 2: The Time-Image*. Translated by Hugh Tomlinson and Robert Galeta. Minneapolis: University of Minnesota Press.
Deleuze, Gilles. 1990. *The Logic of Sense*. Translated by Mark Lester with Charles Stivale. New York: Columbia University Press.
Deleuze, Gilles. 1994. *Difference and Repetition*. Translated by Paul Patton. New York: Columbia University Press.
Deleuze, Gilles. 1995. *Negotiations: 1972–1990*. Translated by Martin Joughin. New York: Columbia University Press.
Deleuze, Gilles. 2004a. *Desert Islands and Other Texts: 1953–1974*. Edited by David Lapoujade. Translated by Mike Taormin. Cambridge, MA: MIT Press.
Deleuze, Gilles. 2004b. *Francis Bacon: The Logic of Sensation*. Translated by Daniel W. Smith. Minneapolis: University of Minnesota Press.
Deleuze, Gilles. 2006a. *Foucault*. Translated by Seán Hand. London: Continuum.
Deleuze, Gilles. 2006b. *Two Regimes of Madness: Texts and Interviews 1975–1995*. Edited by David Lapoujade. Translated by Ames Hodges and Mike Taormina. New York and Los Angeles: Semiotext(e).
Deleuze, Gilles. n.d. "Cours Vincennes: Synthesis and Time. 14/03/1978." *webdeleuze.com*. Accessed July 30, 2018. https://www.webdeleuze.com/textes/66.
Deleuze, Gilles, and Félix Guattari. 1980. *Mille plateaux: Capitalisme et schizophrénie*. Vol. 2. Paris: Minuit, 1980.
Deleuze, Gilles, and Félix Guattari. 1987. *A Thousand Plateaus: Capitalism and

Schizophrenia. Vol. 2. Translated by Brian Massumi. Minneapolis: University of Minnesota Press.

Deleuze, Gilles, and Félix Guattari. 1994. *What Is Philosophy?* Translated by Hugh Tomlinson and Graham Burchell III. New York: Columbia University Press.

Delli Carpini, Michael X., and Bruce A. Williams. 2001. "Let Us Infotain You: Politics in the New Media Age." In *Mediated Politics: Communication in the Future of Democracy,* edited by W. Lance Bennett and Robert M. Entman, 160–81. Cambridge: Cambridge University Press.

Deren, Maya. 1960. "Cinematography: The Creative Use of Reality." *Daedalus* 89, no. 1: 150–67.

Doane, Mary Ann. 1990. "Information, Crisis, Catastrophe." In *Logics of Television: Essays in Cultural Criticism,* edited by Patricia Mellencamp, 222–39. Bloomington: Indiana University Press.

Doane, Mary Ann. 2002. *The Emergence of Cinematic Time: Modernity, Contingency, the Archive.* Cambridge, MA: Harvard University Press.

Dupuy, Jean-Pierre. 2004. *Pour un catastrophisme éclairé: Quand l'impossible est certain.* Paris: Seuil.

Dupuy, Jean-Pierre. 2014. *Economy and the Future: A Crisis of Faith.* East Lansing: Michigan State University Press.

Eco, Umberto. 1972. "The Myth of Superman." *Diacritics* 2, no. 1: 14–22.

Eco, Umberto. 1982. "The Narrative Structure in Fleming." In *Popular Culture: Past and Present,* edited by Bernard Waites, Tony Bennett, and Graham Martin, 242–62. London: Croom Helm.

Eco, Umberto. 1985. "Innovation and Repetition: Between Modern and Post-Modern Aesthetics." *Dædalus* 114, no. 4: 161–84. Republished in *Daedalus* 134, no. 4 (fall 2005: "50 Years"): 191–207.

Eco, Umberto. 1989. *The Open Work.* Translated by Anna Cancogni. Cambridge, MA: Harvard University Press.

Eco, Umberto. 1994. "Interpreting Serials." In *The Limits of Interpretation,* 83–100. Bloomington: Indiana University Press.

Elsaesser, Thomas. 2009. "The Mind-Game Film." In *Puzzle Films: Complex Storytelling in Contemporary Cinema,* edited by Warren Buckland, 13–41. Oxford: Wiley-Blackwell.

Elsaesser, Thomas, and Malte Hagener. 2010. *Film Theory: An Introduction through the Senses.* New York: Routledge.

Esposito, Roberto. 2008. *Bíos: Biopolitics and Philosophy.* Minneapolis: University of Minnesota Press.

"Executive Summary: Digital Millennium Copyright Act; Section 104 Report." n.d. *The United States Copyright Office.* Accessed July 30, 2018. https://www.copyright.gov/reports/studies/dmca/dmca_executive.html.

Expósito Barea, Milagros. 2011. "*Flashforward* o el avance de una muerte anunciada:

Quality popular televisión de saldo." In "Previously On: Interdisciplinary Studies on TV Series in the Third Golden Age of Television," edited by Miguel A. Pérez-Gómez, special issue, *frame* (November): 121–33. http://fama2.us.es/fco/frame/previouslyon.pdf.

Foucault, Michel. 1995. *Discipline and Punish: The Birth of the Prison*. Translated by Alan Sheridan. New York: Vintage Books.

Foucault, Michel. 2008. *The Birth of Biopolitics: Lectures at the Collège de France, 1978–79*. Edited by Michel Senellart. Translated by Graham Burchell. New York: Palgrave Macmillan, 2008.

Freeley, Dustin. 2014. "The Economy of Time and Multiple Existences in *Breaking Bad*." In *Breaking Bad: Critical Essays on the Contexts, Politics, Style, and Reception of the Television Series*, edited by David P. Pierson, 33–52. Lanham, MD: Lexington Books.

French, Alex. 2017. "How to Make a Movie Out of Anything—Even a Mindless Phone Game." *New York Times*, July 27.

Fuller, Matthew. 2005. *Media Ecologies: Materialist Energies in Art and Technoculture*. Cambridge, MA: MIT Press.

Gillan, Jennifer. 2011. *Television and New Media: Must-Click TV*. New York: Routledge.

Gins, Madeline, and Arakawa. 2002. *Architectural Body*. Tuscaloosa: University of Alabama Press.

Gins, Madeline, and Arakawa. 2006. *Making Dying Illegal: Architecture against Death, Original to the 21st Century*. New York: Roof Books.

Grosz, Elizabeth. 2005. *Time Travels: Feminism, Nature, Power*. Durham, NC: Duke University Press.

Grusin, Richard. 2010. *Premediation: Affect and Mediality after 9/11*. New York: Palgrave Macmillan.

Guattari, Félix. 1992. *Chaosmose*. Paris: Galilée.

Guattari, Félix. 1995. *Chaosmosis: An Ethico-Aesthetic Paradigm*. Translated by Paul Bains and Julian Pefanis. Bloomington: Indiana University Press.

Guattari, Félix. 2011. *The Machinic Unconscious: Essays in Schizoanalysis*. Translated by Taylor Adkins. Los Angeles: Semiotext(e).

Hardt, Michael. 1999. "Affective Labor." *boundary 2* 26, no. 2: 89–100.

Hardt, Michael, and Antonio Negri. 2000. *Empire*. Cambridge, MA: Harvard University Press.

Hartog, François. 2015. *Regimes of Historicity: Presentism and Experiences of Time*. Translated by Saskia Brown. New York: Columbia University Press.

Hausmann, Matthias. 2009. "Ein utopie-kritischer Briefroman des frühen 19. Jahrhunderts: Pierre-Marc-Gaston, Duc de Lévis, *Les voyages de Kang-hi* (1810/12)." *Zeitschrift für französische Sprache und Literatur* 119, no. 2: 128–44.

Hongisto, Ilona, and Toni Pape. 2015. "Unexpected Artivism: The Fabulatory Function in *Kumaré*." *Studies in Documentary Film* 9, no. 1: 69–83.

Jacobs, Jason, and Steven Peacock, eds. 2013. *Television Aesthetics and Style*. New York: Bloomsbury.
James, William. 1920. *A Pluralistic Universe: Hilbert Lectures at Manchester College on the Present Situation in Philosophy*. London: Longmans-Green.
James, William. 2003. *Essays in Radical Empiricism*. Mineola, NY: Dover.
Jenner, Mareike. 2015. "Binge-Watching: Video-on-demand, Quality TV and Mainstreaming Fandom." *International Journal of Cultural Studies* 20, no. 3: 1–17.
Jonas, Hans. 2000. *The Imperative of Responsibility: In Search of an Ethics for the Technological Age*. Chicago: University of Chicago Press.
Jones, Steve. 2005. "Virtual." In *New Keywords: A Revised Vocabulary of Culture and Society*, edited by Tony Bennett, Lawrence Grossberg, Meaghan Morris, and Raymond Williams, 367–69. Malden, MA: Blackwell.
Kagan, Robert A. 1997. "Should Europe Worry about Adversarial Legalism?" *Oxford Journal of Legal Studies* 17, no. 2: 165–83.
Kant, Immanuel. 1998. *Critique of Pure Reason*. Translated and edited by Paul Guyer and Allen W. Wood. Cambridge: Cambridge University Press.
Kermode, Frank. 2000. *The Sense of an Ending: Studies in the Theory of Fiction*. Oxford: Oxford University Press.
Keyes, Ralph. 2004. *The Post-Truth Era: Dishonesty and Deception in Contemporary Life*. New York: St. Martin's.
Kobayashi, Bruce H., and Jeffrey S. Parker. 1999. "Civil Procedure: General." In *Encyclopedia of Law and Economics*, edited by Boudewijn Bouckaert and Gerrit De Geest, 1–26. Ghent: Edward Elgar. http://encyclo.findlaw.com/7000book.pdf.
Kovács, András Bálint. 2010. "Notes to a Footnote: The Open Work according to Eco and Deleuze." In *Afterimages of Gilles Deleuze's Film Philosophy*, edited by D. N. Rodowick, 31–45. Minneapolis: University of Minnesota Press.
Lamarre, Thomas. 2009. *The Anime Machine: A Media Theory of Animation*. Minneapolis: University of Minnesota Press.
Lamarre, Thomas. 2018. *The Anime Ecology: A Genelaogy of Television, Animation, and Game Media*. Minneapolis: University of Minnesota Press.
Landau, Neil. 2016. *TV Outside the Box: Trailblazing in the Digital Television Revolution*. New York: Focal Press.
Langer, Susanne K. 1953. *Feeling and Form: A Theory of Art Developed from "Philosophy in a New Key."* New York: Charles Scribner's Sons.
Lapoujade, David. 2013. *Powers of Time*. Translated by Andrew Goffey. São Paolo: N-1 Publications.
Lecercle, Jean-Jacques. 2006. "Introduction: An A-to-Z Guide to *Making Dying Illegal*." In Madeline Gins and Arakawa, *Making Dying Illegal: Architecture against Death, Original to the 21st Century*, 9–23. New York: Roof Books.
Le Goff, Jacques. 1980. *Time, Work and Culture in the Middle Ages*. Translated by Arthur Goldhammer. Chicago: University of Chicago Press.
Lim, Bliss Cua. 2009. *Translating Time: Cinema, the Fantastic, and Temporal Critique*. Durham, NC: Duke University Press.

Logan, Elliott. 2013. "Flashforwards in *Breaking Bad*: Openness, Closure and Possibility." In *Television Aesthetics and Style*, edited by Jason Jacobs and Steven Peacock, 219–26. New York: Bloomsbury.
Logan, Elliott. 2016. *Breaking Bad and Dignity: Unity and Fragmentation in the Serial Television Drama*. New York: Palgrave Macmillan.
Loock, Kathleen. 2018. "American TV Series Revivals: Introduction." *Television and New Media* 19, no. 4: 299–309.
Lotz, Amanda D. 2007. *The Television Will Be Revolutionized*. New York: New York University Press.
Lotz, Amanda D. 2014. *The Television Will Be Revolutionized*. 2nd ed. New York: New York University Press.
Lyotard, Jean-François. 2011. *Discourse, Figure*. Translated by Antony Hudek and Mary Lydon. Minneapolis: University of Minnesota Press.
Manning, Erin. 2007. *Politics of Touch: Sense, Movement, Sovereignty*. Minneapolis: University of Minnesota Press.
Manning, Erin. 2009. *Relationscapes: Movement, Art, Philosophy*. Cambridge, MA: MIT Press.
Manning, Erin. 2012. "The Art of Time." In *All Our Relations: 18th Biennale of Sydney 2012*, edited by Catherine de Zegher and Gerald McMaster, 355–59. Singapore: SC International.
Manning, Erin. 2013. *Always More Than One*. Durham, NC: Duke University Press.
Manning, Erin, and Brian Massumi. 2014. *Thought in the Act: Passages in the Ecology of Experience*. Minneapolis: University of Minnesota Press.
Marker, Chris. 1994. "A Free Replay (Notes sur *Vertigo*)." *Positif* 400 (June): 79–84.
Marker, Chris, Samuel Douhaire, and Annick Rivoire. 2003. "Rare Marker: Interview avec Chris Marker." *Libération*, March 5.
Marx, Karl. 1976. *Capital: A Critique of Political Economy*. Vol. 1. Translated by Ben Fowkes. London: Penguin.
Marx, Karl. 2008. *The Poverty of Philosophy*. Translated by Harry Quelch. New York: Cosimo.
Massumi, Brian. 2002a. "Introduction." In *A Shock to Thought: Expression after Deleuze and Guattari*, edited by Brian Massumi, xiii–xxxix. New York: Routledge.
Massumi, Brian. 2002b. *Parables for the Virtual: Movement, Affect, Sensation*. Durham, NC: Duke University Press.
Massumi, Brian. 2011. *Semblance and Event: Activist Philosophy and the Occurrent Arts*. Cambridge, MA: MIT Press.
Massumi, Brian. 2012. "Buying Out: Of Capitulation and Contestation." In "Out of the Mouths of 'Casseroles': Textes qui bougent au rythme du carré rouge," special issue, *Wi: Journal of Mobile Media* (June 1): 1–6. http://wi.mobilities.ca/wp-content/uploads/2012/06/Buying-Out-by-B-Massumi.pdf.
Massumi, Brian. 2014. *What Animals Teach Us about Politics*. Durham, NC: Duke University Press.

Massumi, Brian. 2015. *Ontopower: War, Powers, and the State of Perception*. Durham, NC: Duke University Press.

McGowan, Todd. 2011. *Out of Time: Desire in Atemporal Cinema*. Minneapolis: University of Minnesota Press.

Mittell, Jason. 2006. "Narrative Complexity in Contemporary American Television." *Velvet Light Trap*, no. 58 (fall): 29–40.

Mittell, Jason. 2010. "Previously On: Prime Time Serials and the Mechanics of Memory." In *Intermediality and Storytelling*, edited by Marina Grishakova and Marie-Laure Ryan, 78–98. New York: de Gruyter.

Mittell, Jason. 2015. *Complex TV: The Poetics of Contemporary Television Storytelling*. New York: New York University Press.

Mottron, Laurent. 2011. "The Power of Autism." *Nature* 479, no. 7371: 33–35.

Mulvey, Laura. 2006. *Death 24x a Second: Stillness and the Moving Image*. London: Reaktion Books.

Munster, Anna. 2013. *An Aesthesia of Networks: Conjunctive Experience in Art and Technology*. Cambridge, MA: MIT Press.

Murphie, Andrew. 2002. "Putting the Virtual Back into VR." In *A Shock to Thought: Expression after Deleuze and Guattari*, edited by Brian Massumi, 188–214. New York: Routledge.

Murphie, Andrew. 2008. "Clone Your Technics: Research Creation, Radical Empiricism and the Constraints of Models." *Inflexions*, no. 1 (May): 1–34. http://www.inflexions.org/n1_murphie.html.

Murphy, Sheila C. 2011. *How Television Invented New Media*. New Brunswick, NJ: Rutgers University Press.

Nelson, Elissa. 2014. "Windows into the Digital World: Distributor Strategies and Consumer Choice in an Era of Connected Viewing." In *Connected Viewing: Selling, Streaming, and Sharing Media in the Digital Era*, edited by Jennifer Holt and Kevin Sanson, 62–78. New York: Routledge.

Nelson, Jenny L. 1990. "The Dislocation of Time: A Phenomenology of Television Reruns." *Quarterly Review of Film and Video* 12, no. 3: 79–92.

Newman, Michael Z. 2006. "From Beats to Arcs: Toward a Poetics of Television Narrative." *Velvet Light Trap* 58, no. 1: 16–28.

Newman, Michael Z., and Elana Levine. 2011. *Legitimating Television: Media Convergence and Cultural Status*. New York: Routledge.

Nietzsche, Friedrich. 1999. *The Birth of Tragedy and Other Writings*. Edited by Raymond Geuss and Ronald Speirs. Translated by Ronald Speirs. Cambridge: Cambridge University Press.

O'Sullivan, Sean. 2010. "Broken on Purpose: Poetry, Serial Television, and the Season." *Storyworlds* 2, no. 1: 59–77.

Pape, Toni. 2012. "Temporalities on Collision Course: Time, Knowledge, and Temporal Critique in *Damages*." In *Time in Television Narrative: Exploring Temporality in Twenty-First-Century Programming*, edited by Melissa Ames, 165–77. Jackson: University of Mississippi Press.

Pape, Toni. 2014. "Preemptive Narratives, Modes of Attention, and the Politics of Perception." *Spectator* 34, no. 2: 63–71.

Pape, Toni. Forthcoming. "Resurrecting Television: Memories of the Future and the Anarchival Politics of Joy in *Arrested Development*." In *Immediations*, edited by Erin Manning, Bodil Marie Stavning Thomsen, and Anna Munster. London: Open Humanities Press.

Parikka, Jussi. 2010. *Insect Media: An Archeology of Animals and Technology*. Minneapolis: University of Minnesota Press.

Pérez-Gómez, Miguel A., ed. 2011. "Previously On: Interdisciplinary Studies on TV Series in the Third Golden Age of Television." Special issue, FRAME: *Revista de Cine de la Biblioteca de la Facultad de Comunicación* (November). http://fama2.us.es/fco/frame/previouslyon.pdf.

Pisters, Patricia. 2011. "Flashforward: The Future Is Now." In "Deleuzian Futures," edited by Nir Kedem, supplement, *Deleuze Studies* 5 (December): 98–115.

Pisters, Patricia. 2012. *The Neuro-Image: A Deleuzian Film-Philosophy of Digital Screen Culture*. Stanford, CA: Stanford University Press.

Posner, Richard A. 2011. *Economic Analysis of Law*. 8th ed. New York: Aspen.

Prigogine, Ilya. 1997. *The End of Certainty: Time, Chaos, and the New Laws of Nature*. With Isabelle Stengers. New York: Free Press.

Raunig, Gerald. 2010. *A Thousand Machines: A Concise Philosophy of the Machine as Social Movement*. Los Angeles: Semiotext(e).

Rizzo, Teresa. 2015. "Television Assemblages." *Fibreculture Journal*, no. 24 (June 3): 106–25. http://twentyfour.fibreculturejournal.org/2015/06/04/fcj-177-television-assemblages/.

Rodowick, D. N. 2001. *Reading the Figural, or, Philosophy after the New Media*. Durham, NC: Duke University Press.

Rodowick, D. N. 2007. *The Virtual Life of Film*. Cambridge, MA: Harvard University Press.

Ruyer, Raymond. 1958. *La génèse des formes vivantes*. Paris: Flammarion.

Sánchez-Baró, Rossend. 2014. "Uncertain Beginnings: *Breaking Bad*'s Episodic Openings." In *Breaking Bad: Critical Essays on the Contexts, Politics, Style, and Reception of the Television Series*, edited by David P. Pierson, 139–54. Lanham, MD: Lexington Books.

Serres, Michel. 2008. *The Five Senses: A Philosophy of Mingled Bodies*. Translated by Margaret Sankey and Peter Cowley. New York: Continuum.

Shaviro, Steven. 2010. *Post-Cinematic Affect*. Winchester, UK: Zero Books.

Sim, Gerald. 2016. "Individual Disruptors and Economic Gamechangers: Netflix, New Media, and Neoliberalism." In *The Netflix Effect: Technology and Entertainment in the 21st Century*, edited by Kevin McDonald and Daniel Smith-Rowsey, 185–201. London: Bloomsbury.

Simondon, Gilbert. 2017. *On the Mode of Existence of Technical Objects*. Translated by Cecile Malaspina and John Rogove. Minneapolis: Univocal.

Snaprud, Per. 2018. "The Consciousness Wager." *New Scientist*, no. 3183: 28–31.

Sobchack, Vivian. 2004. *Carnal Thoughts: Embodiment and Moving Image Culture.* Berkeley and Los Angeles: University of California Press.

Spigel, Lynn. 2005. "TV's Next Season?" *Cinema Journal* 45, no. 1: 83–90.

Spigel, Lynn, and Jan Olsson, eds. 2004. *Television after TV: Essays on a Medium in Transition.* Durham, NC: Duke University Press.

Stengers, Isabelle. 2010. *Cosmopolitics.* Vol. 1. Minneapolis: University of Minnesota Press.

Stengers, Isabelle. 2015. *In Catastrophic Times: Resisting the Coming Barbarism.* Translated by Andrew Goffey. London: Open Humanities Press.

Stern, Daniel N. 2000. *The Interpersonal World of the Infant: A View from Psychoanalysis and Developmental Psychology.* New York: Basic Books.

Stern, Daniel N. 2010. *Forms of Vitality: Exploring Dynamic Experience in Psychology, the Arts, Psychotherapy, and Development.* Oxford: Oxford University Press.

Stewart, Garrett. 2007. *Framed Time: Toward a Postfilmic Cinema.* Chicago: University of Chicago Press.

Stiegler, Bernard. 1998. *Technics and Time.* Vol. 1, *The Fault of Epimetheus.* Stanford, CA: Stanford University Press.

Stiegler, Bernard. 2008. *La télécratie contre la démocratie.* Paris: Flammarion.

Stiegler, Bernard. 2010. "Telecracy against Democracy." *Cultural Politics* 6, no. 2: 171–80.

Stiegler, Bernard. 2011. *Technics and Time.* Vol. 3, *Cinematic Time and the Question of Malaise.* Stanford, CA: Stanford University Press.

Tarkovsky, Andrey. 1987. *Sculpting in Time: Reflections on the Cinema.* Austin: University of Texas Press.

Tessé, Jean-Philippe. 2010. "La série continue." *Cahiers du cinéma* 658: 7. Thain, Alanna. 2010. "Anarchival Cinemas." *Inflexions,* no. 4 (December): 48–68. http://inflexions.org/n4_Anarchival-Cinemas-by-Alanna-Thain.pdf.

Thain, Alanna. 2017. *Bodies in Suspense: Time and Affect in Cinema.* Minneapolis: University of Minnesota Press.

Thompson, Robert J. 1996. *Television's Second Golden Age.* New York: Continuum.

Toffler, Alvin. 1970. *Future Shock.* New York: Random House.

Tryon, Chuck. 2015. "TV Got Better: Netflix's Original Programming Strategies and Binge Viewing." *Media Industries* 2, no. 2: 104–16.

Uricchio, William. 2004. "Television's Next Generation: Technology/Interface Culture/Flow." In *Television after TV: Essays on a Medium in Transition,* edited by Lynn Spigel and Jan Olsson, 163–82. Durham, NC: Duke University Press.

Uricchio, William. 2010. "TV as Time Machine: Television's Changing Heterochronic Regimes and the Production of History." In *Relocating Television: Television in the Digital Context,* edited by Jostein Gripsrud, 27–40. New York: Routledge.

Vancheri, Luc. 2011. *Les pensées figurales de l'image.* Paris: Colin.

Versins, Pierre. 1972. *Encyclopédie de l'utopie, des voyages extraordinaires et de la science fiction.* Lausanne: L'Âge d'Homme.

Virilio, Paul. 1997. *Open Sky.* Translated by Julie Rose. London: Verso.

Virilio, Paul. 2010. *The Futurism of the Instant: Stop-Eject*. Translated by Julie Rose. Cambridge, MA: Polity.
Virilio, Paul. 2012. *The Administration of Fear*. With Bertrand Richard. Translated by Ames Hodges. Los Angeles: Semiotext(e).
Wells, H. G. 1975. *Early Writings in Science and Science Fiction*. Edited by Robert M. Philmus and David Y. Hughes. Berkeley: University of California Press.
White House. 2002. "Saddam Hussein's Development of Weapons of Mass Destruction." *The White House: President George Bush*, September 12. http://georgewbush-whitehouse.archives.gov/infocus/iraq/decade/sect3.html.
Williams, Linda. 1991. "Film Bodies: Gender, Genre, Excess." *Film Quarterly* 44, no. 4: 2–13.
Williams, Linda. 2014. *On The Wire*. Durham, NC: Duke University Press.
Williams, Raymond. [1974] 2003. *Television: Technology and Cultural Form*. London: Routledge.
Wolfe, Cary. 2013. *Before the Law: Humans and Other Animals in a Biopolitical Frame*. Chicago: University of Chicago Press.
Žižek, Slavoj. 2008. *In Defense of Lost Causes*. London: Verso.

Television Series

Breaking Bad. 2008–13. Creator Vince Gilligan. AMC.
Damages. 2007–12. Creators Glenn Kessler, Todd A. Kessler, and Daniel Zelman. FX/Audience Network.
Flashforward. 2009–10. Creators Brannon Braga, David S. Goyer, and Robert J. Sawyer (novel). ABC.
Life on Mars. 2006–7. Creators Matthew Graham, Tony Jordan, and Ashley Pharoah. BBC.

INDEX

abstraction, 90n13
acceleration, 30
actual, 90–91, 95
adversarial legalism, 144–45
aesthetic, 25
affect: preemptive narratives and, 9–12, 46; affective attunement, 29n32, 47, 132, 142; affective fact, 10; fiction and, 125–26
agency, 21–22, 135, 169
amodality (perception), 25n28
anaesthetic, 18, 43, 181. *See also* desensitization
anarchive, 176–82
assemblage, 19
attention, 35, 165–69; participation and, 71; dance of, 71; technic of, 123–24; to life, 165. *See also* ethics

Back to the Future, 77n3
bare activity, 180–81
bare life, 179
becoming, 18–19, 39, 45–49, 82–87; vector of, 73, 165. *See also* interval
binge-watching, 21
black screen, 121–22
brain, 46, 88, 100–101; screen as, 121–23; consciousness and, 122–23
Breaking Bad, 1–6, 14–15, 27–28, 32
Bush, George W., 10–11, 70, 137

Christmas Carol, A, 129
cinematograph, 84
civil law, 143–48
close-up, 155–59
complexity: narrative, 18, 170; experiential, 30–31, 41–44; of the world, 166–69
control (society), 31, 140, 145–49, 167–73
Coronation Street, 61, 65
correspondence, principle of, 75, 93
crime fiction, 12–14; knowledge production and, 109–10; legal drama and, 142–48
criminal law, 143–48

Damages, 38–50, 62–67, 142–74
delay, 103, 128, 158–60
desensitization, 178–82. *See also* anaesthetic
detective, 142–46. *See also* crime fiction
deterrence, 8–9
diagram, 47–48; biotopological, 170–73, 175
disciplinary society, 31–36, 144–45
duplicity, 138
Dupuy, Jean-Pierre, 11n13, 68, 70, 81–82
duration, 39–40, 90
DVD, 57–58

Eco, Umberto, 17n18, 64–65
ecology of practices, 34, 168, 172, 176, 181
ending, 64
ER, 51
ethics, 34, 104; of attention, 124, 128, 139, 171, 179
experimentation, 34, 106
expression, 7n7

faciality, 167
fear, 69
fiction: affect and, 125–26
figural, 25–27, 76, 159
figure of time, 45–50, 100–105, 121–26, 161–62
flashback, 121, 127–29, 152, 155; as bifurcation point, 161
flash-forward, 112–15; sensory-motor schema and, 127
flow, 42–43
form-taking, 46, 66, 105; of thought, 110
functionalist aesthetics, 27
future: visions of, 14, 35, 112–34; future orientation, 77–78, 88–94; future-past, 66–69, 94, 106, 123–35; self-causing, 132

golden age of television (second and third), 51

hypermasculinity, 146n6

immediate experience, 25, 119–20
immediation, 30, 177–82
indeterminacy, 54, 102–5, 123–28, 148–58; of becoming, 69, 113; potential and, 94–95; threat and, 10
insurance industry, 8
intelligence, 87, 94
intertitle, 121–22
interval (of becoming), 66–67, 103, 126, 148–68
intuition, 87, 110; ethics of, 105

James, William, 16, 27n31, 44n6, 66n32, 111, 132n14

Kant, Immanuel, 110–11
knowledge, 87; time as a problem of, 94, 109–10, 128–29; thought and, 109–15

Langer, Susanne, 50n11
legal drama, 142–48
Life on Mars, 24, 73–107, 142–43, 162, 177, 182
loop, 3n1, 66, 139, 172

machine: abstract, 19, 38; serial, 50–56; expressive, 57
madness, 99–106, 113–14
mechanics (Galilean and Newtonian), 110–11
mechanism, 79–80, 110
memory of the future, 104, 121; as potentializing, 162–68
mind-game films, 76
mise en abyme, 115, 125
morality, 32–36; of command, 129–39
mosaic, 132
multiplicity (quantitative and qualitative), 79

narrative, 9–20; complexity and, 18, 57–60, 170; preemptive movement and, 12, 46, 62–67; serial, 64–65; narrative scheme, 13, 64–66, 125, 152; narrative unit, 57–61. See also season
narrowcasting, 54
neoliberalism, 32
Netflix, 20
neuro-image, 119–23, 132
news television, 52

ontogenesis, 39–40, 69–70, 134

pharmakon, 180–82
playfulness, 164
plot twist, 161–65
post-9/11 TV, 135–36
potential and possibility, 94, 138
power, 21–22
preempted ending, 4, 66

preemption, 9–12, 80; creativity and, 137–38; as depotentializing, 93–95, 138–39; news television and, 52–53; moral judgment and, 136–38
preemptive narratives, 12, 62–67
premediation, 29
premise, 75–65. *See also* representation
presentism, 9–10
prevention, 8–9, 80, 111
Previously On segment, 171–72
Primer, 77n3
probability, balance of, 143–45, 158, 167
procedure, 35–37, 168–73, 176–82
progress, 6
prophecy: of doom, 11–12, 82; self-fulfilling, 133–34
puzzle films, 76

quality TV, 55
quasi-cause, 134n18

radical empiricism, 16, 21, 35–36
refrain, 5–9
relation, 25–26, 34–36
relational field, 27, 45–50, 70–71; storytelling as, 102–5, 122
relation-of-nonrelation, 122–23
remix, 177
representation, 73–76; logic of, 24, 74–76, 105
retrospection, 65–66, 121; prospective, 123, 129; teleological, 77
reverse motion, 41
revivals, 55

science fiction, 109–10
season (formats), 58–59
self-differentiation, autopoietic heterogenesis and, 19; enforced, 28, 31; security and, 112–13; time as, 23, 39, 47, 67, 82
sensation, 24–25

sensory-motor schema, 77; flashbacks and, 127–28; delay within, 103, 128, 158–60
seriality, 64–65
sign and signal, 24–25
smoke, 39
soap opera, 22, 60–61
space: smooth and striated, 149–52
spectator, 103–4
storytelling, as relational field, 102–5, 122
subjectivation, vector of, 28
surfer, 139–40, 145, 149
suspense, 123, 127; expectation and, 159–63
syntheses (of time), 119, 132

Tarkovsky, Andrey, 48
technic, 19–20, 123–24
teleological retrospect, 77
television: as machinic assemblage, 16–22, 50–61; cable, 52; industry, 55–57; preemption and, 12–16, procedural, 168–73, 176–82; refrain and, 5–7; technics and, 17–23, 42, 52–57; televisual time, 17–18
temporal critique, 18
temporal displacement, 84, 98–101
tentativeness, 165–68
terminus, 66n32
territory, 7–8
terrorism, 10, 136–38; time and, 113–14
The Sopranos, 59
The Wire, 58
time: as retardation, 104; as self-differentiation, 23, 39, 82; cinematic, 84–87, 170; knowledge and, 109–11; metric, 42, 78; merchant's, 78n5; syntheses of, 119, 132; teleological, 6; televisual, 17–18
time travel, 76–78, 134
transparency: representational, 155–59
tricksterism, 164

Utopia, 78n4

VCR, 57–58
Virilio, Paul, 30
virtual, 88–99

weapons of mass destruction, 70
Wells, H. G., 7

Žižek, Slavoj, 68–70, 81, 113, 186n13, 194nn34,35

www.ingramcontent.com/pod-product-compliance
Lightning Source LLC
Chambersburg PA
CBHW071818230426
43670CB00013B/2493